Changing Software
Development

Changing Software Development: Learning to be Agile

Allan Kelly

John Wiley & Sons, Ltd

Other Wiley Editorial Offices

John Wiley & Sons Inc., 111 River Street, Hoboken, NJ 07030, USA

Jossey-Bass, 989 Market Street, San Francisco, CA 94103-1741, USA

Wiley-VCH Verlag GmbH, Boschstr. 12, D-69469 Weinheim, Germany

John Wiley & Sons Australia Ltd, 42 McDougall Street, Milton, Queensland 4064, Australia

John Wiley & Sons (Asia) Pte Ltd, 2 Clementi Loop #02-01, Jin Xing Distripark, Singapore 129809

John Wiley & Sons Canada Ltd, 6045 Freemont Blvd, Mississauga, ONT, Canada L5R 4J3

Wiley also publishes its books in a variety of electronic formats. Some content that appears in print may not be
available in electronic books.

Library of Congress Cataloging-in-Publication Data

Kelly, Allan, 1969-
   Changing software development : learning to become agile / Allan Kelly.
      p. cm.
   Includes index.
   ISBN 978-0-470-51504-4 (pbk. : alk. paper)
 1. Agile software development. I. Title.
   QA76.76.D47K454 2008
   005.3–dc22   2007035526

British Library Cataloguing in Publication Data

A catalogue record for this book is available from the British Library

ISBN: 978-0-470-51504-4 (paperback)

Typeset in 10.5/13 Times Roman by Thomson Digital, Noida, India.
Printed and bound in Great Britain by Antony Rowe, Chippenham, Wiltshire
This book is printed on acid-free paper responsibly manufactured from sustainable forestry
in which at least two trees are planted for each one used for paper production.

*To Taissia for all her support, understanding and
help with this book and everything.*

*To Mrs. Blyth, Mrs. McQueen, and all the other staff
at Orrets Meadow School for teaching me to read and write all over again. Sometimes you
don't get it right the first time. You unlearn and start all over again.*

Contents

Preface

This book contains two ideas. The first idea is practical and the second more philosophical, but both are essential if we realize the potential of information technology to transform business.

The first is about changing your development team. In the short to medium term, the focus is on making your team *Agile*. In the longer term, it's about making your team into a learning team, capable of learning, changing and improving itself. Such teams are true Agile teams.

Improving the software development process has always been difficult. In part, it's difficult because we haven't known how to do it, and in part it's difficult because any kind of change is hard. Today, we have good models of how to do software development. The Agile community has demonstrated techniques that work. These techniques and ideas are well documented. Consequently, the problem that we face today is less 'How shall we develop software?' and more 'How do we move from the way we do things today to a more Agile way?'

The second idea in this book is a call for us to change the dominant view of software development. Traditionally, software development has been considered an engineering discipline – something to be planned, scheduled and executed. The view presented here considers the process of developing software as an exercise in learning and knowledge creation.

Both ideas are based on a very simple theory: it isn't enough to learn facts alone. For learning to be meaningful, we must take action on what we learn. Learning with action means change, so learning and change are two sides of the same coin.

Acknowledgements

There are many people who I need to thank for helping me directly, and indirectly, to write this book. First and foremost, I must thank Taissia, who not only read the final manuscripts but, more importantly, allowed me the time to write the book.

Many thanks go to the reviewers – Alan Griffiths, Liz Sedley, Jonathon Sefton, Rachel Davies and Giovanni Asproni – and to Nicki Kelly for additional editing.

I am indebted to John Merrells, who as ACCU *Overload* editor encouraged my early attempts at writing. For over four years, John published most of what I wrote, helped me improve and allowed me to move away from technical topics into more reflective management topics. Thanks again to Alan Griffiths, who took over as *Overload* editor when John stepped down.

Thank you to the many members of the ACCU for good conversations and for acting as unknowing guinea pigs for the ideas in this book. Attentive readers will find the prototype of this book in the pages of *Overload*.

In particular, I must thank Kevlin Henney, who introduced me to Pattern writing and to the Pattern community. Although Patterns are not the topic of this book, I have learned much through Pattern writing. So I must thank the Hillside, EuroPLoP and VikingPLoP communities for all the indirect help they have given to this project.

In 2002, I took a year out from IT to attend Nottingham University Business School. As well as being introduced to many new ideas, I also had the chance to rethink the whole software development domain: to everyone at NUBS, and the class of 2002–3, many thanks to you all. In particular, I would like to thank Professors Ken Starkey and John Richards – anyone familiar with their ideas and teaching will spot their influence in this book.

If you are wondering where to get inspiration and good conversation on the topics raised here, I can recommend that you join the ACCU, get involved with the Patterns community or take yourself off to business school.

No book would exist without a publisher. I would like to thank everyone at John Wiley & Sons, Ltd, for their efforts in bringing this book to publication; in particular, Andrew Kennerly, Sally Tickner, Lynette James and especially Rosie Kemp.

Introduction

"We understand that the only competitive advantage the company of the future will have is its managers' ability to learn faster than then their competitors."

Arie de Geus (1988)

Software development, in all its forms, is an exercise in learning. Learning occurs within the teams that develop the software – not just the amongst the managers. Then learning occurs with the people who use the software. If we exploit this learning, we can enhance the competitive advantage for our companies.

In order to recognize the value of learning, it's necessary to change things: to change what we do and the way we do it. Without change we can't truly learn, and we certainly don't exploit our learning. The process of learning and changing is an exercise in knowledge creation. Knowledge itself is learning with action: this action often manifests itself as change. This idea, summarized in Figure 1.1, runs through this book.

Knowledge is the underpinning of our modern economy – hence the 'knowledge economy' – and IT is a key part of this economy. Modern IT wouldn't be what it is without software, and that software needs to be written. Yet the people who develop software, and those who manage them, seldom talk about knowledge and the role that IT can play in enhancing learning. All too often, we prefer to view software development as some sort of factory production line process.

This view runs far beyond the development process. Organizations buy software and other IT products in order to create change. Introducing the

Changing Software Development: Learning to Become Agile   Allan Kelly
© 2008 John Wiley & Sons, Ltd.

Knowledge = Learning + Action

Figure 1.1   Knowledge is.

software creates change for the users, and subsequent changes to the software create more change.

Today's software developers and their managers face three major forms of change. Firstly, there's the need to adopt Agile methods. Agile and Lean development techniques are now established and are moving into the mainstream arena. In order to adopt these techniques, development teams must change the way in which they work.

Secondly, having adopted Agile development, these best-performing teams need to move far beyond the current methods and best practices. Before long, simply adopting the prescribed practices of a methodology such as eXtreme Programming won't be enough. Each team must learn for itself what works best.

Finally, IT is all about creating change in others. IT deployments that inflict change on helpless users don't recognize the true benefits of IT; indeed, many such projects are outright failures. Those developing and deploying software must appreciate the need for change and learning by the end users.

Learning and change are complicated fields. All too often, people see change as the simple application of raw authority: *tell someone to do it differently, tell someone to use a new system, punish them if they get it wrong*. Unfortunately, this technique doesn't work very well. In particular, it isn't effective with knowledge workers who may actually know more about the problem than anyone in a position of authority. So we need a new view of change to help us with these problems.

Fortunately, the best people in IT – and, in particular, the actual software development side – like learning. Much, if not most, IT work is problem solving, which is itself a form of learning. Therefore, we need to help people learn, help them learn the right things and ensure that this learning is maximized through meaningful change.

1.1 Why Read this Book?

Even if you don't wish to embrace Agile software development, there are good reasons to embrace learning and create a learning culture. Building a learning environment and culture can help improve the way in which you create software and benefit your company in many ways.

This book is primarily written for software developers and managers who want to improve the way in which they, and their teams, develop software. Software developers who are making, or have recently made, the transition to team leadership and development management should find the ideas particularly interesting.

There's an additional group of people who I hope will find this book interesting: those dependent on the work of a software development team.

Such people often view IT, and specifically development activities, as a foreign land. Viewing IT as a learning activity, rather than an engineering or scientific activity, can help explain much of what goes on in that land.

1.1.1 Learning for Agility

The book aims to help in three ways:

- *For teams that want to be Agile:* Increasingly, we know what Agile software development is. The problem facing those who aren't Agile is not 'What is Agile?' or 'What do Agile teams do differently?' The problem is rather 'How do we change so that we're Agile?' This book presents learning as a mechanism for creating change.

- *For teams that are Agile and want to improve further:* For teams that have achieved Agility, the challenge is slightly different. Such teams will already be seeing the benefits of the Agile approach. However, there's still a need to improve and become even better. The learning-based approach can help here too.

- *By explaining the role of learning in software development:* During the past 40 years, there have been many attempts to make software development fit within the engineering and process metaphors. Despite this, software projects have continued to fail. In this book, I suggest that software development is an exercise in learning and knowledge management. Changing our perspective offers new insights and approaches. In particular, this perspective allows us to harness the tools and experience of the organizational learning movement instead of the tools of engineering.

This book doesn't attempt to be the last word on any of these subjects. I've tried to point you to many sources for further investigation. Instead, this book aims, firstly, to introduce each of these topics and, secondly, to weave them into a coherent narrative to explain software development as a learning activity.

1.1.2 Learning Creates Competitive Advantage

Modern business is constantly searching for competitive advantage: the ability to out-compete rivals, to sell more products, to sell more expensive products and to increase production. Once upon a time, competitive advantage could be gained by having better physical access than your competitors to some resource, land, labour or capital.

Today, firms seek competitive advantage through better access to knowledge and by their ability to act on this knowledge. Knowledge is the result of learning; therefore, as suggested in the opening quote, a firm's ability to learn may be its only competitive advantage.

By learning, we're able to create better products: we learn more about our customers, we learn more about the technology our products are built from and we learn how to produce the products more efficiently. Using this learning, we're able to improve our products. Learning about our customers, products and manufacturing process may allow us to create better products.

Learning also allows us to increase our productivity. Through learning, we're able to build products faster, more efficiently and with less waste. This allows us to maximize the returns from our investment – whether capital or workers' time – and generate more profit. In these cases, the firm's ability to learn is key to helping the firm improve and succeed. The firm that learns fastest wins.

But learning isn't just essential in order to win: it's also essential in order to survive. Modern businesses exist in a changing environment, new competitors enter markets, customer expectations change, and technologies and regulations change. Firms that don't learn and adapt to a changing environment may not survive.

So, learning isn't an optional extra. Firms and individuals must learn if they are to survive. For those that master learning and can learn faster than others, there are rewards.

1.1.3 Good People Like Learning

Humans are natural learners. Our ability to learn faster than many other animals is one of the reasons why we humans have advanced as far as we have. Within software development, those who enjoy and excel at learning tend to perform better than those who dislike learning new things. There are always new technologies and application domains to learn. Anyone who dislikes learning would be well advised to avoid a career in software development.

The search for competitive advantage outlined above isn't the only reason to embrace learning. People who enjoy learning are more motivated when given an environment in which they can learn more. Motivated people get more job satisfaction and are more productive.

Naturally, when people are motivated and happy with their work they are more likely to remain with the same employer. Therefore, creating a learning environment should help improve staff retention. Recruitment may also become easier, as word spreads of a positive work environment, filled with motivated people who are learning new things.

1.2 Who are Software Developers?

The term *software developer* is most often used to describe the engineers who write program code. In truth, there are many more roles necessary to develop software: testers, business analysts, designers, product managers, architects, deployment specialists, project managers, development managers and others all have a hand in developing the software.

The IT community doesn't have a standard set of job titles and pre-defined roles; what one company calls a 'product manager' is an 'architect' elsewhere, one company's 'project manager' is another's 'development manager', a 'team leader' in one is a 'manager' in another, and so on. All these people are in some way contributing to the development of a software system.

The level of knowledge and experience required to develop a successful system causes the old 'blue-collar'/'white-collar' division to fade. Someone who thinks of a programmer as analogous to a factory worker is making a mistake: the level of knowledge required by a programmer is several orders of magnitude greater than that required by an assembly line worker.

The profile of a modern development team looks more like a group of white-collar managers than a set of blue-collar workers: highly skilled people with specific knowledge who spend their days making informed decisions – not to mention working in air-conditioned offices. Consequently, when looking outside the IT arena, research, advice and inspiration are often to be found in texts that discuss management challenges.

Thinking Point: Why Do You Want To Change?

This book is going to discuss changing the way in which you create software. Specifically, I'm going to describe how you can help your team adopt Agile software practices. Before getting stuck into the task in hand, it is worth taking a step back and asking: *Why? – Why do we want to change the way in which we do things?*

Before you read any further, put this book down and make a list of five reasons why you'd like to change the way in which your organization develops software:

- Try to think beyond immediate reasons such as a recently failed project.
- Try to think about *why*, not *what*.
- Try to think about big reasons rather than small ones.
- Try to think about your company as a whole rather than just your team: *What benefit will this bring?*
- Be honest: if you want to change the team to further your own career, recognize it – you don't have to tell anyone else.

You might also want to think about the opportunities that you can see if you can change.

Now that you've made the list, put it to one side. (If you want to hide it, do so!)

There are various reasons why you might want to change your development practices. Here are a few reasons, all of them legitimate:

- To improve the competitiveness of your team or company.
- To improve the quality of your software.
- To increase the productivity of your team.
- To create new business opportunities, products and/or services.
- To address a problem that you're having today.
- To save your own job, perhaps by preventing your work being outsourced and/or sent off shore.
- To better serve the business.
- To enjoy your job more.

This isn't an exhaustive list; nor are the items in the list distinct – they all overlap. Depending on your situation, some will be cause and others effect: improving the quality may allow you to support your business better and prevent your department being outsourced, thereby saving your job.

In fact, everything could be reduced to the first item: *improve company competitiveness*. However, this is so general as to be of little use. Most of the other reasons can be reduced to either quality or productivity, but to do so means losing useful information about motivation.

1.3 Software Developers are Knowledge Workers

If we look at the definition of knowledge workers, it is clear that it includes developers:

> "Knowledge workers have high degrees of expertise, education, or experience, and the primary purpose of their jobs involves the creation, distribution, or application of knowledge."
>
> Thomas Davenport (2005)

Indeed, writers and experts on the knowledge economy and knowledge workers frequently cite software developers, and IT people in general, as prime examples of knowledge workers. These are individuals who work primarily with their knowledge. Yet it is rare for those in IT, or writers about IT, to discuss software developers as knowledge workers. But then: Why would they? What difference does it make?

This book will argue that by viewing software developers as knowledge workers, and considering development activities as knowledge creation with active learning processes, we gain many useful insights into the process by which software is developed and deployed. By recognizing IT staff as knowledge workers, a rich field of literature and experience opens up from which we may learn from to help improve our own practice.

From the same book quoted above, we can distil a list of knowledge work characteristics:

- Knowledge workers like autonomy: they don't like being told what to do.
- Specifying detailed steps to follow is less valuable than in other types of work.
- Knowledge workers find it difficult to describe what they do in detail: if you want to know, you're better off watching.
- Not only do knowledge workers find it difficult to describe what they do, but they're aware of the value of knowledge and don't share it without a motivation.
- Even though they may not be able to describe what they do, these workers often have good reason for doing what they do and have often thought in advance about the way in which they work.
- Commitment matters and makes a huge difference in productivity.

Looking at this list, two things stand out: firstly, this is a list of developer characteristics too, so any doubt that developers are knowledge workers should be dispelled. Secondly, an individual with these characteristics is unlikely to relish routine, factory-like, work. The traditional view of management isn't applicable to these workers.

Recognizing that IT workers are knowledge workers also recognizes that they're not unique. They share the same characteristics as other knowledge workers. Nor are the problems that they encounter unique. The opportunities and problems faced by IT staff and their managers are quite legitimate, and are shared by other modern knowledge workers. Consequently, it is wrong to think of the 'IT geek' as a class apart.

Once we recognize software developers as knowledge workers, it becomes clear that development activities – specifying, designing, coding and testing new software – are themselves knowledge activities. Such activities are completely different from traditional factory production line processes, where a worker's individual knowledge makes little immediate difference to the end product. Having recognized this critical difference, it becomes meaningless to characterize software development as a factory process.

Many previous attempts to change the way in which IT staff work were misplaced because they failed to recognize the roles of knowledge and the characteristics of knowledge workers. Naive attempts at quality improvement, productivity enhancement and cost cutting that draw on manufacturing experience are simply wrong.

1.4 Drucker's Challenge

Defining software development as knowledge work doesn't allow us to ignore the issue of productivity. Productivity and quality are still very important to the success of a business venture. The management guru Peter Drucker forecast the emergence of this issue as long ago as 1969:

> "Knowledge work is not easily defined in quantitative terms, . . . To make knowledge work productive will be the great management task of this century, just as to make manual work productive was the great management task of the last century."
>
> Peter Drucker (1969)

How you measure productivity in software development is a good question. It is most certainly not lines of code, function points or hours worked. Still, no matter how difficult it is to measure, we are producing something and we can always improve productivity and quality. Perhaps we just have to live with this ambiguity.

Any attempts to quantify software development productivity must make allowance for the multiple results of such work. In developing a piece of software we create a deliverable executable, but there are by-products. The developers themselves increase their stock of knowledge – about their tools, about the subject of the software and about the creation process. Similarly, managers, users and others involved with the specification, implementation and delivery of the software will learn as a by-product.

Despite the problems of measuring productivity, we can still discuss the issues, and we can still ask how we can address Peter Drucker's challenge. Much of this book is directed at addressing this challenge: *How can we make software developers more productive?*

The Agile and Lean schools give us the methods to increase developer productivity, but we still need to apply them. The challenge we face is less 'What can we do to be more productive?' and more 'How can we move from here to there – from where we are today to more productive practices?' and 'How can we continue to improve our productivity?'

In other words: *How do we change? How do we continue to change? How do we go beyond our current stock of knowledge?*

1.5 The Prototype of Future Knowledge Workers

Highlighting IT workers as knowledge workers allows us to learn from the existing body of knowledge on the subject. IT workers are not alone; they are knowledge workers and there's much to learn from other knowledge workers, and from research and literature about knowledge work in general. There's no need for IT managers (and writers) to re-invent the wheel.

Yet, in another way, the existing literature, research and experience can't help IT workers and their managers. This is because IT workers, and software developers in particular, are at the cutting edge of knowledge work. In many ways, they're the prototype of the future knowledge worker; they're pushing the boundaries of twenty-first century knowledge work.

This occurs because, to paraphrase Karl Marx, software developers control the means of production. Modern knowledge work is enabled by and dependent on information technology: e-mail for communication, web sites for distribution, databases for storage, word processors for writing reports, spreadsheets for analysis – the list is endless! These technologies are created by software developers and used by legions of knowledge workers worldwide. The key difference between software knowledge workers and the others is that other knowledge workers can only use the tools that exist. If a tool doesn't exist, they can't use it. Conversely, software developers have the means to create any tool they can imagine.

Consequently, it was a programmer, Ward Cunningham, who invented the Wiki. Programmers Dan Bricklin and Bob Frankston invented the electronic spreadsheet. Even earlier, it was another programmer, Ray Tomlinson, who invented inter-machine e-mail. This doesn't mean that non-programmers can't invent electronic tools. Others can invent tools, but for programmers the barriers between imagining a tool and creating the tool are far lower.

Lower barriers mean that programmers create many more tools than other types of worker. Some tools fail, while others are very specific to a specific problem, organization or task in hand, but when tools do work it is programmers who get to use them first. In addition, because IT people have had Internet access for far longer than any other group, the propensity to use it to find tools and share new tools is far greater. So tools such as Cunningham's Wiki were in common use by software developers years before they were used by other knowledge workers.

Early Internet access has had other effects too: IT workers were early adopters of remote working, either as individual home workers or as members of remote development teams; IT people are far more likely to turn to the Web for assistance with problems and more likely to find it, because IT information has been stored on the Web since the very beginning.

The net effect of these factors and others means that software developers are often the first to adopt new tools and techniques in their knowledge work. They're also the first to find problems with such tools and techniques. Consequently, these workers are at the cutting edge of twenty-first century knowledge work; they are the prototype for other knowledge workers. Other knowledge workers, and their managers, can learn from the way in which IT people work today, provided that we recognize these workers as knowledge workers.

1.6 Software: Embedded Knowledge

When we program, we teach a computer to do something. We use our knowledge of computers and programming to create an automated system that embodies knowledge. For example, accounts software contains knowledge of accounting principles and practices, the software in a telephone exchange contains knowledge of call handling and routing, and so on.

As we shall see later (Section 4.1), software brings together three knowledge domains: knowledge of the technical tools to create the software, knowledge of software creation process and knowledge of the problem that we're trying to solve. Sometimes one person will be accomplished in all three domains – say, an experienced compiler writer. On other occasions, different individuals will embody different knowledge: a programmer knows the tools, a manager knows the process and a product expert knows the problem that we're trying to solve.

At the end of the process we have a piece of software that we expect to function without the presence of any of these individuals. The software itself doesn't know anything; even when running on a computer, it has no self-awareness. However, the software does, to a greater or lesser degree, embody knowledge from all those who were part of its creation.

1.7 Authority and Leadership

One question that inevitably pops up when discussing change is: *Do I have the authority to introduce change?*

This book will argue that change and learning are merely different sides of the same coin, in which case we could rephrase the original question as follows: *Do I have the authority to enhance learning?* This is a much less confrontational question and one that it is perhaps easier to answer *Yes*.

A much more difficult question to answer is: *Does having authority make it easier to introduce change and enhance learning?* Before you rush to answer, consider two facts. Firstly, as already noted, knowledge workers don't like being told what to do. So even if you can order someone to do something, you might not get the results that you wanted.

Secondly, people tend to work better when they're doing something that they want to do. Individuals who choose to do something voluntarily are more enthusiastic, and consequently more productive, more likely to do it well and happier overall.

Consequently, even if you do have a position in the organizational hierarchy that allows you to tell others to do something, you might be better off finding an alternative. Rather than exercising authority, it is better to exercise leadership and to work with people's own motivations. The subject of leadership is itself vast and isn't one that I intend to deal with in depth here. Suffice to say, a position of authority doesn't make you a leader: it does, however, confer on you legitimacy.

Legitimacy is important because it allows you to step forward as a leader; it allows you to create the right environment and remove blockages to learning and change. Legitimacy may also allow you to reward those who follow your leadership. We will return to leadership later.

Authority, leadership and legitimacy manifest themselves differently in different environments. This varies from country to country, from company to company and within companies. There's no guarantee that what works on a German factory production line will work in an American office.

Even in environments in which someone does exercise authority and people do what they're told, there's no monopoly on good ideas. Ideas on how to improve the product, the technology or the process can come from anywhere. Managers who rely on authority to get things done risk missing these ideas because individuals won't speak up and put their ideas forward – and even if they do speak up, the manager may not have time to listen.

This is part of the thinking behind the 'flat hierarchy' (something of a contradiction in terms) and 'empowerment' in the workforce. However sceptical we may be about management commitment and motivation for advocating empowerment, it is of itself a valid idea.

In trying to lead learning and change, we need to consider ourselves empowered – an individual who doesn't will find it hard to lead anything. We need to create change not through our own authority or through borrowing someone else's but, rather, through working with those around us who are receptive to new ideas. Not everyone will be receptive to our ideas, but some will. Sometimes it may seem like throwing mud at a wall: some will stick, some will fall off – you can't tell in advance what will stick and what won't.

On occasions, authority can be useful: sometimes it can be useful to stop people doing something, to ensure that someone takes a specific action or to do something quickly in a crisis. Authority isn't a cure, though, and in many cases you'll find that you don't have the authority to take your desired action. The tools of leadership and legitimacy are more useful and can be acquired and exercised wherever you are in the company hierarchy. If you're in a position to exercise authority, use it judiciously. You can order someone to change, but you can't guarantee that they will, and you certainly can't order anyone to learn.

1.8 Practical Theory

"There is nothing so practical as a good theory"
Kurt Lewin (1890–1947), psychologist, inventor of *action research* and change theorist

During the course of this book, we will look at a variety of theories, mostly about learning and change. For a book that tries to have a practical bent, this might seem unusual. In fact, there are two good reasons to look at theories even when we're trying to be practical.

Firstly, theories allow us to consider and examine the world in ways that are otherwise very difficult. By abstracting away much detail and considering a few key factors, they allow us to look at the issue in hand in a new and potentially revealing way. This provides a grounding for conducting learning and change in practice.

Secondly, we all struggle to understand people and events around us. This understanding then informs our own actions. In order to make sense of the world, we all use our own set of theories. Some of these will be explicit and we will know that we're using a theory; other theories will be implicit and unspoken. By looking at different theories we open our minds to different models of the world: if these models make sense to us, they will inform our actions in the future and change the way in which we act.

Studying theories of learning and change should better prepare us for practising learning and change. Hopefully some of the theories given here will change the way you see the world and might prompt you to discard some of the theories that you're already using. This is the start of the change process.

Terminology

This book draws on a large variety of sources from software development, computing and information technology in general, and from the business world. These sources use different terms for what are essentially the same things. Although sometimes these terms refer to different things, the underlying concept is, from our point of view, the same.

For simplicity, I'm going to consider the terms *Information Technology* (IT), *Information Systems* (IS) and *Information Technology and Communications* (ITC) as synonymous. Some of the authors quoted discuss *Management Systems* (MS) and *Management Information Systems* (IMS). Strictly speaking, the terms refer to subsets of information systems, but the difference isn't important for our purposes.

This book is primarily concerned with the development of software; that is, software development. This is a discipline necessary to all kinds of IT(C) and it is a subset of IT. On the whole, I will use the term *software development* when I am specifically discussing some aspect of the development process and *IT* when I am discussing the wider dimensions.

In addition, I will use the terms *firm*, *company* and *corporation* as synonyms. While these terms usually refer to profit-making entities, for our purposes I include not-for-profit organizations within them.

The word *organization* is a more flexible term that may refer to a large multinational corporation, a division of a large company, a branch office or a single team, depending on the context or your own terms of reference.

> Finally, despite my personal dislike for the term *user* – which has too many negative overtones – there's no more suitable term in widespread use to describe the people who make use of our software. The term *customer* can sometimes substitute, but customers and users aren't always the same.

1.9 Begin with Yourself

The primary objective of this book is to give you, the reader, an understanding of how you can help software development teams improve their ability to learn, allow them to change the way in which they work and adopt a more Agile approach to development. During the course of the book, we will look at various theories of learning and change, we will discuss examples of learning and change and we will suggest some actions that you can take to help teams learn and change.

Naturally, this leads to the following questions: *Where do I begin? What do I do first?*

The answer is: *Begin with yourself.* First seek to improve your own learning and understanding of the situation in which you find yourself.

We will return to this theme again and again, because if you can't improve yourself, then you can't improve your team. Conversely, if you can improve yourself, then you're in a better position to help others and act as a role model and mentor.

Rather than wait until you've finished reading this book, I suggest that you start now. As you read the book, think about the ideas and suggestions presented and how they apply to you and your team.

In order to do this, you'll need to take some time to think about this book, your team, your organization and your current environment. You might like to schedule some time during the week when you can do this. You might also like to undertake your thinking with a partner – in which case the thinking becomes a discussion. It isn't essential that your partner also reads this book, but he or she should share your interest.

If you don't have a partner to work with, you can still do this by yourself. Keeping a personal journal, or diary, can be an effective mechanism for ordering and recording your thinking. You could use an online Blog for the same purposes, but if you do be aware that others – including your team-mates – might read your thoughts. You may not have anything to hide, but knowing that your thoughts are private allows you to express yourself in different ways and to speculate. Alternatively, you could try drawing mind-maps, talking to the dog or just taking long thoughtful baths. Whatever you do, try to think!

Try to think about your organization and environment. Do you understand what the organization is trying to achieve? Or what's happening around you? Or why recent decisions have been made?

Hopefully, such thinking will lead you to inquire more deeply into what's happening. To improve your understanding, ask questions of people around you. It might be that what you think is the case isn't, so it's best not to jump to assumptions. Recognize that different people see situations in different ways: there are multiple ways to see things, so there's no single right way to do things.

In trying to understand the world around you, it is probable that you'll find the need to give up some of your current beliefs and understanding of the way in which the organization operates. This is normal – the process of learning also entails the process of *unlearning*. If you aren't challenging what you think you know, then you aren't learning anything.

Taken together, the process of thinking, inquiring, learning, unlearning and understanding is called *reflection*. It simply means taking time out to think about what's happening.

At some points in the book, I will suggest questions that you might like to think about. These are intended to help you relate the material to your organization. Hopefully, this will help improve your understanding and reveal opportunities.

To help others learn and change, you have to begin with yourself. Nobody can tell you what to do; nobody can give you a recipe to improve your team – you have to decide what you want to do and you have to make it happen. This requires thought and understanding.

1.10 The Organization of the Book

By now, I hope you have a good idea of what this book is going to talk about. We will return to several key points:

- In the modern economy, knowledge is key to all business activities; knowledge can give your business competitive advantage and greater profits.
- Software development is a knowledge-based industry and the workers are knowledge workers.
- Knowledge results from learning and acting on that learning, which involves change.
- Without change we can't capitalize on what we learn, and without change we can't continue our learning.
- Agile methods are rooted in organizational learning; in order to become Agile, we must change the way in which we do things – in order to stay Agile and improve further, we must learn.

Figure 1.2 shows graphically the philosophy behind this book, with learning at the heart. Initially, we start by seeding and motivating learning: most good software developers are eager learners. Frustration sets in when barriers are encountered. Many of these barriers come from implicit assumptions and the

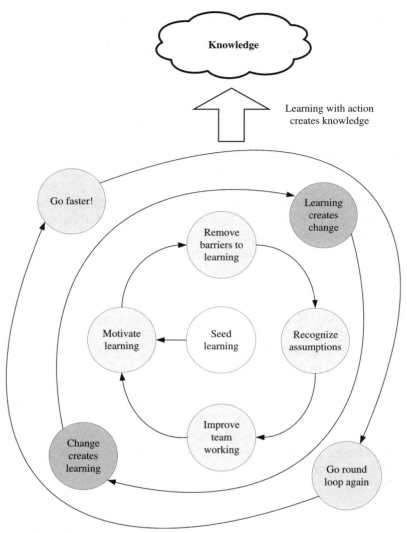

Figure 1.2 The philosophy of the book.

team environment: recognizing these assumptions speeds up and improves the learning process. Active learning leads to and requires change: this change then creates learning, so establishing a virtuous circle of improvement. The alternative is a vicious circle of decay, in which learning without change leads to frustration and delay.

Once we're learning and changing, we need to keep doing it. We can't simply declare our work done and stop. We need to do it again and again, each time getting better and faster. And out of this work knowledge is created.

In the chapters that follow, we will explore these points in more depth and consider what you can do to learn, how you can improve your organizational learning, how learning can create change and how to manage change to create learning.

We start by looking at Agile software development in Chapter 2. Those of you who are already familiar with Agile may prefer to browse this chapter rather than read it in full. If you are new to the ideas of Agile, you should read the chapter more thoroughly.

The next three chapters look at knowledge and learning in more detail. Those anxious to start doing something soon might want to skip ahead and read Chapter 4, which discusses different types of learning and how we can enhance learning in our organizations. Chapter 5 expands on this to look at learning in organizations, and specifically the ideas of Peter Senge.

Having grounded ourselves in knowledge and learning, in the second half of the book we turn our attention to change specifically. Chapter 6 starts by looking beyond development at the wider picture of business change, and considers how software requirements change and how IT changes the people who use it.

Chapter 7 considers how we can classify change so we can recognize different types of change, and Chapter 8 follows this up with some theories of change. Taken together, these chapters help us to understand the nature of change and why it is difficult.

Chapters 9 and 10 try to pull learning and change together by discussing what action we can take to create learning and change in our organizations.

If you're happy in your understanding of learning and change, then you might want focus on Chapters 3, 8 and 9, where most of the hands-on advice for day-to-day action can be found. Chapters 10 and 11 contain some more involved techniques for promoting improvement.

Finally, Chapter 12 pulls everything together and considers where you can start turning ideas into action.

Understanding Agile

"Agility is the ability to both create and respond to change in order to profit in a turbulent business environment."

Jim Highsmith (2002)

The first programmable computers appeared during the first half of the twentieth century. Programming them was a challenge, because nobody had ever done it before. As the capabilities of the machines expanded, more and more complex tasks were asked of them. By the late 1960s it was already apparent that large-scale programming wasn't easy. The challenge now lay in the complexity of the thing being built.

A NATO conference in 1968 coined the term *software crisis* to describe the problems that companies, governments and the military faced. The new industry responded by inventing software engineering and attempting to make programming into an engineering discipline. Since nobody really knew the right way to programme or manage a development effort, multiple methodologies and notations were proposed in an attempt to bring discipline and engineering rigour to the problem.

The crisis was never really resolved and after 20–30 years the term fell into disuse – after all, most crises last for hours, days or maybe months, not decades. But software engineering and methodologies stuck. The problem was that software projects were still unpredictable, still delivered late – if at all – and regularly over budget. If anything, the problem had got worse because computers, and thus software, were far more widespread than in 1968.

Changing Software Development: Learning to Become Agile   Allan Kelly
© 2008 John Wiley & Sons, Ltd.

In the late 1990s a new stream of thought appeared. Several different figures in the software development community came up with similar ideas at about the same time. Kent Beck, Ward Cunningham, Alistair Cockburn, Jim Highsmith, Ken Scwaber and others proposed a new breed of 'lightweight' methodologies.

Many of the lightweight proponents had previously been involved in the software Patterns community, and before that the object orientation movement. This meant that many of them knew each other and had been exposed to similar ideas and thinking. For example, Cunningham's EPISODES pattern language had lain the basis for eXtreme Programming five years before Beck published *eXtreme Programming eXplained*.

It quickly became apparent that although some of the details differed, the new methodologies had a lot in common. Eventually, many of the key movers in the lightweight methodology movement came together and proposed the Agile manifesto (see topic box). So Agile software development was born. The proposed methodologies still existed in their own right, but they had a collective name.

A Manifesto for Agile Software Development

We're uncovering better ways of developing software by doing it and helping others do it. Through this work we have come to value:

- Individuals and interactions over processes and tools.
- Working software over comprehensive documentation.
- Customer collaboration over contract negotiation.
- Responding to change over following a plan.

That is, while there's value in the items on the right-hand side, we value the items on the left-hand side more.
Source: http://www.agilemanifesto.org/

2.1 The Roots of Agile Thinking

The thinking behind Agile methodologies isn't hard to find. Indeed, much Agile thinking is simply common sense or good management practice. In the pursuit of engineering rigour, modern management thinking had sometimes been overlooked.

The first thing that the lightweight methodologies did was to simplify the development activities. The previous generation of methodologies had tackled complexity with complexity, so simplicity was high on the list of influences.

Agile development has also been influenced by the arguments of Phil Crosby (*Quality is Free*[1]) and W. Edwards Deming (see the topic box). Agile developers seek to find faults early in the development cycle. In doing so, costly and disruptive re-work can be eliminated from the later stages of development.

The next aspect to be embraced concerned the dirty little secret of software engineering: people. While architecture, engineering, process, notation and tools tend to dominate the literature and teaching of software engineering, there has always been an understanding that it is people who make the real difference. Even by the 1960s, it was apparent that some programmers were simply far more productive than others.

Authors such as Fred Brooks, Tom DeMarco, Timothy Lister and Gerald Weinberg have long written about how to get the most from programmers and teams. Most of this writing parallels similar ideas in common management literature, such as the work of Peter Drucker. However, organizations frequently fail to put this advice into practice, preferring instead to buy bigger machines, fancy tools and brand name methodologies. The Agile manifesto and methodology writers took notice of these ideas and put people centre stage in lightweight methodologies.

Other ideas that had been seen to work found their way into the mix too. The Agile development cycle looks a lot more like the classical maintenance cycle than the waterfall model often used for new development work. Maintenance work was often considered the poor relation of big new developments, but it had a better delivery record. Fixing faults and adding new features to software that already works entails less risk than developing something new.

Similarly, prototyping had long been practised, but it was often considered bad form to evolve prototypes and so they were usually thrown away. In the original edition of *The Mythical Man Month*,[2] Fred Brooks said:

> "Where a new system concept or technology is used, one has to build a system to throw away . . . The only question is whether to plan in advance to build a throwaway . . .
>
> Hence, plan to throw one away; you will anyhow."

Less well known is his change of mind 20 years later. In the anniversary edition,[3] he said:

> "This I now perceive to be wrong, not because it is too radical, but because it is too simplistic. . . .
>
> The biggest mistake in the 'Build one to throw away' concept is that it implicitly assumes the classical sequential waterfall model of software construction . . . derive[d] from the GANTT chart layout"

[1] See Crosby (1980).

[2] See Brooks (1975).

[3] See Brooks (1995).

So Agile has embraced prototyping too. Teams develop some aspect of the product, show it to customers, listen to the feedback and then decide what features to develop next. If customers don't like a feature, it might be dropped or replaced. Outside of the software community, this approach has been described as *expeditionary marketing*.[4]

The thinking that started to emerge from all these influences has much in common with *Lean manufacturing* and later *Lean product development*. This is hardly surprising, since Deming's theories had their greatest influence in Japan, the home of Lean manufacturing, and specifically the Toyota Production System. Not only do Agile and Lean share a common ancestor, but Lean has influenced Agile and, as we shall see, Agile can be considered a type of Lean.

Hidden away inside all of these influences was one more: *learning*. It was implicit in Deming's points, it explained why some people and teams excelled, and it was why refinement through iteration and market testing worked. Learning was what the lightweight proponents had been doing when they joined the object-oriented movement and when Patterns emerged from object-orientation. The emergence of Agile from Patterns was a repeat of the process.

Deming's Fourteen Points

W. Edwards Deming was an American statistician, who used statistical techniques during the Second World War to improve American manufacturing output. Following the war, he taught the same techniques to Japanese managers and engineers.

Deming proposed 14 points that he thought would lead to quality improvement:

1. Create consistency of purpose.
2. Adopt new philosophy.
3. Cease dependency on inspection.
4. End awarding business on price.
5. Improve constantly the system of production and service.
6. Institute training on the job.
7. Institute leadership.
8. Drive out fear.
9. Break down barriers between departments.
10. Eliminate slogans and exhortations.
11. Eliminate work quotas or work standards.

---

[4] See Hamel and Prahalad (1991).

12. Give people pride in their job.
13. Institute education and a self-improvement programme.
14. Put everyone to work to accomplish it.

2.2 Positioning Agile

Agile software development started as a term for a collection of lightweight methodologies, such as eXtreme Programming (XP), Crystal, Scrum, Dynamic Systems Development Method (DSDM) and others. It has evolved into something more than that. Agile embodies a philosophy about software development, a set of common beliefs and some practices. The methodologies themselves are more prescriptive about how development is done and contain specific practices.

For example, teams that follow Scrum are Agile, but not all Agile teams are Scrum teams; the same goes for other teams following XP or Crystal. Other teams will have found their own ways of working, using the Agile philosophy and practices that work for them. Figure 2.1 demonstrates how specific methodologies are refinements of Agile.

Agile itself is a form of Lean. Many organizations outside of software development have applied Lean principles to improve their processes and practices. While Lean recommends a few specific practices – for example, value stream mapping – it is itself a way of thinking about business processes and it embodies certain ideas and concepts. These concepts lie behind much of the Agile philosophy.

Agile teams are practising a form of Lean. However, it doesn't follow that all Lean teams are Agile, because some teams may find alternative solutions that are compatible with Lean thinking but not present in Agile practices. For example, a high-performing Lean team may decide to abandon the iteration model if it finds a better model for its environment.

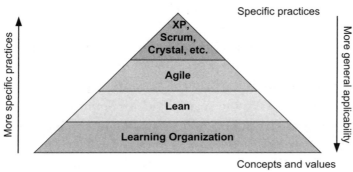

Figure 2.1 How methods stack up.

Lean in turn is an embodiment of many ideas found in organizational learning. Through learning, individuals and teams can improve their working environment. Organizational learning, however, prescribes even fewer practices than Lean, much of the literature on learning being rooted in principles, values and ideas. Each learning organization needs to find its own way to learn. Learning occurs in different ways in different companies and in groups within organizations.

For Lean to be implemented successfully, teams must learn, and Lean thinking embodies some specific practices to enhance team learning. So, all Lean teams must be learning teams, but not all learning teams are Lean teams.

There are few hard and fast practices that are shared between learning organizations. Consequently, we can't tell if an organization is learning just by looking at the practices. This couldn't be said about an XP team, which is defined by the XP practices that it's using.

Still, all Agile teams – whether following XP, Scrum, Crystal, some other process or one that they created themselves – need to learn. Problems occur when teams adopt practices without a learning culture. When this happens, teams can't adapt to changing environments and team members are denied a voice in change.

The Principles behind the Agile Manifesto

We follow these principles:

- The highest priority is to satisfy the customer through early and continuous delivery of valuable software.
- Welcome changing requirements, even late in development. Agile processes harness change for the customer's competitive advantage.
- Deliver working software frequently, from a couple of weeks to a couple of months, with a preference for the shorter timescale.
- Business people and developers must work together daily throughout the project.
- Build projects around motivated individuals.
- Give individuals the environment and support they need, and trust them to get the job done.
- The most efficient and effective method of conveying information to and within a development team is face-to-face conversation.
- Working software is the primary measure of progress.
- Agile processes promote sustainable development.
- The sponsors, developers and users should be able to maintain a constant pace indefinitely.
- Continuous attention to technical excellence and good design enhances agility.

- Simplicity – the art of maximizing the amount of work not done – is essential.

- The best architectures, requirements and designs emerge from self-organizing teams.

- At regular intervals, the team should reflect on how to become more effective, and then tune and adjust its behaviour accordingly.

Source: http://www.agilemanifesto.org/principles.html

2.2.1 What is Lean?

The term *Lean* was originally used to describe a form of working found at Japanese manufacturing plants, and specifically at Toyota. Lean embraces ideas such as *Just In Time* (*JIT*) production, *stockless production*, *kanban* cards and *Kaizen* improvement processes.

Fundamentally, Lean is driven by a focus on removing waste, a belief that those who do the work are best placed to improve the system and an unremitting drive to continually improve and remove more waste. As one source of waste is removed another becomes visible; when that is removed a third is revealed; and so on.

The original work on Lean concentrated on *Lean manufacturing* as derived from the *Toyota Production System*.[5] While software developers can learn much from Lean manufacturing, a better source is *Lean product development*. This also derives from Toyota, in this case the *Toyota Product Development System*. While it embodies the same principles and values as Lean manufacturing, it is better described as *knowledge-based product development*.[6]

More recently, the authors responsible for introducing the world to Lean manufacturing have attempted to apply the same ideas more widely. In the book *Lean Solutions*,[7] they show how Lean thinking can be applied to healthcare, retail, transport and other business sectors.

Examples of Lean teams and organizations striving to be Lean exist outside of software development. While Toyota is the obvious example, less well-known examples are the Seven-Eleven and Tesco retail chains. It is possible for elements or teams within a business to be Agile or Lean without the whole organization being so. Such differences can be the source of friction.

Mary and Tom Poppendieck have applied Lean thinking directly to software development.[8] Rather than suggest Lean as another development methodology, the Poppendiecks suggest that it expands the theoretical foundations of

---

[5] See Womack, Jones and Roos (1991).

[6] See Kennedy (2003).

[7] See Womack and Jones (2005).

[8] See Poppendieck and Poppendieck (2003, 2007).

Agile and provides thinking tools to help translate Lean principles into Agile practices.

All Lean organizations are by definition learning organizations, because the process of identifying and removing waste requires the organizations to learn. However, not all learning organizations are Lean – both the Royal Dutch/Shell oil company and the US Marine Corps have been called learning organizations, yet neither is Lean – let alone Agile.

2.2.2 What is a Learning Organization?

The idea of learning organizations appeared in the 1980s and grew during the 1990s. The concept is somewhat nebulous, and if you ask different people, you're likely to get different answers. Chapter 5 goes into more detail about learning organizations and organizational learning.

It is reasonably straightforward to define an organization. In this context, such an organization is usually a company, a department or a team. The organization itself doesn't need to be commercial: it could be a government unit, a hospital or a charity.

On first consideration, learning is also quite straightforward. Learning is the process by which we acquire new information and knowledge. However, as this book argues, merely learning facts is of little use. For learning to be truly useful, it must also lead to some action and some change.

While each of us can learn in our own particular way and act on whatever learning we like, things get more difficult when we consider learning at the group level. Not everyone will recognize the same facts, draw the same conclusions or decide on the same course of action. And just because some action is decided on doesn't mean that the action is taken.

To build on and act on what they learn as a group, learning organizations need mechanisms. Learning and acting as a group can be more difficult than working individually. As individuals, we all know how to learn and how to think; yet doing the same thing in a group can be more difficult. Members of a group need to find new ways of learning and collectively thinking together. This is what distinguishes a *group* from a *team*.

Agile teams need to overcome the obstacles that stop them learning together. As the team improves, some problems will be beyond the boundaries of the team. In order to improve further, they will need to spread the message so that those around them become Agile too. Over time, Agile will spread out from software development to the wider enterprise.

2.3 Common Practices of Agile Teams

There is a set of common practices found in most of the Agile methodologies. These practices embody Lean principles, but are ready-made for teams to adopt without needing to re-invent existing work. These practices are interlocking and tend to support one another. Several of the practices could be placed in more than one of the categories outlined in the following sections.

2.3.1 Quality

As already noted, Agile development fully embraces Philip Crosby's *Quality is Free* argument. By maintaining a high standard of work during development, faults (bugs) are significantly reduced, thereby reducing the amount of re-work required. In software development, the need to re-work adds three types of costs: firstly, all work must be extensively tested; secondly, once problems are found, re-work takes time in addition to the original work; and, thirdly, re-work is disruptive.

Many software projects focus on completing the required feature set and then declare themselves 'feature complete' or 'code complete'. At this point, software testing begins in earnest. Each fault that is found must be fixed or a lower quality accepted. Yet because there's no way of knowing how many bugs will be found – let alone how long it will take to fix them – it's impossible to predict when the software will be finished.

In such conditions, the number of bugs found may simply be a function of the number of testers employed. More testers report more bugs, requiring more work. All too often, the only way to resolve the situation is to accept a lower standard of work. This adds more costs – and this time the costs are borne by the customer who has to work with the product. Eventually, this cost will be passed back to the producer in terms of lost orders or lower prices.

In order to reduce re-work and improve quality, Agile software development teams adopt a number of specific practices:

- Code reviewing: it has long been known that one of the most successful ways of finding faults is for other developers to review the code that is written.

- Pair programming: this is an extreme form of code reviewing. Two programmers share one keyboard and screen. They discuss the design and the approach: while one codes, the other reviews, and periodically the pair switch roles.

  Pair programming is controversial for two reasons. Firstly, sceptics doubt productivity claims, because both programmers could be writing code separately. It is hard to quantify the productivity benefits of pair programming. However, anecdotal evidence supports the assertion that quality is improved and suggests that two programmers working together are more focused and less prone to interruptions.

  Secondly, developers accustomed to working alone find it difficult to accept a co-developer. This problem is compounded on small teams (less than four developers), where there is less variety in the partners available. In small teams, social interactions are the dominant factor in deciding whether or not pair programming works.

- *Automated testing:* Wherever possible, developers and testers seek to introduce automated tests to the system under development. Such tests can be run many times a day with little or no overhead added to the workload. Such tests serve not only to check new features added to the system but also to ensure that changes don't break existing features.

- *Automated unit tests/Test-driven Development* (TDD): Unit testing is a practice performed by developers on their own code. This is done before the code is submitted to the testing group for formal testing. However, in some environments unit tests have been skipped or performed on an *ad hoc* basis.

  Agile development not only insists on developer unit testing, but also recommends that such testing is automated and that the test is added to the reoccurring test suite. TDD – also called 'test first development' – goes further and recommends that developers write tests before writing any feature code.

- *Continuous integration:* All large systems are developed in many small pieces, which are brought together to deliver the final system. Naturally, these pieces need to work together when finally delivered. However, on some projects these pieces are kept separate until late in the project. Agile practice is to integrate all pieces of software at the earliest opportunity, in order to detect any conflicts or problems. Coupled with an automated test suite, this becomes a powerful quality assurance check.

- *Quality before features:* In the event that a fault slips past these various checks and is detected after the code has entered the main code base, then teams should fix the fault before continuing with new features.

- *Malleable design:* Agile teams take a different approach to design – as described below. This approach helps teams to maintain the internal quality of the software.

Taken together, and with other quality assurance practices, these techniques can eliminate the final phase of a project where developers race to fix bugs to allow the software to ship. Such 'bug-fixing' phases – which may be euphemistically called 'testing' or 'stabilization' – are unpredictable, with deadlines missed more often than not.

By following these practices, the software can be kept in a state where it is ready to be released without a big bug-fixing phase. Some specified features may be missing, but those that are implemented are completed and require no more work.

2.3.2   Business Priorities

During the software development process, Agile teams involve customers as much as possible. Sometimes actual customers are seconded to the team; on other occasions, proxy customers play the role. Proxy customers are usually either product managers or business analysts, depending on the nature of the software products.

The role of customers is the source of business knowledge on the project and the authority on what work is undertaken. They are responsible for devising the requirements, prioritizing the work, elaborating on the requirements during development and accepting the solution delivered by developers. By keeping the voices of the customers inside the development process, the team is better informed about the requirements, ambiguities and disputes are resolved sooner and teams are more focused.

Consequently, customers are much more involved with Agile teams than is traditionally the case, and they carry a heavy workload. If the role isn't adequately staffed, the customer can become the bottleneck for development or suffer overwork and burnout.

2.3.3   Design

In traditional software methodologies, the design phase of a project occupied a large chunk of time at the start of the project. This approach has been characterized as *Big Up-Front Design (BUFD)*. During this time, designers and architects evaluate the requirements, technology and possible future demands on the system. They then produce a set of designs describing how the software is to be built. Sometimes these designers will then switch to implementing their designs, or they may turn the designs over to programmers to implement them.

Unfortunately, designs completed before coding began are never perfect and usually change during implementation. Unforeseen requirements emerge, technical restricts are found, developer ability varies and new insights offer better design solutions.

Traditional development techniques – as described in textbooks – demand up-front requirements and coding. However, in reality many software projects start with vague requirements, an uncertain future and very little design. Those paying for the project want to see people coding and software being produced. Time is often limited, so coding begins before any design is available. In polite circles this has been called *No Up-Front Design (NUFD)* – and in less polite circles as *hacking*.

In both the textbook cases and in reality, the software design emerges over time, and in both cases the internal quality suffers. The code quality declines as requirements change, team members come and go, and short cuts are taken to meet deadlines. Developers often conduct experiments in code to learn about what works and what doesn't. This is necessary in order to allow a design to emerge and create insights into better design, but it also detracts from consistency and leaves some failed experiments in the code.

Such factors mean that a perfect design isn't possible. Nor is it desirable, because if developers acted to rectify each of these failings when it first appeared, then projects would never complete. Fortunately, software code doesn't need to be perfect to work, but each time a compromise is made the internal quality of the code suffers. Over time, this loss of quality makes the code more difficult to maintain and develop.

Agile software developments starts with several assumptions that lead to a different approach to design:

- Requirements are at best vague and at worst unknown.
- Change is valuable and should be accommodated.
- Delivering working software is the highest priority.
- Quality is important both internally and externally.
- Design is emergent.

Given these assumptions, Agile teams typically set out to develop *the simplest thing that could work* given the current known requirements. This often leads to a NUFD approach. Alternatively, because doing the simplest thing isn't always simple, teams may engage in a little design and planning – sometimes called *Rough Up-Front Design (RUFD)*.*

By forgoing BUFD, teams can start to deliver working software earlier in the project and allow business value to be recognized. However, teams still have to cope with internal quality, which if ignored will – over time – hinder development and affect external quality.

To address this problem, Agile teams use a technique called *refactoring*. This is a process whereby developers revisit existing code and improve the internal qualities without affecting the external functionality. At first sight this may look like re-work, but it isn't, because refactoring is triggered not by failure of the code itself but by a change in the surrounding environment, usually as a result of changes in requirements.

Software is by its nature soft. Unlike hardware, software should be easy to change. However, increasing complexity in a software system increasingly makes it difficult to change the software. Accepting emergent design and practising refactoring allows teams to keep software malleable. This in turn improves the team's ability to deliver.

2.3.4   Predictable Schedules and Time Boxes

Agile methods deal with schedule overrun by working in short time-boxed iterations. An iteration may last from one week to three months, although two

---

* I am indebted to Kevlin Henney for introducing me to the terms BUFD, NUFD and RUFD.

or three weeks is more usual. All iterations are the same length of time, and iterations are not extended. Unlike traditional development where schedules could be lengthened, the iteration length never varies – hence the term *time-boxed*.

Each iteration starts with a planning meeting and ends with a release of working software. Work that won't fit into a single iteration is divided into smaller chunks and carried out over several iterations. Teams are encouraged to break all work down into small pieces that can be accomplished in a day or less with the desired quality. Individual pieces of work are self-contained entities that are either completed or not completed at the end of the iteration.

Teams transitioning to Agile development need to learn the skills of breaking work down into small chunks. This can be difficult at first and requires support from the customer, product manager or business analysts working with the team. Once mastered, this skill – combined with time-boxed iterations and high quality – is a powerful means of scheduling and tracking work.

At the end of each iteration, working software is delivered. For some teams, this means that the software is actually deployed to a live server for users to use: for other teams, the end of the iteration is an opportunity to show customers the new features of the software, receive feedback and adjust requirements and priorities.

2.3.5   Feedback and Communication

Modern software development efforts involve many different people in different roles. Having more people involved in a project means that more communication is needed. In particular, teams and individuals need to provide feedback to one another, so that corrective action and improvements can be made. Agile teams seek to improve feedback and communication in a number of ways:

- Teams make use of various visual indicators to track progress and focus work efforts. White boards and index cards (or Post-It Notes) are used to display current status and work in progress to a wide audience.

- Iteration planning meetings are supplemented with short daily meetings. These are held standing up to help keep them short, and they provide opportunities for team members to report on progress, focus on the work of the day and identify blocks.

- Short iterations allow teams to stay focused on the work in hand and make it easier to communicate progress.

- Iteration and project retrospectives (Chapter 11) provide teams with an opportunity to collectively reflect on the progress of the project and adjust their working practices and processes.

- Teams frequently present their work to customers who provide feedback on the software ('show and tell') – what they like, what they don't like and what new requirements they would like to see emerging.

2.3.6 The New Bargain

The practices of Agile software development represent a bargain between the business that wants the software and the team developing it. Both sides agree to do away with the illusions that have dominated traditional software development:

- That requirements could be known in advance.
- That documentation is complete.
- The illusion of SMOP:[9] programming is complex and the detail in particular is difficult.
- Control: work estimates, GANTT and PERT charts may appear to show a project under control, but this is seldom the case.

With these illusions out of the way, the business and the development team enter into a new agreement. The business agrees to:

- Work closely with the development team to define requirements and guide work.
- Trust the developers to do the best work possible and allow time for quality to be built into the system.
- Provide the resources (tools, space, cooperation etc.) needed to build the system.

In return, the development team agrees to:

- Only work on features that the business actually wants.
- Allow the business to prioritize.
- Deliver working software early and often.
- Work to unlock the greatest business value first and mitigate risks.

The new bargain removes defences behind which both sides have traditionally hidden. Instead, it creates an environment that demands more from both sides. The new environment is more productive, because it more accurately reflects what actually happens and allows conflicts to be resolved within the system rather than destroying the system.

---

[9] The acronym 'SMOP' stands for 'Small Matter of Programming'.

An Example of an Agile Process: Blue-White-Red

Blue-White-Red is a simple Agile system, invented by Liz Sedley and myself, for a London company that was transitioning to Agile development. The system was mainly derived from XP with Scrum influence and was modified as we went along.

The whole system revolved around a large magnetic white board, upon which index cards were placed to represent work. The cards themselves were blue, white or red. The board was marked with information such as the iteration deadline and a record of how much work had been done in previous iterations, and was divided into four columns: *work to do*, *in progress*, *waiting for test* and *completed work*.

Product managers still produced Product Requirements Documents (PRDs). Pieces of work from these documents, usually features, would be written on blue index cards. The information on these feature cards only needed to be brief – perhaps a title and a document section.

The nature of the product and the existing code base meant that one blue card usually represented more work than could be done in a short space of time. Developers would break the work down into a set of tasks written on white index cards. So for every blue feature card there would be multiple white task cards. The breakdown was usually done during the bi-weekly planning meetings. If the feature was very complicated or poorly understood, a special meeting might be held to discuss the work and break it down into task cards.

Developers could also add white task cards to the work pile if they felt that some piece of remedial work was needed – typically, this was larger refactorings.

In the bi-weekly planning meeting, the product manager would select the features to be implemented during the next iteration. During the iteration, the team would focus on only these features and their associated tasks. Other blue cards would be held offline in an index card box.

Work estimation was done in abstract numerical points. At first this caused some confusion, but teams quickly came to a shared understanding of how much work could be accomplished in a single point. Estimates usually ranged between half a point and two points. Occasionally, zero-point cards would be written to remind us of things, or for trivial tasks.

Although each team placed a slightly different value on a single point, we normally found that a card with a point value of more than two needed to be broken down further. We also found that the more words were used on a white card to describe the task, the more accurate was the estimate. Cards with brief descriptions were usually poorly understood and poorly estimated.

The first task in the planning meeting was to clear the board and count the point value of the cards completed in the previous iteration. This was recorded and used as a guide for the coming iteration's capacity. The team could accept slightly more points into the iteration than had been completed in the previous week on the understanding that some might not get done.

With blue cards and white cards prepared and our estimate of the work that could be done, the product manager would prioritize all the white cards. Developers would advise of any dependencies between cards, risks, opportunities and suchlike, but prioritization was the product manager's decision alone. All cards were prioritized in absolute order, so that it was clear which one was the top priority and which the last. No two cards were allowed the same priority. Once prioritized, they would be placed on the board in the *work to do* queue.

Each day, the team would hold a short stand-up meeting and select the cards they would work on from the *to do* queue. Some developers would choose to pair on some work, but we didn't pair all the time. If work was completed without pairing, it would be subject to a short desk-based code review before checking into source code control.

Developers tried to write unit tests for the new features. However, due to the existing legacy code base this wasn't always possible. There were no unit tests for code that already existed, so refactoring existing code was difficult. All unit tests were run each night after the nightly build was completed. Should the build or any tests fail, the whole team received mail and the first person in began to investigate the failure.

Each team had a software tester, who was responsible for accepting a completed white card. When the developer felt that a card was complete, it would be moved to the *waiting for test* column on the whiteboard and the developer would take another card. Only when the tester was satisfied that the work was completed would it be marked and moved into the *completed* column.

Testers had a variety of ways of testing cards: they could perform a manual test, they might ask to verify that the unit tests were working and they might ask for proof that the code had been reviewed. If they were not satisfied, or a defect was found, then the card would move back to the *in progress* queue, with a high priority.

Finally, if a fault did slip into the system, or was reported by another team and was added to the team's workload, it would be written up on a red card. Red cards automatically took priority as the next piece of work to be started. Unfortunately, the nature of the system meant that it was difficult to eliminate such tasks, but over time the number did fall.

Several projects successfully used this process and each team modified it in different ways. No team was able to eliminate all manual testing,

> because it wasn't possible to retrofit unit tests to parts of the legacy code base. Over time, unit test coverage increased, but never covered the whole application.

2.4 Applicability Outside of Software Development

Agile software development isn't always easy, but for those teams that master it the rewards are great. It is reasonable to ask: *Could Agile be applied to other domains?* The intuitive answer is Yes.

Such a company would be highly responsive to its customers: it would understand the core value of its product and most likely deliver products in incremental pieces, each addressing some part of the customers' need. Needless to say, quality would be high and the company would listen to feedback from customers and workers alike.

Implicit in this description is the need for the company to be a learning organization. Without the ability to learn, the firm would be deaf to feedback, unable to meet customer needs and unable to deliver the quality improvement necessary to maintain high quality.

Having defined what an Agile company would look like, the next question is: *Do any such companies already exist outside of the software world?*

This is a more difficult question to answer. While I'm aware of companies that fit this description, none of them would describe themselves as Agile. Instead, these companies and the commentators who describe them prefer to call them Lean or learning organizations. Examples might include Toyota, Dell, Southwest Airlines, the Tesco retail chain, the US Marine Corps and the Royal Dutch/Shell oil company. Learning organizations are as different as they're alike, and exist in many different industries and environments.

You might like to argue that these companies are Agile, but then they're also learning organizations and some are Lean. Because of the shared values inherent in Agile, Lean and learning organizations, it can be hard to draw a line between them.

While it might well be possible for non-software companies to be considered Agile, there is, for the moment, little point in adding another term when suitable ones are already in use. For the moment, Agile means *Agile software development*.

Whatever collective term we use to describe these companies, we need to remember that they're the exception. Most companies either don't try to reach these standards or fail to do so. For the companies that do succeed, the rewards are considerable.

2.5 Conclusion

Being an Agile software development team isn't about specific practices such as pair programming, or employing a certified Scrum master. It means being a learning organization. The true hallmark of an Agile team is that it learns and it changes. You can't achieve true Agility without learning.

You might be able to jump-start a team by adopting specific practices, but if you don't build in learning your agility will be fragile; most likely, it will depend on one or two individuals. The team may go through the motions of Agile development without understanding why, and will never develop its own Agile method to match your business needs.

True Agile software development is Lean development done by learning teams. It is unimportant whether it is done under the name of Crystal, XP, Feature-driven Development (FDD) or any other methodology. The rest of this book is aimed at helping make teams Agile through learning, and through sustaining that learning so that teams can continue to improve.

Knowledge

"Error 1: Not Developing a Working Definition of Knowledge
If knowledge is not something that is different from data or information,
then there is nothing new or interesting in knowledge management."
Liam Fahey and Larry Prusak (1998)

We don't know how many knowledge workers there are in the world today, but in 2003 Bill Gates claimed there were over 95 million such workers in America alone. So we know that there are a lot of knowledge workers. However, while we talk about knowledge a lot, it isn't always clear just what we're talking about.

Software engineers are accustomed to shunting bits and bytes about. We call this data, and we may even accept that this represents information, but is it *knowledge*? In fact, are there any real and important differences between data, information and knowledge? And are these differences of any importance to us when we develop software?

Unless we develop an understanding of what *knowledge* is, how can we even attempt to understand software development as a knowledge industry?

3.1 The Difference between Knowledge and Information

In everyday language data, information and knowledge tend to be interchangeable terms. Many dictionaries define each one in terms of the others. However,

Changing Software Development: Learning to Become Agile   Allan Kelly
© 2008 John Wiley & Sons, Ltd.

if there's no difference between these terms, what's the point of having three different words?

In fact, there are many more words that we could consider: *wisdom, skills, intelligence, proficiency* and *facts*, just to name a few. We could subdivide the whole concept of knowledge and information into even smaller chunks and ever increasing subtlety. It is possible to define a three-way division – *data, information* and *knowledge* – that's both useful and succinct, but we still need to distinguish between these three terms. We start with the working definitions provided by two of the leading writers on the subject of knowledge, Davenport and Prusak:[1]

- Data claims to be some objective facts about events.

- Information is a message intended to change the receiver's perception of something: it is the receiver rather than the sender who decides what the message means.

- Knowledge is a fluid concept, incorporating experience, values and the context that exists inside an individual's mind or in the processes and norms of an organization.

Another leading writer on the subject of knowledge is Ikujiro Nonaka; he assigns three attributes to knowledge:[2]

- Knowledge is about beliefs and commitment: it is a function of perspective and intention.

- Knowledge is about action: creating knowledge requires action and knowledge is embedded in our actions.

- Knowledge and information are about meaning and are context specific.

Later, Nonaka[3] extended these ideas to place knowledge within a concept called *ba*. *Ba* is a Japanese term used to describe the *space* in which knowledge exists. A single piece of information doesn't exist in isolation but, instead, within a space that contains experience, reflections and ideas, about events and people. While you can write down a simple fact, it is harder to capture the space it resides in, which is intangible. If you separate the fact from the *ba*, what you're left with is mere information.

For example, computer languages have their own *ba*. There's more to knowing a computer language than simply knowing the keywords and syntax. Each language has its own idioms and norms, which are more difficult to articulate than the keywords and syntax. Communities of people form around languages to share experience, practice and advance the understanding of the language. These communities have values, ethics and beliefs that influence the way in which the language is used.

Knowledge can be a delicate thing: if we don't use it, we forget it. So, we need to consider the environment in which we keep and grow our knowledge – some

[1] See Davenport and Prusak (2000).

[2] See Nonaka and Takeuchi (1995).

[3] See Nonaka (1998).

people like to refer to this as the *ecosystem*. Knowledge won't grow in a hostile environment; if we want knowledge to grow and spread, it must be supported and nurtured.

Again, knowledge differs from information. Knowledge is rooted in our beliefs and values; it is the result of our interpretation of events and as such depends on our perspective and our intentions. Information is more objective and less subjective.

As we have already suggested, knowledge also implies action: we use knowledge to create action. Information may rest passively – in, say, a book or a database – but knowledge is active: it is used and the use creates more knowledge. This also makes knowledge more delicate than information: stop using some knowledge and you risk losing it. The need for action also means that knowledge exists in the present and in the present context.

Knowledge doesn't automatically create action, nor do all actions create knowledge. In order to use knowledge meaningfully, and derive meaningful knowledge from action, we must engage in thinking. The connection between knowledge in our heads and physical action is the thinking process. Without conscious thought, knowledge remains passive.

To summarize, our working definition of knowledge has the following characteristics:

- Knowledge exists within an ecosystem that we will call *ba*.
- Knowledge is more than simply the possession of information: it implies action.
- Knowledge implies some act of creation, such as thinking.
- Knowledge exists in the present: its value may increase or decrease with time.

3.2 Knowledge into Action

The above definition of knowledge specifically included action, because without action we can have as much knowledge as we like, but it doesn't mean anything. Unfortunately, many organizations regularly have problems turning what they know into action.

We cut corners because we're rushed or because doing it right involves doing more work. Maybe the work is dirty – or nobody else does it right, so why bother? Or perhaps we think 'they want it done this way'. Sometimes our definition of 'the right way' isn't necessarily what others think is *the right way*'.

Software developers are not alone in this. Pick up a newspaper and you're sure to find a report of some incident that could have been avoided if people had only listened to advice from the government, from consultants or from the newspaper itself.

For example, in the manufacturing sector Toyota is widely admired and many companies seek to emulate the company's productivity and quality. In theory, this isn't difficult: Toyota's production methods are far from secret and they have opened their plants to suppliers and competitors alike. The company has been studied and documented for decades, business schools teach their ideas and at least one book on the topic is a bestseller.[4] The difficulty is not information on Toyota's practices: it is turning that information into lasting action.

This gap between what we know and how we act has been called the 'knowing–doing gap' and is the subject of a book by that name.[5] Frequently, individuals, teams and companies know things but don't act on them. For example:

- They know why product quality is low, but they don't fix it.
- They know customers aren't buying their product, but they keep making it.
- They know how to improve their operations, but they prefer to keep doing things the way they always did.

Thinking Point: What Do You Know That You Don't Act On?

Make a list of the problems and opportunities that you see in your organization and what you regard as the best thing to do. Now work out what stops you from turning this knowledge into action.

When you've done this, look at the list and see what assumptions you've made. Also look for ambiguities and generalizations – specifically anywhere you have written 'they' or 'them' – exactly whom do you refer to?

Try to remove any assumptions, ambiguities and generalizations – if you have to ask others to clarify and confirm things, then do so.

Many organizations fall into this trap to a greater or lesser degree. However, there are companies that do act on what they know and do improve. Perhaps surprisingly, the companies that close the gap don't seem to have any special secret ingredient, or magic bullet – they don't necessarily do anything other companies don't know about. What these companies do is to actually act on what they know. It's simple, really.

If we're to address *Drucker's challenge*, as set out in the introduction, it isn't sufficient to know what we must do; we must actually do it, and having done it we must find the next thing and implement that. There needs to be a constant learning and changing cycle. One of the barriers to improving software development – perhaps the biggest, in fact – is simply failure to act on what we know.

---

[4] See Womack, Jones and Roos (1991).

[5] See Pfeffer and Sutton (2000).

[6] Peters first found fame with *In Search of Excellence* (Peters and Waterman, 1991) and revisited many of the topics, including *bias for inaction* in *Re:Imagine!* (Peters, 2003).

The management writer Tom Peters[6] claims that successful firms have a *bias for action*; however, all too many firms have a *bias for inaction*. This is as true in software development firms as elsewhere.

There are plenty of books describing how best to run a software project. There are plenty of theories and case studies to draw on. And there's a whole science of organizational learning and knowledge management introduced here. Again, we see that information isn't the block.

Nor can we merely copy Toyota or Dell, or only implement the things that well-known writers such as Alistair Cockburn, Kent Beck or Martin Fowler think are a good idea: we need to move beyond the low-hanging fruit and find our own ideas.

3.3 Explicit and Tacit Knowledge

Knowledge itself can be subdivided into two types: explicit and tacit. We're aware of explicit knowledge: that is, *we know we know it*. Consequently, we can codify explicit knowledge and communicate it in books, manuals and working procedures, copy these documents, share them or store them in a library or database.

However, because we can codify this knowledge we can get a false sense of security: reading a copy of *The C++ Programming Language*[7] may look like learning C++, but it leaves much unsaid about the language and its idioms, styles and norms. Expecting someone to maintain a C++ program after reading a book, or even going on a short course, is about as reasonable as expecting someone who has been on a car maintenance course to change the tyres during an F1 pit stop.[8]

There's a second, more subtle, form of knowledge at work, which is *tacit knowledge*. This is more difficult to codify and write down. We normally learn it by some process of osmosis. Much of this knowledge is embedded in our work environment, culture or skills, or just the way we work. Often, we don't recognize that we know something special.

The classic example is riding a bike, an everyday thing that most people can do. However, nobody ever learned to ride a bike by reading a book – learning to ride a bike is a process where we learn through experience.

Tacit knowledge can be communicated and it can be taught, but the process of doing so operates at a more personal level. We can acquire tacit knowledge through personal experience, conversation and training courses – which often involve exercises to gain experience and conversations with others who are also learning or have already mastered the skill. Provided that you have the time and their permission, watching other people can help you to acquire tacit

[7] See Stroustrup (1997).

[8] Thanks to Alan Griffiths for this analogy (private correspondence).

knowledge, particularly if you can ask questions – so-called *legitimate peripheral participation*.

Acquiring and learning to use this knowledge requires time. We need to be immersed in it and let it lap around us. Eventually we may try to do something, and from this we learn some more. Again, we need time: time to observe, time to question, time to reflect, time to make mistakes and time to think.

Just because we can't write down our tacit knowledge doesn't make it any less valuable than explicit knowledge – quite the reverse. Because it is difficult to codify and communicate, tacit knowledge it is worth more than explicit knowledge.

Within corporations, we find tacit knowledge embedded in the company culture and 'the way we do things around here'. This can make it both harder and easier to change the way in which people do things. People have reasons for doing things in a particular way; there's knowledge behind their actions. If we don't appreciate why they do things in a particular way, then changing things will be harder and riskier. Conversely, where processes are tacit they can be easier to change because we only need to work with the people who undertake the processes. There's no official process manual to be changed through lengthy procedures.

Tacit knowledge is hard to codify, but it isn't always impossible to do so. Often, this involves a second person to help identify what's important and what's missing.

If we do try to write down everything we know, we face an additional problem: we know an awful lot of stuff. We know too much to write it all down: it would take too long to write, let alone read. So, what's worth writing down and what isn't? And who decides?

The difficulty of writing down tacit knowledge is one reason why so many requirements and specifications documents are inadequate. Such knowledge is like jelly: you can't nail it down; it isn't in the specification because it is hard to codify. Only when you come to use the specification do you find gaps that are hard to fill. Unlike specification documents, computer code is inherently explicit and any gaps or ambiguity will be exposed.

Did You Ever Hear the Story about the Photocopier?

Just about every modern office has a photocopier and most of us will have experienced the failure of the machine at some time or other. When a copier fails, it is a technical problem: we call out the engineer and expect them to fix the machine. The companies that employ these engineers want the engineers to fix the problem as quickly as possible, so they supply them with diagrams, fault-finding charts and other explicit documents to quickly fix those technical problems.

However, this is only part of the story. Julian Orr spent time with a group of copier engineers in Silicon Valley and he found that fixing a copier is a lot more complicated than you might think.

Many of the problems that engineers see aren't covered in the documentation, so the engineers need to find their own solutions. An engineer may have been called to fix a technical fault, but the cause of the fault might be very non-technical.

The engineers tell each other stories about individual machines, about different models of machine and about the companies where the machines reside. These *war stories* contain their knowledge of the machines.

The stories go further: when engineers encounter a particularly difficult problem, they create a story about the machine. Rather than following the purely logical process of checking individual parts of the machine or following a chart, they conduct tests. They will talk to the people who use the machine regularly. Over time, they will create a consistent story that helps them find the fault and the cause of the fault. Once done, the story will allow the engineers to share their experiences with others who may one day run into the same problem. Source: Orr (1990)

3.4 Sticky Knowledge

It is because knowledge is more than just information that it is important. If we treat knowledge as simply another form of information, we ignore its true value and risk losing it. For managers, it is the practical implication of this insight that makes knowledge important. Failure to recognize *knowledge* as distinct from *information* leads to problems.

Information can be bought and sold. The sum of just £1 buys a copy of the *Financial Times*, which is full of information. We can't treat knowledge in the same way. Sometimes knowledge stays in one place and refuses to move; at other times it flows right just where it wants to go. This has been characterized as 'sticky' and 'leaky' knowledge. Why some knowledge sticks and other knowledge leaks poses a 'knowledge conundrum', but managing this problem is key to managing knowledge.[9]

The Xerox PARC Story

The story of how Xerox PARC originally developed the graphical computer interface and how Apple built on this work for the MacIntosh is well known and shows many of the issues involved in knowledge management.

---

[9] For a full discussion of sticky and leaky knowledge, the knowledge conundrum and the Xerox PARC experience, see Brown and Duguid (2000).

The researchers at the Palo Alto Research Center (PARC), who developed graphical interfaces, the laser printer, network protocols and so on, were based in California. The development engineers who would turn these into commercial products were in Dallas, and the managers responsible for authorizing the programme and business strategy were located in New York.

Xerox gave demonstrations to Apple Computer in nearby Cupertino. The CEO of Apple and his engineers recognized the significance of the graphical user interface developed at PARC, and subsequently produced the Apple Lisa and MacIntosh.

While the knowledge at PARC was 'sticky' and failed to spread within Xerox, the same knowledge was simultaneously 'leaky' and spread easily to Apple a few miles away in Cupertino. Simply having the knowledge inside Xerox wasn't enough: it wasn't in the right place in the company, and the action needed to capitalize on the knowledge took place outside the company.

So why was it that the knowledge flowed so easily out of the organization? It seems that there were several factors. Firstly, Apple formed a strong, clear vision of what was possible. It wasn't necessary for Apple to acquire the technical blueprints of the Star microcomputer; all that was needed was a communicable vision.

The geographical proximity of Xerox in Palo Alto and Apple in Cupertino also helped. Scientists and engineers were able to meet and exchange ideas formally and informally, and many of them belonged to the same networks of practice. Proximity also made it easier for individuals to move from Xerox to Apple. The engineers at the two companies shared the same ecosystem – the same *ba*. Conversely, the Xerox engineers in Dallas and managers in New York lacked all these opportunities and existed in a different *ba*.

At the time, Apple was a young innovative company that had yet to experience business failures. It needed, and valued, a supply of new ideas. Ideas from PARC found a receptive home. Like Xerox, Apple's first attempt was a commercial failure, but after the Lisa failed Apple learnt and tried again with the Macintosh. In contrast, after the failure of the Star, Xerox didn't try again.

Indeed, Apple did nothing that Xerox couldn't have done itself: Alan Key (Chief Scientist at PARC) had a vision that was in fact stronger than Apple's. Kay's *Dynabook* vision influenced a generation of computer scientists and engineers.

By creating PARC in the first place, Xerox had already shown itself open to new ideas. The stream of pioneers who left Xerox to bring their ideas to market shows that their people were every bit as receptive as those at Apple. Xerox could, had it so chosen, have incubated Bob Metcalf (founder of 3COM), and Charles Geschke and John Warnock (the Adobe founders), but instead they left PARC to pursue their visions elsewhere.

The researchers' knowledge stuck in Palo Alto and never made it to the engineers in Dallas. Xerox did eventually produce a commercial product based on the work, but it wasn't a commercial success.

Nor did the knowledge reach the managers in New York, who had established PARC to research technologies for the company's long-term strategy. These managers didn't comprehend the implication of the technologies coming out of Palo Alto, and consequently the company failed to exploit its initial lead in these technologies.

Source: Brown and Duguid (2000)

3.5 Problems with Knowledge

Before we look at the role of knowledge in software development, it is worth considering the more general implications of the schism between *information* and *knowledge*. There are things you can do with information that you can't do with knowledge. For example, you can mass-produce information, but you can't mass-produce knowledge.

While we can identify these differences and discuss them one by one, we need to remember that knowledge is holistic. These issues are all interrelated and we can't simply fix one. Similarly, the management of knowledge is not separate from knowledge itself: knowing how to manage knowledge is knowledge itself.

3.5.1 Knowledge Can't be Mass-produced

Knowledge transfer is difficult – as Xerox found out. Information transfer is a known problem that is solved daily in millions of classrooms and electronic networks worldwide; but knowledge is entwined with beliefs and commitments that can't be transferred so easily, let alone mass-produced. However, we can produce, package and sell products based on our knowledge, we can embed our knowledge in products or we can use our knowledge to create new products.

We don't need to own knowledge in order to use it; one alternative is to rent the knowledge that we need. Organizations can hire knowledgeable consultants to assist them with some tasks; this doesn't mean that they acquire the knowledge automatically. One option is to have the consultant perform the task, and then when the task is done and the consultant leaves, the result of the knowledge remains. This is a direct use of a consultant. However, if we wish to perform the task again by ourselves, it is desirable to manage the consultant so that the knowledge is passed on.

Those consultants who endeavour to pass on knowledge, rather than just perform a task, come closer to being knowledge producers. Still, these firms can't mass-produce knowledge: managing the transfer process is a task in its own right. Likewise, as we have seen, even knowledge transfer within an organization requires careful management.

There are no *silver bullets* to bring about knowledge transfer – although this has not stopped countless vendors attempting to sell knowledge management tools. Foremost amongst these have been IT companies. While IT can automate routine processes and help capture information, it is a mistake to equate this with knowledge. No technology can replace humans, because humans can exercise judgement through their skills.

Still, this hasn't stopped companies from trying to use IT to store and produce knowledge: e-mail systems, collaborative software, databases and 'knowledge bases' are a few of the tools used. Simply installing the technology won't make knowledge flow and spread, and it certainly won't create new knowledge.[10]

What must be considered is the social dimension. Technology alone isn't enough to facilitate knowledge flows. Software can make the flow of information and knowledge easier, but it must be viewed in the social context.

3.5.2   Knowledge Flows

Although we talk of transferring knowledge, the transfer process can enrich both sides. Givers of knowledge will retain the knowledge that they had beforehand; they may even understand it better, having engaged in the transfer process. The knowledge receivers have not only increased their store of knowledge, but by combining it with their existing stock may have generated more knowledge.

In knowledge terms, there's no loss of knowledge: if anything, the total amount of knowledge has increased. From a business perspective there is a loss, as knowledge shared gives others opportunities and reduces your own options. After showing Apple their technologies, PARC hadn't reduced the stock of knowledge held by Xerox, but they had enabled a potential competitor in the shape of Apple. It was only because Xerox had failed to capitalize on its knowledge that Apple was able to.

(According to some reports, Xerox received Apple stock in return for demonstrating their technologies, so perhaps it wasn't a complete loss.)

In business, knowledge represents a potential advantage. Once Apple had this knowledge they were able to act, and in doing so they changed the playing field. Xerox had the same knowledge that they'd had before they shared any (less a few engineers), but the commercial environment had changed.

The important lesson from this tale is that knowledge doesn't respect organizational boundaries. It will flow as easily between different firms as it

---

[10] For a longer discussion on the pitfalls of using technology to manage knowledge, see Davenport and Prusak 2000).

will within an existing firm. The challenge for managers is to ensure that knowledge flows freely within their organization, and not out of it.

Effective knowledge transfer is itself a key skill. Even for firms that are regarded as good knowledge managers, such as Hewlett-Packard, there's a continual challenge – hence the much cited quote: 'if only HP knew what HP knows'.

3.5.3   The Uniqueness of Knowledge

Every time knowledge is transferred, it is changed. Rather than being digital in nature, it is analogue and, like a cassette tape, each copy is slightly different. The application of the individual's vision and values modifies the knowledge. This introduces a random variable that mutates the knowledge, for better or for worse.

The net effect is to create unique knowledge. In the same way that no two people ever see exactly the same rainbow, no two people will ever share exactly the same knowledge. However, they may see similar enough rainbows to compare notes; and where the vision is clear, distortion will be less.

The clearer and sharper the vision, the easier it will be to communicate and share. Alan Kay's vision of the Dynabook was clear enough to influence not just the scientists at PARC and Apple, but a whole generation of computer scientists and engineers.[11] Yet this exceptionally clear vision was still not enough for the Xerox managers, who observed the vision from a very different perspective – for them, the developments at PARC were passive information, not active knowledge.

The very uniqueness of knowledge makes it the ideal basis for giving a company a competitive advantage. Where a firm bases its competitive advantage on vision and knowledge, it can't be copied. Others can approximate it with similar vision and learning capabilities, but it will never be exactly duplicated.

3.5.4   Business Strategy and the Form of the Organization

If we accept that knowledge can't be mass-produced and can't be stored in a database, then we see the importance of individual knowledge. Knowledge exists inside an individual's head and is communicated from one individual to another; it can only be communicated if the individuals know one another.

Therefore the size of a knowledge-based corporation is limited by the ability of individuals to know other individuals in the same organization. Some writers have suggested that this limit is as low as 200–300 people.[12] Beyond

---

[11] Kay's vision was undoubtedly furthered by the novelist Douglas Adams (Adams, 1979), who independently envisaged a strikingly similar kind of *book* in the *Hitchhiker's Guide to the Galaxy* and other novels.

[12] See Davenport and Prusak (2000).

this size, firms will see rapidly diminishing returns on their knowledge base. Corporations encountering this limit need to adapt their strategy accordingly. Some companies may accept this limit, while others look for ways to continue growing. One possibility is to break the business into a set of smaller units, each with its own knowledge. But then we need to find a way of helping these units work together; otherwise, they might as well be separate organizations.

The future knowledge-based economy may well consist of a large number of small to medium-sized firms, each with its own knowledge base providing core competencies. Since new product development frequently requires skills and knowledge that can't be provided by one such firm, these firms would need to cooperate with one another.

At each level of organization, the key is cooperation. In the small firm, the cooperation is between individuals. In the network model, it is between firms; and in the corporate model, it is between units within a firm.

Clearly, knowledge-rich organizations such as HP, Southwest Airlines and SAS Institute have managed to grow beyond 300 people, so the ceiling isn't absolute, but breaking through this limit requires skilful management. The key point is that techniques and practices used in a small firm don't scale to large firms, thereby creating another set of problems for us to tackle.

3.6 Where is Knowledge in Software Development?

The whole software development process is an attempt to codify knowledge. We start with some vague idea of what a system should do and, through successive processes of specification, design, implementation and testing, try to turn that knowledge into a useful working model.

Our problem is that knowledge is difficult to codify. As software developers, our skills and knowledge reside in our own domain, our own field of *ba*. We take a problem domain, with its own *ba* field, and attempt to produce a product that

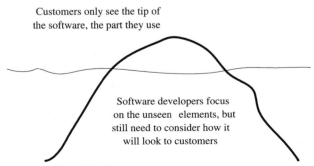

Figure 3.1 Software is like an iceberg.

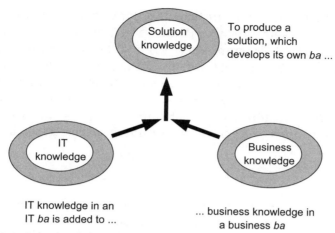

Figure 3.2   Solutions develop their own *ba*.

will exist in both domains, satisfying the requirements of the problem domain while meeting the engineering requirements of our own solution domain. (Chapter 4 will look more closely at the different domains.)

Software needs to exist simultaneously in these two environments. Commercially, it is the part seen by customers that tends to get priority. However, this often represents only the tip of the iceberg (Figure 3.1). As engineers, we see the bigger, more complex, problem beneath the waves.

Once our software is developed and given to users, an interesting thing happens: the software develops its own *ba*. In any community of software users, we can find tips and suggestions for using the software being passed from person to person. Much of this information isn't in the manuals: it relates to the way in which the software is used. Particularly in offices that use bespoke software packages, we find old hands advising new colleagues – for example, 'Oh, if it says *invalid telephone number*, it's usually because . . .'

Knowledge about the software product combines with knowledge from the business to create new knowledge about the technology (as shown in Figure 3.2). Subsequent changes to the software can benefit from this new knowledge and must also respect it as changes are made.

3.6.1   Codification

As if this weren't enough, much knowledge is actually tacit. It is uncodified, and not written down anywhere. We may not realize that we have this knowledge until we attempt to write it down or do things differently. Usually, it is just 'the way we do it around here'.

When we deliver a program, it enters into the users' domain. It becomes part of their *ba*, so we must respect what users know and expect. If we embed values and judgements into our software that are different to those in use by our users, they will find the system difficult and unnatural to use. If, on the other hand, we tailor our system to their norms, they will find the system easier to use.

Of course, often the whole point of introducing software is to disrupt current practices so that they can be changed. However, we should be sure that we know which practices we're attempting to change and which we want to keep. There's no point in introducing software that forces doctors to measure temperatures in degrees Kelvin if we're trying to change their prescribing practices.

3.6.2   Specification

It is when we come to write the specification that we start to grasp the difficulties that are presented by both *ba* and tacit knowledge. Specifications have a tendency to grow and never seem to be complete. Indeed, it is usually quite easy to pick holes in specifications. If we attempt to write a complete specification, we must codify not only the system requirements but also the context, the *ba* in which they exist.

Specifications are themselves abstractions, and in making the abstractions we have to leave out detail. But the attempt to leave out detail leads to incompleteness, because we rely on context to provide it. It is always possible to add more explanation to a specification. Thus we end up with thousand-page specifications.

Specification documents also need to tackled as tacit knowledge. As we write the specification, we'll uncover more and more undocumented rules of thumb, methods of working, common practices and so on. This continues as the system moves to implementation and we see how the different bits interact. Testing invariably throws up undocumented assumptions, missed function points and incompatible implementation.

Where end-users are involved in the development process and the testing cycle, insights into the very business process being modelled are common because the different groups are combining their *ba*. This is especially true where the software development team is part of a business unit and not an external group.

When we write a program, we attempt to codify everything. For the machine to complete the task, we must encode the assumptions, we must encode the *ba* and we must encode the tacit knowledge. If we skimp, our program will be less than complete. (See Chapter 6 for more on requirements and specifications.)

3.6.3   Hand-over

Anyone who has worked on a large software system will have seen project hand-overs where one developer attempts to dump the contents of their brain, their knowledge, on to a new team member. For the new team member, trying to absorb a million and one facts about a system can be intimidating.

Documentation is of limited help. Like many developers, I've experienced the mountain of documentation that lies in wait when you join a new project. Because it has been written down, many people expect that simply reading it will make you as knowledgeable as the writer.

When you're new to a project, the documentation can seem very abstract and difficult to comprehend. Until you've been immersed in the project, spoken to other developers, tried to understand the problem and the solution and generally entered the project environment, large parts of the documentation are meaningless.

Again, we see tacit knowledge and *ba* at work. The documentation can't possibly contain everything that the last developer knew about the system. Even if he or she divided his or her time equally between documentation and coding, there are assumptions that will never make it to paper.

3.6.4   The Documentation Myth

The role of documentation in project hand-overs is one aspect of the documentation myth. This is the idea that we can put on paper everything that we need to know about a project.

In fact, writing documents can often be a way of hiding information and ensuring that it isn't widely disseminated. In the case of the photocopier repair engineers described before, the documentation designed to simplify tasks was largely ignored; the engineers came to see the documentation as overly simplified and devaluing of their skills. Yet managers believed that the documents told the engineers what they needed to know. As a consequence, the documentation actually served to drive management and workers apart.

On many projects, large piles of documentation – sometimes called *Victorian novels* – go unread. Time taken reading documentation means delaying the moment when actual work is done. Further, reading documentation is an exercise in diminishing returns, since it is unlikely that the fiftieth page will be read with the same attention as the first.

Reliance on written documentation is based on several false assumptions:

- The documentation is comprehensive and accurate.
- All system knowledge is explicit and can be captured.
- The role of tacit knowledge and *ba* is minimal.
- Writing and reading documentation is the most efficient means of transferring technical knowledge.
- That documentation will be read.
- Most importantly, when it is read it will be fully comprehended.

The more we try to make the documentation comprehensive, the more complex and larger it becomes – making it less likely to be read and fully understood.

Documentation assumes that people learn well from written documents. This may be true for some people but, as we'll see in our discussion of learning styles in Chapter 4, people learn in different ways. In particular, engineers are likely to learn better from concrete experience.

Taken together, these assumptions constitute the *documentation myth*. The more we believe the myth, the more self-reinforcing it becomes.

'We need more documentation' is the call of so many managers and developers on so many projects. Yet projects survive without documentation. If documentation was as vital as many of its proponents claim, it would get written and it would get used.

3.7 Knowledge Creation

In producing a solution to a problem, we need to create new knowledge about the process and about the solution. There's a knowledge creation process at work. So far, we have discussed the communication, transfer and codification of knowledge, but we have said little about the creation of knowledge.

Nonaka suggested that we think of knowledge creation in four stages, as shown in Figure 3.3. This model starts with what we already know, namely tacit

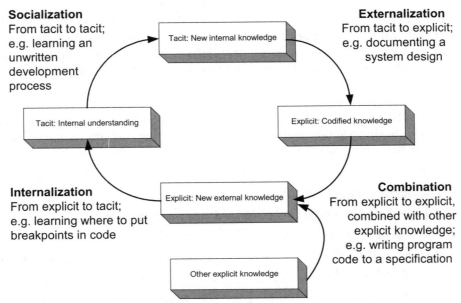

Figure 3.3 Four modes of knowledge conversion.
Source: Based on a diagram from Nonaka and Takeuchi (1995)

knowledge. This is turned into explicit knowledge, combined with other explicit knowledge and then turned back into tacit knowledge. At each stage, thought is needed for the transformation. This is known as the SECI model (*socialization, externalization, combination, internalization*). Knowledge creation is a continuous process, completion of one stage starting the next.

With each conversion, knowledge is extended. This may mean that it is combined with some other knowledge to create new knowledge, or it may mean that more people understand the knowledge; it may also mean that individuals have a better understanding of existing knowledge.

This model is at work when we develop software. Written specifications are often the first attempt to codify business processes. Such processes are usually passed from person to person by socialization: in writing the specification, we externalize this knowledge. Next, we combine this with specialist IT and software development knowledge to produce a solution that forms part of a new business process. This new business process creates a new *ba* that is again communicated between users by socialization.

While this model helps explain how knowledge can be created, it isn't the only way to do so. The SECI model is only one among many. Nor should we think that it always necessary to make tacit knowledge explicit before we can combine it – so there's no need to write everything down.

Thinking Point: What Knowledge Do You Use?

Make a list of all the knowledge you need to do your job: technical knowledge, knowledge about your organization, managerial knowledge and knowledge about the problems you work with:

- How much of this knowledge is tacit?
- Which knowledge is unique to your organization?
- What would a competitor like to know about your company?

3.8 Conclusion

Software development is fundamentally a knowledge-based activity. We see tacit and explicit knowledge around both projects and technologies, we see knowledge creation and we see knowledge flow – and failure to flow – between people and organizations.

Knowledge itself is fundamentally different from information. Failure to appreciate the difference will prevent successful execution of knowledge-based activities such as software development. However, appreciation of this fact alone isn't enough to guarantee success.

While the implications covered here aren't exhaustive, they're enough to show that simply having knowledge alone isn't enough: we need the ability to use knowledge, manage knowledge and ensure that it flows within the organization, to give the company competitive advantage.

The challenge for managers is to ensure that knowledge is created, shared, flows where it should and doesn't flow where it shouldn't. This is difficult. However, if it were not difficult, then there would be no competitive advantage to be had. Because it is difficult, this is a very valuable skill.

Looking at software development as learning and knowledge creation highlights why it is difficult to communicate and codify what we want from a piece of software – the old 'do what I want, not what I say' syndrome.

While software is key to the knowledge economy and is used by knowledge workers, we should also consider software development itself as knowledge creation. The software development community tends to look inside for answers to problems, but there's much we can learn from elsewhere. The writers quoted here aren't specifically interested in software development, but their ideas are highly applicable. However, these are not technical problems and we should not expect technical solutions.

Everything software developers do concerns the application of knowledge and learning. From specification through design to delivery, we're concerned with using knowledge and developing products through the application of our existing knowledge and the creation of new knowledge. Understanding this should help to improve the development process.

Learning

"Everyone thinks of changing the world, but no one thinks of changing himself."
Leo Nikolayevitch Tolstoy, writer, 1828–1910

Think back over the last ten years. What have you learned? What have we, the programmer community, learned? Maybe you learned C# or Java – or relearned C++ in the ISO version, with the standard library and meta-programming. Or maybe you've learnt Python, JavaScript, Perl, Ruby or some other scripting languages that didn't exist in 1998. Perhaps you're not a programmer, but you've picked up bits of technologies such as HTTP, FTP and XML somehow.

If you're a manager, you may have learnt PRINCE 2, ITIL or balanced scorecard techniques. And you still need to learn the consequences of technologies such as .NET, even if you're only managing people who use them.

Whatever your speciality is if you work in IT, the chances are that you've learned a lot of new technologies in the last ten years. If change is the only constant, then learning is the only real skill you need – the corollary being as follows: *If we can't learn, can we change?*

4.1 Three Knowledge Domains

As if technological change wasn't enough, IT people also learn about the business side of things. There are two well-known domains of knowledge:

- *The application domain:* Also called the *problem domain*, this describes the business knowledge involved with a project. Our users and customers are concerned with this domain. Examples include finance, telecoms, utilities, energy, transport and so on.

- *The solution domain:* This is our domain: it is the knowledge of the technology that we'll use to solve the problems in the application domain. In this domain we find Unix, Windows, C#, Apache and so on.

It is just about impossible to create software with only solution-domain knowledge. Developers who lack application-domain knowledge need help from those with such knowledge, which may be supplied by users, business analysts, product managers or other subject matter experts. Over time, developers acquire this knowledge for themselves, and consequently many end up being minor experts in an application domain as well as the technical domain.

There's another less commonly recognized domain that we can add to these two:

- *The process domain:* This is the body of knowledge concerning the software development process. How we go about creating software, how we track issues, manage projects and so on? This is where we find knowledge of Agile methods and improvement techniques.

All software developers have some knowledge of the process domain, but only a few delve in deeply and try to understand how we can change it, improve it and advance the process.

While these domains are separate, they also overlap (see Figure 4.1). Some people will specialize in one domain and have little knowledge of the others, while other people will be more general in nature, with significant knowledge in more than one domain.

As we develop software, we're constantly learning; sometimes in one domain, sometimes in another, sometimes in two domains at once. So too are

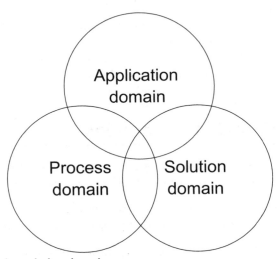

Figure 4.1   Three knowledge domains.

our customers: they learn as they use our product, as they make requests for changes and as we ask them for information and preferences. Learning happens whether we intend it to or not. Our only choice is whether we work with the learning process and encourage it, or work against it and discourage it.

When we harness learning, we can generate knowledge. This allows us to produce better software and better businesses. When we resist this learning, when we try to stop it happening or ignore the results, not only do we miss an opportunity to improve, but we create frustration, distrust and disappointment in those who are learning.

4.2 Developing Software is Learning

If we look at the software development process, there are at least four key learning activities:

- We learn new technology.
- We learn the application domain.
- We problem solve by applying our technology knowledge to the application domain.
- Users learn to use our application and learn about their own problem – which changes the application domain.

Each one of these points reinforces the others: in our efforts to solve a problem we need to learn more about the problem; our solution may use a technology that is new to us. When the users see the end product, their mental model of the problem will change too. They too will learn, through the software, and acquire new insights into the task that may lead to changes to the software.

Learning is thus inherent at every stage of software development. We can either choose to ignore it and muddle through somehow, or to accept it and help improve the learning process.

4.3 Learning Benefits Your Business

Of course, some might wonder why a business should foot the bill for continual learning. After all, businesses hire people for the skills that they have. They may have hired you because you already know Java, so why do you need time to learn more Java? There's a straightforward answer to this question, and it returns us to the quote with which we opened Chapter 1.

Although we can buy the fastest machines on the market, only hire people with an IQ above 160, expand our teams endlessly and work to ISO-9001, we aren't actually doing anything that our competitors can't do. All we're doing is proving that we can spend money. Worse still, none of this guarantees that we'll actually develop good software.

If, instead of viewing software development as a problem task, we view it as a learning activity, we gain some new insights. Firstly, we can recognize that most developers actually want to make customers happy and – what's more – they like learning new things. It is just conceivable that a firm that encourages its staff to learn will find it easier to retain staff, hire new staff and at the same time see the capability of existing staff improve.

Secondly, every time employees learn something, they have increased the resources available to the firm. The staff members have become more valuable to the firm because they know something new, whether this be about technology, the business problem or the way in which we're doing things. Potentially, they can spread this knowledge to other team members.

We can think of this as investing in the firm's human assets. The more you invest by way of training and time, the more valuable your assets will become. Unlike most assets, human assets don't depreciate with time: because us humans continue to learn while we work, our assets increase in value rather than diminishing.

Thus, learning can give your organization an advantage over competitors that don't recognize their assets, or that don't invest in them. Of course, it may be that the opposition isn't in a position to learn. For example, once a corporate IT department has been outsourced, it can be difficult to acquire the knowledge required to change the service provider or bring the department back in house.

Even if one of our competitors is in a position to learn, this doesn't mean that they will. Some companies discourage learning through physical restrictions: they may eliminate spare time or remove resources such as books or Internet connectivity. In other places, the corporate culture may discourage the risk taking and occasional failures that are required for active learning.

On the other hand, companies can actively encourage learning through quite simple mechanisms and create a culture within the company that values learning. Such a company will learn faster than its peer group – such companies are the subject of this book.

For learning to be effective, we need to put it into action. If you walk into a good bookshop, you'll find racks of books on ideas for improving the software development process, but how many companies are actually able to implement even a fraction of these ideas?

If we can't implement well-known ideas, then what chance have we of producing any new ideas of our own? The ability to learn is a prerequisite for successful innovation. So if we can't learn, we can't innovate.

Since software development is intrinsically a learning process, it is logical that recognizing it as such, removing barriers to learning and promoting learning within our team will improve our software. Once we do this, we have something that competitors can't copy, because we'll create our own environment. Competitors can copy the actions, but they won't learn the same things because they're different companies employing different people.

4.4 Learning Theories

Before we talk about actual things that we can do to improve learning, we need to consider how learning happens. Examining the learning process produces useful insights and helps inform our actions.

There are many theories about how learning happens and we can't cover them all here – even if there were enough space, diminishing returns would quickly set in. Instead, we will look at a few theories that are visible in the software development field.

4.4.1 Single-loop and Double-loop Learning

Hopefully you're now convinced that you need to learn and you're ready to create an environment in which learning is actively promoted. But what happens when some of your developers come back from a training course and suggest that your basic underlying way of working is wrong – and they question the very reason for developing your application?

This could be a surprise to you. After all, you sent them on a course to improve their UML and they've come back questioning many different aspects of the project. Education can be a dangerous thing.

This little example demonstrates the difference between single-loop learning and double-loop learning.[1] In single-loop learning, we increase our stock of learnt things and act on what we already know. In double-loop learning, what we learn leads us to question our assumptions and our understanding of the world.

The usual example is that of a thermostat. A thermostat set to 20 °C will switch the heating on when the temperature drops below 20 °C, and turn the air conditioning on when it goes above. Such a thermostat operates a single loop: it checks the temperature and does one of three things: nothing, turn the heating on or turn the air-conditioning on.

Of course, the thermostat is a simple mechanical device. It can't question why the temperature should be 20 °C: it can't consider whether 20 °C is a pleasant temperature or whether it is the *right* temperature. Answering these questions requires a second loop to allow consideration of what's to be achieved and what we value.

In double-loop learning, people question their underlying assumptions and mental models. Single-loop learning doesn't detract from what has been learnt before – we're still increasing our stock of learnt things – double-loop learning changes our understanding of how the world works and may cause us to reconsider things we have learnt before (Figure 4.2).

Single-loop learning has also been called 'exploitation', because we're exploiting the knowledge and learning that we already have. Similarly,

---

[1] The terms *single-loop* and *double-loop* learning are from Argyris (1994).

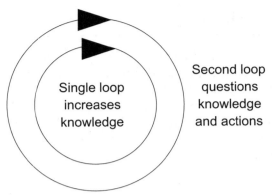

Figure 4.2   Two loops of learning.

double-loop learning has been called 'explorative', because it is more of an exploration of our thoughts, values and understandings.

Double-loop learning represents a deeper form of learning. We need both types of learning and should value each – it isn't merely a case of 'single-loop good, double-loop better': these are different types of learning. Sometimes we need single-loop learning – say, when learning a new computer language. On other occasions, such as learning reflection in Java or exception handling in C++, we need double-loop learning to question the way in which we have done things before and the new possibilities that these paradigms open up.

Thinking Point: Single-loop and Double-loop in the Workplace

Try to think of examples of single-loop and double-loop learning in your workplace. When you design software, how much is single-loop? And how much double-loop?

Sometimes relying on single-loop can create problems: we think we know the answer and we jump to assumptions, but in reality things aren't what they appear. Deeper thinking – the application of a second loop – can provide better answers.

Single- and double-loop learning start to become apparent when we try to create change in our organization. Application of single-loop learning can look attractive: we can send the entire team on eXtreme Programming training courses and insist that everyone works to the XP practices. In the short term, this may well improve our results and we might see this as *good enough*.

However, we have also created a number of problems. Firstly, a team that has simply adopted someone else's 'best practice' may become stuck when it encounters a problem that isn't covered in the documentation. Such a problem may well require deeper thought and reasoning, but the team has never been challenged like this before.

Secondly, we have done nothing that our competitors can't do. They too can send their developers on the same XP courses and follow the same practices. If we become markedly more productive, then the competitor can use the same tools to close the gap. From a business point of view, the advantage is temporary.

Only if we move beyond exploiting current knowledge and start to explore and develop our own knowledge can we do something that others can't do. Allowing our teams to find their own solutions will enable them to overcome future problems and improve their practices in a way that competitors cannot.

Competitors who attempt to do the same thing will find that they have different insights and different practices. These practices may be better or worse than ours, but they're the subject of genuine competition. Rather than competing to see who can adopt third-party advice fastest, we're competing on our firms' own abilities. The game has moved beyond *adopting best practice*; instead, it has become one of *creating new practice* – new best practice, above and beyond current best practice.

Relying too heavily on single-loop learning and exploiting current knowledge can be dangerous. If we rely on what we currently know, then we don't allow for changes in the environment.

Consider the manager who learns that his software developers are always about a month late. His solution is to set the deadline early. What happens next is anyone's guess. But without a second loop of learning – an explorative examination of what has happened – we have no way of knowing why the team was always late and whether he has taken the right action.

Triple-loop and Identity

There's a temptation to extend beyond double-loop learning. After all, if single-loop is good and double-loop is better, then what about the third-loop, fourth-loop and the fifth-loop?

Well, as far as I know, nobody has proposed fourth- or fifth-loop learning, but people have proposed a third loop. Some writers attribute properties of double-loop learning to triple-loop. Other writers suggest that the third loop is about improving the ability to learn, and still others suggest that the third learning loop is about identity. In short, there's no widely agreed definition of what the third loop constitutes.

Perhaps the most interesting suggestion for the third loop is the idea of identity change. For example, many software developers won't consider reading this book because it looks too much like a management book: conversely, there may be managers who don't read this book because it looks too much like a programmers' book. Similarly, some software testers are suspicious of *Test-driven Development* (*TDD*) because they don't believe that programmers know how to test software.

Conversely, some programmers resist writing unit tests because they believe that is a tester's job.

In all these cases, it is identity that is guiding the argument and the learning people with different roles. Their role and identity is more than just a title on a business card; it is part of who they are.

Identity is a very strong force and is often the root of why we do things. People hired as software testers will expect to test software and will act accordingly even without being told what to do, because they're driven by their identity. Similarly, identity also stops us from doing things – as in the case of the programmers who object to writing unit tests.

Questioning our identity can be scary, but it can also lead to significant learning. What does it mean to be a *software tester*? What does it mean to be a *project manager*? Considering these labels leads us to consider our own identity and engage in deep learning.

4.4.2 Learning Styles

The loop learning models are just one explanation of how learning happens, and there are many other models we could look at. One particularly interesting one is from David Kolb[2] and this is interesting for two reasons. Firstly, Kolb's model can be mapped on to the software development process to describe how learning happens as we deliver software.

Secondly, Kolb recognizes that different people learn in different ways. Initially, it can come as a surprise that people learn in different ways but after a little thought it is quite obvious. Some people prefer to learn from books, and others from watching, reflecting or experiencing.

The different ways in which we learn are categorized as one of four *learning styles*. Each learning style excels in one part of Kolb's learning cycle (Figure 4.3), but all learning styles are needed to complete a learning cycle. Learning is a continuous process that involves different stages and different skills: as we learn one thing, we move on to another.

Concrete experience forms the basis for observation and reflection, which in turn allow us to create abstract concepts and generalize about what we have observed for future use. These concepts and generalizations need to be tested in new situations to see if they're useful, which in turn represents more concrete experiences for us to work with. Each time we go around the cycle, our understanding improves.

To be effective, we need different abilities in each part of the cycle. In order to have concrete experience, we must open ourselves to new experience and be prepared to engage with our environment. In order to maximize the benefits of

[2] See Kolb (1976).

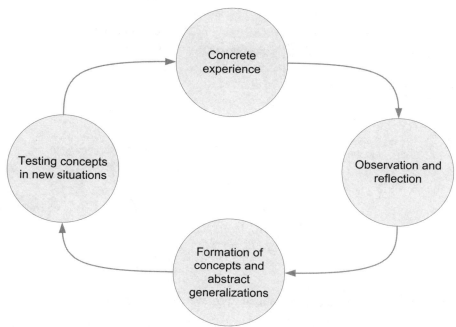

Figure 4.3   Kolb's experiential learning model.

observation and reflection, we need to consider the issues from different perspectives and create theories that are logical and sound. Finally, we must be prepared to test our theories in decision-making and problem solving.

Figure 4.4 shows how we can map this model directly on to the software development process. For a given requirement – say, processing insurance claims – we undertake a development cycle:

- We look at how claim processing is done – *concrete experience*.
- We write a description and specification – *reflective observation*.
- We develop software functionality to model the process – *abstract conceptualization*.
- We test it and deliver the software – *active experimentation*. Figure 4.4

In some software development models, that's it – one cycle. Such models adopt a 'get it right first time' approach. Such methods assume that all the necessary learning can be captured in one cycle. In reality, these models usually feature a 'maintenance' or 'stabilization' phase at the end, which allows more learning and modification to be conducted.

Developing software in iterations allows us to exploit the learning cycle: with each iteration around the cycle, we deliver a little, we see the results and we repeat the cycle. This allows developers and users to constantly re-evaluate

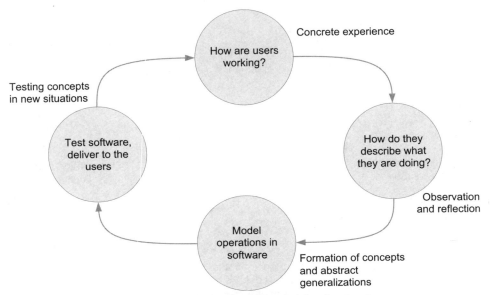

Figure 4.4   Kolb's learning cycle mapped to software development.

what they're seeing, adjust hypotheses and test their revised understanding through concrete experience, reflection, generalization and testing.

In order to learn, each of us must pass through all four stages of the model. However, each of us also has a preferred learning style; that is, each of us prefers some aspects of learning over others. This means that each person will prefer some parts of the cycle, where they will perform better than at other parts (see Figure 4.5).

To determine your preferred learning style, you need to take a 'learning style inventory' test. Unfortunately, these tests are marketed commercially, so it usually costs to take one. These tests group people into one of four categories: converger, diverger, assimilator and accommodator (as summarized in Table 4.1).

It is hardly surprising that when we correlate this with people's employment choices, we find that some learning styles lend themselves to one job more than another. Convergers are often engineers, while divergers occupy human resources posts; assimilators gather in planning and research, while accommodators are found in sales and marketing. This also starts to explain why these groups have difficulty communicating.

When faced with a problem, our learning style will influence how we tackle the problem and how we communicate it. Two engineers with a converger learning style will find it easier to work together and discuss the problem and possible solutions. When asked to explain it to a diverger – say, a human resources manager – communication is more difficult.

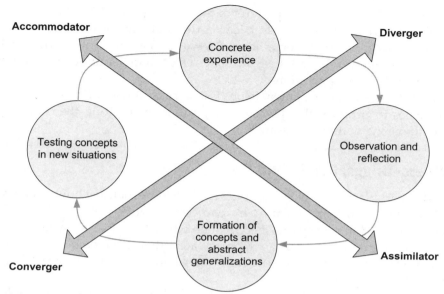

Figure 4.5 The four learning styles.

Table 4.1 Learning styles and preferences.

Learning style	Good at	Characteristics	Typical roles
Converger	Abstract conceptualization and active experimentation	Good with the practical application of ideas; unemotional; prefers dealing with things rather than people	Engineers
Diverger	Concrete experience, and observation and reflection	Imaginative and emotional; interested in humanities, culture and the arts	Counsellors and personnel managers
Assimilator	Abstract conceptualization, and reflection and observation	Good at creating theoretical models, inductive reasoning and integrating different explanations into a common understanding	Planning and research
Accommodator	Concrete experience and active experimentation	Good at implementing plans and new experiments; greater risk takers than other styles	Sales and marketing

Even though we will have a preference for some aspects of the learning cycle, we still need to complete the cycle to learn. Although our natural tendency may be to work with people of a similar style, we can benefit from working with people of different styles, because this helps create a richer understanding of a problem and possible solutions.

The challenge for development teams is to harness these different talents and approaches to produce the best solution, rather than letting the differences create divisions within the group.

Myers–Briggs, Belbin and Co.

In the workplace, Kolb learning styles explain more than just how a person learns: they can help explain why two people work well together and another two don't. They can shed light on why a team is dysfunctional or why some groups seem to antagonize each other. Kolb wasn't alone in creating these theories. Two, perhaps better-known, techniques are Belbin and Myers–Briggs.

Meredith Belbin studied how teams worked and suggested that people take on one of nine roles within a team. These roles are: implementer, shaper, completer/finisher, plant, monitor/evaluator, specialist, coordinator, team worker and researcher. A balanced team needs each of these roles to be filled: having too many of one type and not enough of another would unbalance a team. Some individuals can fill more than one role, so teams don't need to be composed of nine people exactly.

One of the best-known profiling techniques is Myers–Briggs. This approach is based on the ideas of psychiatrist Carl Jung, and while it was initially aimed at understanding individuals, it can also be used to analyse teams. In particular, human resources departments and recruitment managers often seem keen on Myers–Briggs.

Myers–Briggs rates individuals on four scales: *introvert and extrovert, sensing and intuition, thinking and feeling* and *judging and perceiving*. A person taking the test is scored on these criteria, which are then combined to give one of 16 personality types. Again, these types can be used to understand team dynamics or interpersonal relationships.

Although widely used, all three techniques have been criticized for various reasons. The tests used to categorize people aren't always consistent. Personally, Myers–Briggs tests have sometimes categorized me as an introvert and on other occasions as an extrovert.

Myers–Briggs is also open to criticism because it is based on Jung's ideas of psychology. These ideas contain within them a model of the world and humanity that isn't universally shared.

Whatever test we use, there's always a danger that once we pigeon-hole people, we start to expect them to conform to type, we restrict our expectations and we limit their opportunities.

Plenty of books and web sites devoted to Kolb, Belbin, Myers–Briggs and other profiling schemes are available for further research. The point of presenting the ideas here, and specifically Kolb's, is not to suggest that you use them but, rather, to shed light on the learning process and the differences between individuals.

4.5 Learning, Change, Innovation and Problem Solving

An old philosophy question asks: *If a tree falls in the forest and nobody is there to it hear it, does it make a sound?*

You may also like to yourself: *If I'm told something and it doesn't change my behaviour, have I really learnt anything?*

If you never learnt anything after today, would you behave differently from the way you behaved today? Unless you lived your life by a roll of the dice, there seems little reason to assume that you would. If you wore a big coat today because the weather was cold, then tomorrow you'd wear a big coat again, and the day after that. Unless you're able to learn that the weather is now warm, you'll keep wearing a big coat.

In the film *Groundhog Day*, Bill Murray's character is learning: he is aware that the day repeats itself and he learns a little bit more piano every day until he is a virtuoso. But nobody else learns: nobody else notices that the day is repeating, so they all behave in exactly the same way every day.

Informed choices such as what coat to wear, what supermarket to shop at or what brand of shampoo to buy are all the result of learning something that changes our behaviour. Sometimes this is single-loop learning – the weather is warm, so I wear a different coat – and sometimes this is double-loop – say, I become a vegetarian and decide to shop elsewhere for a greater variety of vegetables.

The relationship is even more obvious if we turn the question around: *Why should we change anything*? We only behave differently because new information has come into our possession that causes a change in behaviour. Otherwise, without new information, the decisions that I made today will be good for tomorrow.

When we change our behaviour, we're innovating. We're trying something new. Sometimes we change our behaviour as the result of something we learn, and sometimes we change our behaviour and learn something as a result.

Learning, problem solving, innovation and change are just different aspects of the same thing. Figure 4.6 shows how when we solve a problem we learn, when we innovate we change, when we change we learn, and what we learn helps us solve problems. Single-loop learning and action allow us to react

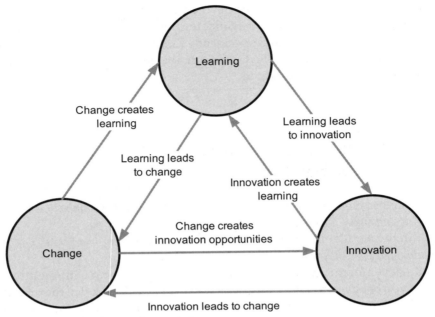

Figure 4.6   Learning, innovation and change.

quickly: double-loop learning and action allow for more innovation and change.

4.6 The Role of Leaders

Most software projects have multiple leaders, who may include:

- Product managers or business analysts, who lead the understanding of the application domain and what's required of the software.
- Technical architects and designers, who lead thinking in the solution domain to create the software.
- Project planners and project managers, who control the schedule and reporting to other managers.

In a proactive, motivated team, there's little need of a central manager to tell people what to do. People know what to do and set about doing it without being told to. In such a team, people are specialists and lead in their own field. Team members respect and support specialists who lead in one field but not in others. This leaves traditional manager and team leaders with a question:

What's left for management and leaders to do?

In a learning environment, the leader's role is no longer one of 'command and control', in which they ensure that everyone is doing what they are 'supposed' to do. Nor is their role to ensure on-time delivery. There may be technical authorities, but they are there to inform the decision-making of the whole team.

In a learning environment, the leader's role is one of enabler and learning director. The leader needs to ensure that the team works together and that there are no artificial obstacles placed in the way. Leaders may use their legitimacy and authority to obtain resources for the team, or they may use authority to protect the team, but they are not exercising authority over the team.

Within the team, the leader's role is to develop individuals and the team. Individuals need to be learning, they need to be given opportunities and they need to feel that they're advancing.

The people on the project are the leader's primary responsibility. These people need the resources and environment in which they can learn and grow – not just as employees or team members, but as individuals. These are the individuals who will learn the application domain: they will apply their technical knowledge to problem solving, and in the process they will learn more both technically and business-wise. These are the people who will innovate.

To do so, these people must learn. The leader's task is to help them learn: once the organizational obstacles are removed, the leader needs to help individuals to remove their own obstacles – to help people challenge their assumptions, think in new ways and innovate.

The leader also needs to ensure that the team works together: that team members trust and value one another, that they agree on what needs to be done and that the whole team moves forward as one – learning, developing and improving as they go.

4.7 Seed Learning

So far, we have looked at how learning happens and why developing software is an exercise in learning. Chapter 5 will build on these foundations and explore how we can build learning organizations. Before we close this chapter, we need to look at how you can start to seed learning and knowledge creation in your own organization.

Doubtless people in your organization are already learning and already creating knowledge. Still, it is possible to speed up this process and ensure that they're learning the right things to benefit your team. We can actively encourage people to learn more and learn more worthwhile things.

While we can't force anyone to learn – nor should we – there are some things that we can do to encourage the process. The ideas that follow carry two messages. The first message is direct: the thing you study can have a direct application. The second message says that the organization values learning.

Whatever the technique you choose, make it accessible, get people thinking and get them talking. Firstly, get them learning and thinking, and then build on their ideas to create change.

Embracing learning and change is itself a learning and changing experience. Some of this change is about changing our own mindset: trusting people, accepting that mistakes will happen, recognizing tacit knowledge and creating a culture of change and improvement in our organization.

What Learning Is Occurring Already?

The developers in your organization will already be learning. Some will be direct learning, some will be indirect (things implied from others actions) and some will be *on-the-job* learning about the work they're undertaking:

- Make a list of the learning that you can see going on around you.
- Then make a second list of the things that you think people would benefit from learning, and that would benefit the organization.

Compare the two lists:

- Are people learning the right things?
- Are they learning them quickly enough?

4.7.1   Personal Reflection

Section 1.9 suggested that you take time consider the ideas in this book and the world around you. More formally, this skill is known as *reflection* and has already been mentioned in our review of Kolb's learning cycle.

Reflection is a key skill to ensuring that you can learn and change. At the simplest level, reflection is about taking time to consciously think about the world around you. In our busy lives, it is too easy to neglect this habit because it requires some time. Of course, we can think about the world in spare moments, but once in a while we need to take time to have a good think. For me, the writing of this book has been a major exercise in reflecting.

We could spend all day thinking about the world – about current events, global warming, politics, our holidays and so on. So we need to focus our reflection on matters that are important to us. In the context of *Changing Software Development*, this could be making sense of this book, understanding our work environment or considering a course of action.

The act of reflection is about making sense of the world around us, connecting all the different pieces of information that reach us and trying to create an sensible understanding. Our understanding will be informed by our own values, principles and beliefs, and in turn our values and beliefs will be informed by our understanding. Therefore the understanding that we reach as individuals may be quite different from the understanding that others reach. No one person is right; nobody is wrong.

It can be difficult to find time to reflect in our modern world. We can snatch moments of reflection during the daily commute or walking the dog, but if we are to do it regularly we need to set aside some time and organize some triggers to provoke thinking.

Personally, I try to keep a journal of professional related events and thoughts. The process of writing forces me to structure my thoughts and forces some logic on to the environment around me. I can also rehearse conversations, actions and scenarios in my journal. Again, writing it down forces me to work through the structure and logic of my ideas.

On other occasions I've created mind-maps – or similar diagrams – to help me think through situations; and I'm aware of people who use audio recorders to speak their thoughts. In the office, simply writing up notes on a meeting, or preparing notes for a meeting, can also be a useful trigger to take time to reflect.

Taking time to actively reflect is completely within our own power. Whether we do it at home or at work, we simply need to find the time and do it. Yet we can't force another person to reflect: each person must find his or her own motivation and approach. Some of the ideas outlined below can be used to spark reflection if used in the right way. For example, talk to the individuals who attended a course and ask them what they thought: take time to listen and enquire into what they thought.

The busier I am at work, the more difficult it is to find the time to keep a journal, but I still try to make at least one or two entries a week. Paradoxically, I find that the times when I am in most need of my journal and reflection are the times when I am busiest.

Bug Journal

One developer I know kept a very specific type of journal. For a period of several months he recorded details of every bug that he found or that was reported in his code. His intention was to analyse the type and cause of the problems so that he could work to avoid them in future. However, after only a few weeks a very clear pattern became evident: string handling problems quickly emerged as the source of many problems.

In this case, the journal notes allowed a hidden problem to be exposed and fixed. I don't know if he continued the journal as planned, but I do know that he quickly changed his approach to string handling and stopped many problems before they happened.

4.7.2   Training Courses

Training courses can be good at seeding learning, but often less effective at changing the way people work. Traditional training can be expensive and actually dis-empowering to individuals, because they're expected to sit quietly and learn. When faced with a training class, some people automatically lapse into 'school mode' and expect to passively receive information.

More innovative training classes can alleviate some of these problems. You may be more likely to find such training courses run by small independent experts than by large corporations that sell training as a regular product. So if you're looking for a training course, shop around.

Once a course has taken place, look for opportunities to act on what has been learned. You may talk to the individuals on the course and try to stimulate some reflection, perhaps by asking for their thoughts on the course or what they plan to do differently now. If several people have attended the same course, you could convene a meeting to discuss how they and the organization can put the learning into action.

4.7.3   Talk Programmes

A regular talk programme can be a good way of introducing new ideas, spreading change stories and encouraging people to talk about learning and change. In technology companies these often go by the name of 'TechTalks' and usually take the form of a dedicated slot (say, an hour) on some regular basis (weekly, fortnightly, monthly etc.). In the first instance, these can be a good way to get people talking about their projects and spreading knowledge within the company.

With a regular slot there's no need to stick to the lecture format with PowerPoint – sometimes called 'talk-and-chalk' presentations. The slot can be used for discussions, brainstorming and the introduction of new ideas.

Such a programme should include corporate communication, strategy and marketing as well as hard-core technology subjects such as language and libraries. This adds variety to the schedule and encourages people to look beyond their immediate area of concern. Typically, many IT people are glad to know more about the company, the problems it faces and how the managers are solving their problems.

Talk programmes achieve three objectives: firstly, as a direct communication channel for spreading knowledge and ideas; second, as a sign from management that they value this dissemination; and, thirdly, presentations help the presenters themselves, allowing them to develop their own communication skills and make their voices heard.

A talk programme can also be a cheap way of giving people training. You can bring in an outside expert for a couple of hours to introduce the topic, or have one of your own people give a talk on some technique that you'd like to see used more widely. Guest speakers also add to the feeling that the talk programme is important, as well as introducing ideas, experience and opinions that are not available internally.

4.7.4 Conferences

While the broad theme of a conference is directed by the actual sessions, those who attend a conference are free to find their own theme. Attending a conference can improve motivation and help expose people to new ideas.

Conferences differ: some are tightly focused on a single topic, while others are broad; some run a single track and others multiple tracks. Many business conferences are actually less about learning and more about networking and opportunity hunting, so look carefully and speak to people who have attended the conference.

4.7.5 Company Libraries

Books can be a great source of new ideas, and building a corporate library gives you a chance to put those ideas right in front of people. By removing the need for individuals to purchase books with their own money, some risk is removed.

Unfortunately, books go missing from libraries, but this isn't necessarily a bad thing. I used to get annoyed when a book went missing from my corporate library, but one day I realized that if someone likes a book enough to take it home, then something good has happened. That individual has come to value and associate with the book. So what if it cost £30, £50 or even £70? It's a cheap way of getting a new idea accepted.

Don't confine yourself to books in the library. Magazines and journals can be a useful way to get new ideas into a company. In an IT company you probably want journals on the latest tools and techniques anyway, but seek out those that contain a variety of information.

4.7.6 Book Study Groups

Some companies run internal book study groups. These might take place over a lunch hour (perhaps with the company buying pizza) or immediately after work. The participants agree to work through a book together, perhaps at one chapter per meeting.

The format that I've found works best is for one or two participants to summarize a chapter, perhaps with PowerPoint slides or perhaps on a white board. This gives the gathering some structure and allows those who didn't get around to reading the chapter to join in. The presentation forms the basis of a discussion, which is often more interesting than the book itself.

Again, by creating discussion around the book and its contents, people are encouraged to think about the ideas and relate them to their own environment. This may take the form of 'Hey! Why didn't we think of that?' or 'That will never work here.'

Book groups work on several levels. At the simplest level, they provide a reason to read a book and to spread the ideas of an author. At the same time, they allow the participants to create a shared understanding of the topic and approach. Were individuals to read the book on their own, they would each gain their own understanding: by discussing it in a group, the whole group creates a common understanding and, at its best, engages in collective reflection.

4.7.7   Wikis

Book groups and talk programmes are good, but they require everyone to participate at the same time. Web sites allow you to post information, but can be difficult to change. Such barriers reduce contributions.

This is where Wiki web sites fit in. Because changing a Wiki is easy, barriers are lowered and everyone is able to participate, record information or provide links for others. Wikis aren't so good for debates, particularly ones where people disagree, but they're useful for capturing information.

Wikis also score good points for promoting participation. Because anyone, at any level, can add to a Wiki, they're egalitarian and they enable contributions.

4.7.8   Blogs

Like Wikis, Blogs can be good for capturing knowledge and information. When combined with Really Simple Syndication (RSS), they're also good for disseminating ideas and spreading information between groups. In order to work as an effective long-term store of knowledge, Blogs need to be combined with search engines so that information can be found later.

Probably because of their history, Blogs have something of an anti-establishment air about them. It is a little too early to tell exactly what role Blogs will play in the future but, again, by lowering the barriers to participation they encourage people to participate and share their thoughts.

Blogs are an important part of what's becoming known as *personal knowledge management*. They allow people to manage their own knowledge: to record the things that are important to them, link to things that are useful and share this information with others.

4.7.9   Searchable Intranets

Intranets can host many useful applications to promote learning. At the simplest level, a Wiki will help coordinate activities and allow everyone to contribute ideas. Intranets can also be repositories for information that is written down. Storing documentation on the intranet in an easy-to-access format greatly speeds things up.

Having information on an intranet, Wiki or Blog is only half the story. For people to make the most of this information, they need to be able to find it. On the Internet we do this using search engines and you can do the same with your corporate intranet. Google, Autonomy, Oracle and others all sell search engines that you can use to make your own intranet as searchable as the public Internet.

Making information available on an intranet is good, but it isn't enough. In order for information to be useful, people must be able to find it when they need to. If information can't be found in a timely manner, people will assume that it isn't online.

4.7.10   Welcome Debate

Each of the activities outlined in this section is also an opportunity to debate. When a discussion starts, let it run. Don't worry about the agenda in these sessions, because the debate can often be far more valuable, and you can come back to the original topic at a later date. Debate is similar to reflection in that we're actively thinking and challenging ideas.

Debate works in various ways: simply explaining your own position often helps improve your understanding. Like writing a diary, you're forced to structure your argument so that others can understand. Similarly, listening to another person's point of view can help you both understand their thinking and further illuminate your own. Discussing two or more different, possibly opposing, ideas can also help bring about a synthesis of a better idea.

Some debates need a moderator to ensure balance and to allow each party to have a fair say. Moderators need to remain fair to each side even if they aren't neutral themselves. This means that they need to moderate themselves: if they fail to do so, the group will cease to respect the moderator and treat him or her as just one more participant.

Unfortunately, cultural differences can inhibit debate: some cultures aren't accustomed to open questioning, particularly of someone in authority. People from such cultures may construe discussion as disrespectful. In such circumstances, silence doesn't represent agreement. If you're moderating a discussion, you need to be aware of such factors and make allowances for them.

Is Learning in Your Corporate Mission Statement?

A friend of mine was hired to turn a small development team Agile. I was coaching her through this process and after a few weeks in the job she asked if I could give an 'Introduction to Agile' presentation to the team. I happily agreed and a few days later found myself at their offices.

On the wall was a series of modern art pictures with a couple of words each. The one that struck me said 'learn more'. I asked what the pictures were about – my mind was figuring out how to refer to them during the presentation.

'Oh', she said, 'they are supposed to be the company values' and went back to what she was saying.

What? The company values learning? The company wants its employees to learn more? Brilliant!

Really, it wasn't about making her team more Agile. It was about making the company values come alive, making them mean something more than just some modern art on the wall. I knew at that moment that she wouldn't fail. What she was doing was completely aligned with the strategy and values of the company.

Too many people have become cynical about company mission statements and values. Statements get read, but go in one eye and out of the other. People think that they apply to someone else and not them. Many managers know this – they probably think the same thing! What's a poor CEO supposed to do?

Find out if your company has a values statement, mission statement, strategy description or any other kind of statement about what they're doing. Read it carefully and see if you can find any support for what you'd like to do.

Does it talk about change? Serving customers better? Learning? Adapting? The chances are it does – these things are important to senior managers.

This might be all the support you need to get started on Agile. Of course, you might find that your manager has become cynical about the mission statement too, but if you have the CEO on your side, you're off to a flying start.

4.8 Conclusion

Learning is happening all the time. Our challenge is to harness the learning for change and knowledge creation. This means that we need to ensure that learning is occurring in the right direction – we don't need to work out everything that needs to be learned; just that learning is happening in the general area. And it means that we need to speed up the learning process to bring business benefits.

There's much that we can do to seed learning and provide learning opportunities, and this all starts with the individual. Beyond the individual, we need the team, the group and the organization to learn. This is the subject of the next chapter.

CHAPTER 5

The Learning Organization

"In the accumulation of over 20 years of studies, they [organizational learning writers] have not developed a comprehensive view on what constitutes 'organisational learning'."

Ikujiro Nonaka and Hirotaka Takeuchi (1995)

So far, I have described the role of learning and knowledge in the creation of software development and suggested some means of enhancing learning. During this discussion, the ideas of *organizational learning* and *the learning organization* have arisen. In this chapter, I want to explore these ideas in more detail and consider what such an organization would look like and what it would do.

As I noted in the introduction, Agile teams need to be learning organizations in their own right. The term *learning team* is probably a more accurate description of an effective Agile team. Such teams need to learn together to create large pieces of software in the application, solution and process domains. Learning teams need to help individual members learn and learn collectively. Such learning teams form building blocks of the bigger learning organization.

For those working in a large organization, it can often seem that the company is determined to restrict our learning. A constant focus on *making money* deprives us of time to learn, and the need to *drive down costs* stops us getting the resources we need. Corporate organization and internal politics seem to create barriers to our learning.

Changing Software Development: Learning to Become Agile   Allan Kelly
© 2008 John Wiley & Sons, Ltd.

It seems that we have a contradiction: we need to learn to create products and deliver services, but our company seems intent on stopping us from learning. This is what makes business hard.

If we didn't face these kinds of problems, then there would be no need for a book on the subject. If these problems were easy to solve, then everyone would be able to solve them and there wouldn't be any competitive advantage to be had. It is because these problems are hard that the value in solving them is much greater.

Again, IT people aren't the first to face these problems. Others have tackled the building of learning teams and organizations before, and there's much written for us to work with. However, this does mean stepping outside the IT world to find the answers. Unfortunately, as the above quote demonstrates, there's no magic recipe for creating a learning organization. While we can learn from others, we must find our own path to build our own learning teams and organizations. The concept of a learning organization is itself more abstract than concrete.

5.1 Defining the Learning Organization

All organizations learn to one degree or another. It is simply a case of whether the learning is improving the organization or damaging the organization. In some organizations, the spiral of learning is negative: people learn how to avoid nasty managers, how to keep their jobs and how to avoid blame.

Software development abounds with examples of negative learning, whether it is program code that should not be touched or time estimates that are padded – or reduced – to make them more acceptable regardless of the work required. Negative learning can be considered sub-optimal because it creates other problems.

Positive learning occurs when people and teams are learning to improve the way in which they work in an optimal fashion. One example is the points-based work estimates used by Agile teams. Over time, teams converge on an understanding of the work value of a *point* without any rigid definition of what a point is.

Both positive and negative learning can be self-reinforcing. We can think of them as spirals (Figure 5.1). Negative learning tends to lead to more negative learning – problems multiply because our solutions create more problems. Positive learning, on the other hand, leads us a greater understanding and reveals further opportunities for learning and improvement.

In a negative spiral, each badly solved problem is not completely solved. Problems are stored up for the future and, most probably, people lose motivation. Future problems come from existing solutions. Positive learning leads to the reverse spiral: as problems are solved and people learn, more new problems are uncovered and existing solutions revisited. However, with each improvement overall performance increases and people are more motivated.

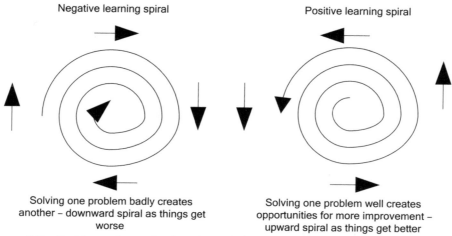

Negative learning spiral

Positive learning spiral

Solving one problem badly creates another – downward spiral as things get worse

Solving one problem well creates opportunities for more improvement – upward spiral as things get better

Figure 5.1 Positive and negative learning spirals.

Most companies are active at learning, but few would consider themselves *learning organizations*. Indeed, it may be better to keep such a term to yourself lest people get the wrong idea or jump to assumptions. A few organizations do consider themselves learning organizations – names such as the Royal Dutch/ Shell oil company, 3M, Hewlett-Packard, Toyota and even the US Marine Corps come up again and again.

It probably matters little if organizations are conscious or unconscious of the learning that is occurring in the workplace. It is more important that the learning occurs than what it is called.

Thinking Point: Identify Positive and Negative

Look at the lists you made of learning that is already occurring in your workplace. Look also at the list of single-loop and double-loop learning. Identify which items you think are positive and which are negative. Add more items if you think of them:

- What future problems or opportunities may arise from each of these items?

5.1.1 Companies Learn through People

Fundamentally, a company is a legal entity set up to undertake business – to trade, to buy, to sell and do whatever it takes to make money in the process. It is hard to see a company – or any other organization – actually learning itself. *How does a company learn? Which corporate entity learns? Does it learn on the balance sheet?*

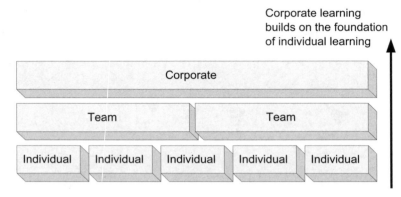

Figure 5.2   Learning begins with the individual.

The answer, of course, is that the people in the organization learn. Individuals learn, and groups of individuals learn together as teams, hence forming the foundation of learning in the whole organization, as shown in Figure 5.2.

Just because people are working doesn't stop them being human, and when humans gather together they form communities. They share experiences, agree normalities and learn together. People within companies learn and talk to each other: they observe each other and learn what works with their colleagues, their bosses, their team and the organization.

Even the most automated factory needs people and these people form a community. These individuals are capable of learning and passing on their learning. So if I learn that my boss expects me to be at my desk by 9 a.m., I'm likely to act on that information and pass it on to new recruits.

When this happens, it can appear that a firm is learning – think of it as a Turing test for companies. Although the firm can't learn, if its employees can learn, they're capable of giving the firm the appearance of learning. Outside, the firm appears as a single entity. An outsider can't tell how many people are inside – one or many – or whether the work is performed by machines or by people (Figure 5.3). Inside the firm, it's the people who are learning – because only people can learn – but to the outsider, this is indistinguishable from the firm itself actually learning.

It follows that a firm that encourages learning by individuals and groups can benefit. To facilitate the learning process, the organization must do more than simply advocate learning: it must be prepared to invest in mechanisms to encourage learning, record that learning and disseminate learning to a wider group.

This, then, is how an organization learns. First the people learn, then the community learns and finally the firm learns. Organizational learning isn't just how the corporation learns: it is about learning at every stage, from individual to multinational corporation.

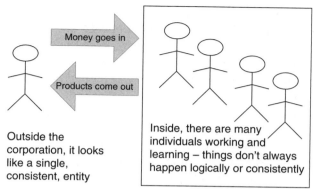

Outside the corporation, it looks like a single, consistent, entity

Inside, there are many individuals working and learning – things don't always happen logically or consistently

Figure 5.3 The Turing test for organizational learning.

The Turing Test

Proposed in 1950 by Alan Turing, the test is one attempt to answer the question 'Can machines think?' Turing hypothesized that if investigators couldn't tell whether they were communicating with a machine or a person, then the machine could be said to be capable of thought.

To perform a test, an investigator is placed in a room with a simple communication device – say, a Teletype. The other end of the connection is in another room, where it might be connected to a machine or to another Teletype manned by a human. The communication mechanism removes any clues as to who or what is on the other end. If the investigator believes that he or she is communicating with a human when in fact he or she is talking to a machine, then the machine is said to have passed the Turing test.

5.1.2 The Role of IT in Organizational Learning

Much has been written on the role of technology in the learning process. Most writing breaks down along one of two streams: *computer-assisted learning* or *IT as an agent of change*.

The first stream dominates the discussion by volume of literature. This stream considers IT a learning tool (e-learning) and a repository for documented knowledge. During the 1990s, many believed that software was the answer to knowledge management. Once documented, knowledge could be stored in databases and repositories. This assumption lay behind the early popularity of Lotus Notes and other tools marketed as knowledge management solutions.

For many people, knowledge management is still intrinsically tied up with software tools such as Notes. However, this view overlooks the role of action and tacit knowledge. While tools may provide useful facilities, they represent at best only part of the answer to knowledge management.

The second stream of thought takes a different point of view, by considering IT as an agent of change. The introduction of new IT systems into an organization not only requires new learning (e.g. training in the software) but can also be the catalyst for additional learning. By introducing new technology, the existing environment is changed and new learning opportunities arise for the technology users.

This second stream lacks the same volume of writing (and marketing) as the first stream, but has an equally long history. One of the founders of the organizational learning movement, Chris Argyris, wrote about 'Organizational learning and management information systems' over 25 years ago.[1] Since then, the theme has been revisited by many researchers,[2] but it has never become mainstream in the development community.

5.1.3   Technology Domination

The popular literature of software development again reveals two streams of discussion. The dominant stream is concerned with technology, which includes methodology, process and other formalisms. This stream assumes that development is an entirely rational process, and that therefore getting it 'right' is simply a case of using the right tools with the right process.

While the technology stream has long dominated the teaching and approach to software development, there's also an alternative description. This stream describes development in terms of people, internal politics and emergent behaviour. While far fewer books exist describing this stream, the ones that do include some of the best known: *Peopleware*,[3] *The Psychology of Computer Programming*[4] and *The Mythical Man Month*.[5]

These authors espouse the idea that it isn't so much the technology, methodology or the programming language used that brings success. Rather, it is the people and the way in which they work together. To a degree, these books have won the argument and few people today would directly challenge the idea that people make a difference to software projects. However, we still prefer to discuss technologies, methodologies and defined processes, so this view of software development has been neglected.

These two streams of thought are not incompatible. Indeed, they both help us understand how software systems are created and how we can improve the process. Unfortunately, the first stream dominates our literature and teaching.[6]

---

[1] In an academic journal piece entitled 'Organizational learning and management information systems' (Argyris, 1977).

[2] Authors include Ang, Thong and Yap (1997), Holt (2001), Huysman (2000) and Robey, Boundreau and Rose (2000).

[3] See DeMarco and Lister (1987).

[4] See Weinberg (1971).

[5] See Brooks (1975).

[6] For a deeper discussion, see Truex, Baskerville and Travis (2000).

The emergence of Agile practices goes some way to offsetting this domination. By putting people at the centre of the development activity and recognizing that development teams are not staffed with emotionless automatons, more reality has been injected into the literature. However, excessive emphasis on following any methodology, Agile or not, can limit our view.

A learning view changes this. Rather than focusing on process and technology, we look at what's being learnt, what knowledge is being generated and what's inhibiting our learning and forward movement.

5.1.4 The Search for Good People

Fortunately, one message from the second stream has largely been absorbed: people are important. People make the biggest difference to the success or failure of a project. Having absorbed this message, it is only natural that organizations strive to get the best people. This approach has two consequences.

Firstly, an organization's ability to perform is dependent on its ability to hire the best people. Since all organizations have learnt the same lesson, they're all pursuing the same strategy. Consequently, hiring becomes more difficult – the so-called *war for talent*. However, hiring good people isn't enough by itself, because since all your competitors are pursuing the same strategy, there's no advantage.

Secondly, the best technical people don't always have the best team skills and vice versa. Sometimes this plays itself out as a battle between technical managers and Human Resources (HR) departments. Consequently, some development teams are less teams than they are groups of individuals. (Section 5.5.4 has more to say on this subject.)

In fact, when it comes to staffing, companies face a classic buy versus build decision. Most IT companies choose the buy decision and try to hire experienced people. The alternative is to build your own people, or rather to hire people and help them grow into good technical people. This approach has the advantage that is allows you to grow fully rounded people who are both good technical and good team workers.

Learning organizations are better placed to develop their own people. However, they still need to hire people. When this happens, the team needs to rethink its priorities. For example, rather than seeking to hire the world's best JavaScript programmer, you may choose to hire someone with the *ability* to become the world's best JavaScript programmer. Values and beliefs become more important and technical skills less so.

Eventually, Agile teams will need to hire people, either because people leave or because teams expand. Agile teams need to take the long-term view and hire people who will contribute to the learning and develop themselves over time as part of the team.

5.2 The Infinite and the Finite Game

According to writer James Carse,[7] there are two types of games: those that are *finite* and those that are *infinite*.

Finite games have a defined start and end; at the end of the game, one of the players is (usually) declared the winner. All players share the same objective, namely *to win*. We can play the game again, in which case there may be a different winner, and we might play the game in rounds. Cricket, football, tennis and chess are all finite games.

Infinite games, on the other hand, don't have a start or an end. The game continues with new players joining and existing players retiring. There's no winner, because the only objective is to continue playing the game. Nor are there any losers; only those who no longer play. Within the game, players seek to survive and they may have additional individual objectives. Examples of such games are life, careers and sports such as rock-climbing.

Software development and business are infinite games that are sometimes played in rounds. Within each round there may be winners and losers, and it is possible to lose and play again in another round. In these cases we need to balance the need to win a round with the need to position ourselves for the start of the next round. Good players not only pay attention to the immediate game, but also position themselves for future play.

For example, the Microsoft XBox games console was introduced in 2001 to compete against the Sony PlayStation 2 and the Nintendo GameCube. In terms of market share, the XBox lost to the PlayStation, but Microsoft valued the experience gained. This allowed Microsoft to position itself for the next round of competition, against the Sony PlayStation 3 and the Nintendo Wii, with the XBox 360.

Business too is an infinite game. Despite the sporting metaphors and talk about defeating competition and winning market share, the real objective of every company is survival. The business writer Arie de Geus[8] describes companies as living entities that exist to survive; their objective is to continue playing the game.

Similarly, software development is a game with finite elements:

- *Finite:* We want to ship software – our customers expect us to deliver within a given time frame, according to prescribed rules.
- *Infinite:* Successful players get to play again – even if we aren't successful, we may play another round as long as we don't mess up too badly.

Consequently, we need to position ourselves for the next round even as we aim to win the current round. These objectives can and do come into conflict, which

[7] See Carse (1986).
[8] See de Geus (1997).

is one of the reasons why software development is so difficult. Again, because this is difficult, it can be the source of competitive advantage.

When survival gets harder, it is more difficult to win rounds. Similarly, when we try to win rounds we make it more difficult to position ourselves for the next round. However, if we don't concentrate on survival and winning the occasional round, we won't be able to compete in the future rounds.

In building learning organizations, we face the same demands. Spending all our time in learning activities may help to position us for the next round, but we need to survive the current round too. Conversely, working flat out to win this round is great, but may leave us poorly positioned for the next round of competition. There's a need to balance the two demands.

In the past, software development groups have often tried to position themselves for forthcoming rounds by future proofing their work. This takes the form of development frameworks, generic or reusable code and designing for requirements that are only imagined. Agile development dispenses with this kind of work and instead focuses teams on the project in hand. (Alistair Cockburn has a longer discussion on software development as an infinite game in *Agile Software Development*.[9])

The learning view suggests that rather than preparing for the future through technology, we prepare for the future through people. Instead of future proofing our technology, we invest in people so that they can respond to new challenges.

5.3 The Layers of the Organization

There are many dimensions to a positive learning organization. Some authors emphasize one dimension, others a different dimension. At times, it can seem that we need to hold many ideas in our heads simultaneously. However, most of these ideas are not contradictory, but merely represent different aspects. As with a software system, we can view these different aspects as layers, each one building on the layers below and supporting higher levels of functionality.

Figure 5.4 shows a layered model of a learning organization. Before any organization can start to learn, trust and honesty must exist. Without trust and honesty, employees can't openly discuss problems and opportunities within the organization. Unfortunately, some organizations will fail at this first hurdle.

Assuming that we have trust and honesty in the organization, we need to allow time and resources for learning and change to occur. This implies that we can't run our organization at 100 % usage all the time. Rather, we need to allow some *slack* in the system to provide learning opportunities.

[9] See Cockburn (2002).

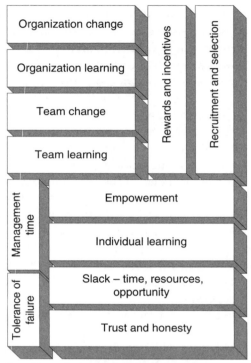

Figure 5.4   Organizational learning contains many layers.

Once we have trust, honesty and some slack, we create the opportunities for individuals to learn. There are many different ways for individuals to learn, and it is wrong to assume or mandate one way. Each individual needs to find his or her own path to learning.

The management of an organization must be prepared to let individuals put their learning to use in order to change the way in which they work as individuals and affect those immediately around them. Management needs to accept and empower individuals to learn and act on their own initiative.

These four layers constitute the heart of a learning organization. Taken alone, employees will start to learn and effect change to improve the organization. However, an organization can still block learning and change if it is risk averse and intolerant of failure. Individuals won't truly be empowered if they fear failure and restrict their actions to those they know are safe. Failure is a subject that appears in several different disguises in this book.

Responsible employees will naturally want to talk to others about things they have learned and opportunities they see for change and improvement. Managers must make themselves available to talk to employees about such ideas. Without management time, two things will happen. Firstly, employees won't feel valued by their managers and organizations, and they will be less forthcoming with ideas and suggestions for improvement. Secondly, managers themselves will lose, because they will no longer be in contact with front-line workers. They won't have an accurate picture of the business and won't have access to the ideas that are circulating in the front line. Over time, the two groups will diverge in their views of the organization, and empowerment and trust will suffer.

With these basics in place, organizations can advance from individual learning and change to team learning and change, and beyond that to organizational learning and change. The philosophy of this book is to use learning as the precursor of change, rather than forcing change and learning later.

Organization management can show the value attached to learning and change by ensuring that incentive and rewards (e.g. pay reviews and bonuses) recognize learning and change. Doing so explicitly demonstrates corporate commitment and directly encourages people to learn and change themselves and as part of a bigger group.

Initially, a learning environment is established with the people already in an organization. These are the people who know the work and the challenges best. In the longer term, opportunities will arise to hire new staff. Selection criteria for new staff should include willingness to learn themselves and the ability to contribute to team learning.

5.3.1 Trust and Honesty

Trust and honesty are mutually beneficial and difficult to separate. Without honesty, there's no basis for trust and without trust we can't assume honesty. Both trust and honesty are things we decide on as individuals, for ourselves: *Do I trust this individual? Shall I be honest in this situation?* However, honesty is about our outgoing communications – *Are we telling the truth?* – while trust is about the incoming communication – *Do we trust this person?*

If we don't trust others to be honest with us, then we must suspect every comment and message. Similarly, if we aren't honest with others, we'll wrap ourselves in lies and deceit, and others won't trust us. Obviously, neither situation is conducive to learning.

The same is true at an organizational level. Organizations that don't trust their members won't be able to confront problems or recognize opportunities. Without a clear and honest account of what the problem or opportunity really is, positive action isn't possible. Obviously, trust and honesty are incompatible with secrecy.

Organizations that culturally don't trust employees will spend time and energy checking the truth and honesty of those employees. Such effort is not only wasteful in itself, but it detracts from undertaking the real work of the organization. In such an environment, it is difficult for learning to grow and difficult to imagine people wanting to take risks and try new ideas.

5.3.2   Slack

Learning organizations need to make time to learn and they need to provide the resources to learn. Consequently, we can't expect a learning organization to operate at breakneck speed. People who are working 60-hour weeks simply don't have the time to attend talks and discussions. Nor do they have the energy or separation to reflect usefully on what's happening in their organization.

Companies that want to learn and improve need to allow some *slack* in the workplace. They need to allow time for people to reflect, think, discuss and take part in activities that don't immediately contribute to the company's output. Over time, the benefit of engaging in these activities will repay the investment many times over. Time must be taken from the finite game to ensure that the company improves its position in the infinite game.

The term *slack* was introduced by Tom DeMarco.[10] The same concept exists in *The Seven Habits of Highly Effective People*,[11] where Steven Covey distinguishes between our *productivity* and our *productive capacity*. Both authors suggest that we need to invest some of our time and resources in improving our organizations and ourselves. (This is another example of *infinite* and *finite* games.)

Time is just one aspect of slack. Being a highly specialized individual or an efficient organization brings a different danger. As in nature, the organizations that are most highly adapted to their environment tend to be less adaptable. In order to prepare for change and undertake change, we need some spare capacity. We need this capacity to allow for mistakes, to allow for experiments that don't work out and to give people space to undertake change and learning.

Slack includes more than just time. We need physical resources too, such as books and actual space. Staffing levels also have a role to play. Companies that employ only the absolute minimum number of workers lack the flexibility to conduct trials.

Teams need space for new recruits. The people who will staff the company tomorrow need time to become part of the company today. Initially, new recruits will be less productive and may reduce the productivity of existing staff, but this is all part of learning. Slack time is needed by both those doing the teaching and those doing the learning.

We also need slack management structures. Although flat organizations may improve communication between the top and bottom of a company, they can result in the exact opposite. Overworked managers lack time to listen and talk to employees. Managers can become cut off from workers, operations and the market, not because of layers of hierarchy but because they lack time to listen. Without middle managers there may be nobody to support a new idea, to coach staff in self-improvement or to encourage new ideas.

---

[10] See DeMarco (2001).

[11] See Covey (1992).

5.4 Learning in Practice: Senge's View

The Fifth Discipline[12] is a seminal work in the application of organizational learning to the workplace. The next few pages very briefly cover the five 'component technologies' that Peter Senge believes help us understand and encourage learning. If you've read *The Fifth Discipline*, you might want to skip these pages.

5.4.1 Personal Mastery

" 'Personal mastery' is [. . .] the discipline of personal growth and learning. People with high levels of personal mastery are continually expanding their ability to create the results in life they truly seek. From their quest for continual learning comes the spirit of the learning organisation."

Peter Senge (1990)

Personal mastery[13] is concerned with individuals' desire and ability to grow through learning. Those who have the discipline of personal mastery are actually 'masters of personal learning'; people who value learning and who act on what they learn.

This kind of *mastery* implies a more active form of learning, a desire to find out more and to act on what we find out, turning it into knowledge, and in the process improving our lives and moving us closer to our objectives.

Achieving true *mastery* involves a constant search for priorities. Prioritizing is itself a form of learning, which requires awareness, honesty and continual questioning. We must be prepared to note changes in ourselves and our environment, and re-prioritize accordingly.

Learning organizations are built by people with personal mastery. Without people who will question and re-prioritise, any organization risks pursuing the wrong goals and constantly playing catch-up with the opposition. In return, organizations need to value those who value learning. Companies need to provide opportunities to learn and act, and they need to seek ways to align the individual's goals and objectives with those of the firm.

According to Senge, not only will those who possess mastery learn faster, but they will be more committed and more prepared to take the initiative. Enlightened companies will seize upon these attributes and harness them to the firm's goals. This can only be a win–win situation: individuals are given opportunities to learn and are happier in their work. Meanwhile, the firm reaps the returns from new ideas, commitment and improved operations.

---

[12] See Senge (1990).

[13] Think *mastery* as in 'master of' rather than 'dominate'.

It is frequently these characteristics – an eagerness to learn and take the initiative – that separate the average developer from the highly productive developer. Those with personal mastery are valuable to software development teams and are great assets to Agile teams. These are the people who seek out new ideas and technologies.

Thinking Point: Look For Master Learners

Think about your team-mates and work colleagues:
Which of these people do you think exhibit personal mastery?
Who are the enthusiastic learners?
Having identified these individuals, think about what it is that they do that marks them out.
What are their behaviours?
How can you encourage these behaviours in others?
Can you, or those you have identified with personal mastery, teach these behaviours to others?

5.4.2   Shared Vision

"At its simplest level, a shared vision is the answer to the question, 'What do we want to create?' Just as personal visions are pictures or images people carry in their heard and hearts, so too are shared visions pictures that people throughout the organisation carry."

Peter Senge (1990)

Sharing a common goal is what distinguishes a team from a group of people. Simply putting people in a room and telling them that they are a team doesn't make them a team. Similarly, hiring six developers who have worked well in six different teams before and calling them a team doesn't make them a team. Each team is different, because each team contains a different mix of people and each team needs to find its own way of working together, its own strengths and weaknesses.

Participating in the shared vision means that individuals accept that they won't create the whole themselves. Instead, individuals are offered the opportunity to create something bigger than they could create alone, and something that will be bigger than the sum of its parts.

For this to happen, each individual must hold a personal stake in the vision. In order to build a personal stake, it helps if each person is allowed to take part in the vision formation. This will help them internalize the vision and make it part of their identity, thus creating a sense of belonging and focus for actions.

Simply handing a team a ready-made vision and asking them to adopt it as their own is the antithesis of true shared vision. People who are handed a ready-made vision won't feel the same attachment, and consequently they will be less motivated to bring the vision to reality.

For a shared vision or mission statement to really motivate individuals and teams, they must be able to associate closely with the idea. It is not enough for a manager or planner to explain how vision affects an individual. In order to create a close personal relationship with the vision, individuals need to hold a stake in it.

Thinking Point: Visions

Think about the vision present in your team or organization. If you have no visions, then look for the plans, goals, objectives, strategies and mission statement of the organization. Look at software designs and architectures. Each of these contains a form of vision:

- Does your project have a clear vision of what it is doing?
- Can team members articulate the vision?
- Do team members articulate the same vision?
- Do they feel motivated to make the vision come true?

5.4.3   Team Learning

"Team learning is the process of aligning and developing the capacity of a team to create the results its members truly desire."

Peter Senge (1990)

In any development team, many members will have specialist skills and knowledge. For the team to work well together, the members need to respect one another and maximize individual's specialities, but also support the needs of those with less experience or knowledge.

For Senge, there's more to *team learning* than just ensuring that a team works well together. Team learning goes beyond good teamwork. Team learning builds personal mastery and shared vision, to create highly effective motivated units.

Team action and learning are guided by the shared vision that helps the team to direct its thinking. The shared vision helps the team to know what to investigate and what to pass over.

When a team works well together, guided by a shared vision that all members believe in and work towards, then a phenomenon of *alignment* is seen. This occurs when all team members are pulling in exactly the same direction, without diversion. Unfortunately, there's a danger that effective individuals working with the best intention but not working in alignment can pull in different directions. This makes management more difficult.

Team members need personal mastery to keep their individual learning moving, but for team learning there needs to be more. There needs to be sharing of learning amongst team members and between teams. Individuals can be great learners themselves, but if they don't share their learning then team learning won't occur.

Effective teams are open to learning as a group. The team needs to be able to engage shared reflection and what Senge calls *dialogue and discussion*. Senge differentiates between dialogue – which he considers a creative exploration – and discussion, which he describes as the presentation and defence of different views.

The team should inquire into opportunities and problems, and recognize potential conflicts rather than avoiding them. These mechanisms help the team learn, build team knowledge and identify improvements to work practices.

Thinking Point: Teams

Identify the teams in your organization and the people who comprise those teams. Think about the successes and failures of each team. Compare the team members with those who you consider possess personal mastery:

- Which teams hold a shared vision? And where did it come from?
- Which teams do you consider most successful?
- What are the differences between the most successful teams and the less successful ones?
- What opportunities exist for teams to reflect together?
- What happens when someone is a member of two teams at the same time?

5.4.4   Mental Models

"Our 'mental models' determine not only how we make sense of the world, but how we take action."

Peter Senge (1990)

Mental models are the ideas, preconceptions and assumptions that we all carry around in our heads. We need these models to help us function every day, and they are valuable short cuts that enable us to skip over first principles and get things done.

When we're aware of these models, there's little problem. If our assumptions are out in the open, are explicit and we're aware of them, then we can selectively switch them off when dealing with new problems or seeking new solutions. Problems set in when we're unaware that the models are governing our actions, or when we fail to recognize that our models don't apply.

Senge goes further than just pointing out that mental models exist. He advocates a discipline that seeks to expose the models and open them to questioning. Recognizing that these assumptions exist allows them to be questioned and rethought.

Mental models exist throughout the software development process. They exist in specification documents, in manager's models of how development works, in the code that developers write and in the tests run against the system. Some inaccurate assumptions lead directly to bugs found by customers.

At every stage in the development process, we use our mental models to make assumptions. Advocates of voluminous documentation and strict methodological processes can claim that documentation will help overcome the problem. But as we write longer documents, and add extra rigour to our processes, we encourage individuals to take short cuts and rely on their mental models all the more.

Mental Models in Action

A team of developers based in Chicago developed a software system for an international financial institution. So successful was the software that the company decided to deploy it in the London office as well. Unfortunately, the developers hadn't provided any support for currencies other than the dollar. These developers had a mental model about how the software was going to work, in dollars, and that was that.

This model was quickly exposed and the developers added support for the multitude of currencies that were traded in London – sterling, euros, Swiss francs, and so on. Unfortunately, the developers had thrown aside one mental model and replaced it with another faulty one.

The developers had taken the message to heart, and the new software updated valuations several times a minute to reflect changes in exchange rates. However, the traders using the system didn't need this level of accuracy and found the constant updating distracting. For them, a single daily exchange rates update was enough.

Thinking Point: Finding Models and Assumptions

Finding assumptions and mental models can be difficult, because we're often unaware that we're making decisions based on mental models. It can be easier to see mental models when things go wrong. Think about recent problems and bug reports:

- Were any of these caused by incorrect assumptions?
- How could you have identified those assumptions before the problem arose?

5.4.5   Systems Thinking

"System thinking is a discipline of seeing wholes. It is a framework for seeing relationships rather than things, for seeing patterns of change rather than "snapshots"."

Peter Senge (1990)

Systems are not just computer systems. They are any kind of device or process where a number of different pieces need to work together to produce an end result or product. *Computer systems* are just one type of system, namely the type relating to computers. Modern society and business are full of systems.

Traditional Western science emphasizes breaking things down into small parts and understanding the operation of each small piece. We consider substances made up of atoms, and atoms made up of electrons, protons and neutrons; protons in turn are made up of quarks and so on. Systems thinking takes the opposite approach. It seeks to understand how larger entities interact and inter-operate. Rather than looking at individual actions – and explaining how each one came to occur – we look at the overall system and try to understand the drivers for whole systems.

Issues arise because although all the individual pieces may be working faultlessly, when they work together – in the system – unintended results occur. Identifying the problems can be difficult because our training, as engineers and scientists, leads us to decompose the problem and examine individual pieces. To overcome this, we need to engage in *systems thinking*.

Diagnosing problems is only half the story. Once identified, these problems need to be addressed. Again, the complex interaction between multiple pieces makes solutions harder. Fixing a problem may require several coordinated changes. What may appear to be a retrograde step in one piece may actually resolve a far larger problem.

Exercise: Recognizing Systems

Systems surround us:

- *Transport systems:* Cars, roads, filling stations, repair centres, buses, trains, . . .
- *Retail systems:* Shops, shopping malls, window displays, . . .
- *Food:* Restaurants, kitchens, order-taking, food delivery, . . .

And systems exist within systems: food moves to shops via a transport system, to be sold through a retail system and cooked in a kitchen system.

Identify the systems at work in your team or organization. Attempt to draw the systems and link the different parts together. Think about how the different parts interact, and about the forces that are supporting the system and those that are working against it.

5.4.6 And Reflection

Finally, although Senge doesn't give it the same up-front emphasis as his other 'technologies', there's an additional discipline that underpins much of his discussion. This is *reflection*, and it has already been mentioned in Sections 1.9 and 4.7.1:

> "Skills of reflection concern slowing down our own thinking processes so that we can become aware of how we form our mental models and the ways they influence our actions. Inquiry skills concern how we operate in face-to-face interactions with others, especially in dealing with complex and conflicting issues."
>
> Peter Senge (1990)

In practice, reflection simply means 'taking time to think about things'. It is very easy in a hectic environment to be so concerned with *getting stuff done* that we never stop to think about what we're doing, why we're doing it and whether we may actually be making everything worse with the fixes we apply.

Reflection is key to personal growth and development. Actively practising reflection can substantially improve our own learning process and help us achieve our aims and objectives. Team reflection can also help with enhancing team learning. Some of the ideas outlined in Chapter 10 can help improve team reflection and learning.

> ## Thinking Point: Reflection
>
> If you followed the suggestion in Chapter 1 to keep a journal, then you've probably been doing some reflection already. *What have you discovered so far?*
>
> If you haven't been keeping a journal, then consider what has blocked you from doing so and take time to think about how you could overcome those blocks.
>
> If you don't like the idea of keeping a journal, then identify other mechanisms you can use to promote reflection.

5.5 Blocks to Learning

There is another route to improving learning: removing the obstacles that block learning. Such learning inhibitors come both from within ourselves and from outside. Likewise, for an organization some inhibitors are self-made, while others are external.

Some blocks to learning are simply the flip side of Senge's disciplines. For example, the opposite of systems thinking leaves us seeing parts, not wholes. Other blocks, such as camouflage, are distinct in their own right. In the sections below, I describe some general blocks and some blocks that are common in the software development field.

> ## Thinking Point: Your Blocks to Learning
>
> This section looks at a few ways in which learning can be blocked. Make a list of the things that stop you from learning more.

5.5.1 Invisibility

Many of the most valuable learning experiences come from solving problems. However, you can only solve a problem if you can see it. Similarly, it isn't possible to capitalize on an opportunity if you don't recognize that the opportunity exists. Sometimes problems and opportunities are just invisible.

For large problems and opportunities, especially those that concern the team or organization, it is necessary that more than one person sees the issue. Trying to fix a problem that nobody else recognizes will be very frustrating. Therefore, one of the first things we can do is to expose problems and opportunities and let people see that they exist.

Problems can be hidden in a multitude of ways. Some examples include:

- *Electronic bug databases:* Bugs aren't visible; bugs get talked about by reference number – *'Is bug 432 fixed yet?'* – which makes them all seem equal. When bugs become numbers they become less visible.

- *Lack of communication:* If teams don't talk to each other and to management, then there's little chance that issues will be discussed. Even when individuals and teams do talk about problems, there needs to be someone there to listen. Communication isn't just about talking – it's about listening too.

- *No forum to talk about issues:* There can be things that are known – even widely known – but if nobody feels able to talk about them, especially to senior people, then they're never exposed.

- *Pub- and coffee-only conversations:* Many problems are discussed by teammates over a beer or a coffee, but once back in the office nothing is done.

Some problems are hidden simply because there's no information on them. For example, if nobody actually asks customers what they think of a product, the team will never know that the customers are looking for an alternative. Yet even if this information is available, it needs to be highlighted and acted upon.

Helping other people see a problem or opportunity can make it easier to address. However, there's a danger that when faced with problems – particularly those that they don't feel able to solve – people will become defensive and deny that problems exist, or act to isolate themselves.

5.5.2   Camouflage

Problems become camouflaged[14] when they are partially solved or solved in such a way as to create other problems. A partial solution may appear to resolve the problem, but in fact it makes things worse elsewhere. Such solutions are often found in program code, where removing one problem exposes another that was hidden by the first. Similar problems exist in processes and organizations.

There's a propensity for one solution to create problems elsewhere: Senge refers to these as solutions that 'shift the burden'. Such solutions may appear to work for a while, but eventually they make the situation worse.

Many development groups add time at the end of a schedule to fix bugs. Sometimes this is honestly called 'bug fixing'; at other times it is given euphemisms such as 'stabilization', 'beta release' or 'testing'. This allows products to ship closer to the scheduled date, but they still ship later than they need to. Over time, these phases have a tendency to increase in length.

The real solution is to avoid creating the bugs in the first place. If bugs can't be prevented from entering the code, then they should be removed as soon as

---

[14] The term 'camouflage' comes from Argyris (1997).

possible. Unfortunately, too many people have bought into a mental model that says 'Bugs are inevitable. We just have to live with the fact.'

Partial solutions often come about when the problem isn't fully appreciated. This can happen when we don't enquire into the problem and the effects that it is having. Instead of enquiring, we jump to assumptions and rely on our existing mental models – in effect, a form of single-loop learning.

5.5.3   Personal Defences

One of the bigger blocks to learning and change comes from our own personal defences and those of other people. We all create defensive ways of thinking and acting in order to protect ourselves, and our families and teams. As such, defences are usually created with best intentions in mind; however, they can slow down and prevent learning and change.

Defences are a little like wearing blinkers so that we don't see problems that might hurt us. A defence may be something that we do, or something that we don't do. We might be aware of our defence or it might be subconscious. Our defensive behaviour allows us to stay in our comfort zone and just keep on doing things the way we always have.

Personal Defences in the Code Review Process

One company that I know set up a code review system driven by source code control check-ins. When a piece of code was checked, the designated reviewer would receive an e-mail prompting her to review the code. The reviewer would send an e-mail to the originator, with comments for revision. No discussion took place – developers weren't allowed to explain their decisions or ask for more information. The reviewer's word was final.

Unfortunately, this made for an adversarial system. Comments would be short and possibly abrupt, without explanation. Developers couldn't respond and sometimes they felt personally hurt by the comments. Consequently, they delayed and reduced the number of check-ins that they performed by batching changes into fewer and bigger check-ins. As deadlines approached, reviewers would be overwhelmed by code for review. Under these conditions, it could take reviewers weeks to review all the code.

The code reviewers had created a defence in a highly automated system that took as little of their time as possible. The developers responded with a defence to limit the instance of hurt they felt. As a result, a system designed for efficiency became highly inefficient and ineffectual.

Sometimes we consciously create defensive behaviours. On other occasions, we subconsciously adapt our thinking and actions to avoid pain. Over time, these changes can escalate, as defences in one person or group cause a response in another group, and this in turn triggers a new defence in the first group.

Some researchers have suggested that the emphasis on development techniques and methodology is itself a form of defence.[15] By adopting a formal process, development project failures can be attributed to failings of the process or failure to follow the process. Consequently, the real reasons for project failure may not be examined. Rather than debating what individuals must do to improve next time, the discussion centres on process improvement. The process serves to shield individuals from failure and prevents learning and change.

Many of the same tools that we have been discussing can be used to tackle and remove defences; namely, team learning, recognizing mental models and system thinking. Before we can tackle defences, we need to establish trust and honesty – discussed in Section 5.3. It will be harder to persuade someone to drop a defence if he or she fears the consequences.

Defences are a form of assumption that governs our behaviour. However, they are more than just an assumption, because human emotion is involved. It is quite legitimate for people to have these feelings, even in the workplace. Considering how other people will feel and react when we're trying to dismantle their defences will make our task easier in the long run.[16]

When Action is the Wrong Thing

The need for action is a reoccurring theme in this book, but action isn't always the right thing to do. In fact, action can itself be a form of personal defence that we use to avoid hard decisions, and which stops us engaging in more thoughtful activities such as reflection. Sometimes we use a *bias for action* to do the wrong things. This happens when we're so busy *doing things* that we have no time to make decisions, to think or to spend time with our colleagues deciding on the right things to do.

Constantly doing things, such as writing program code, reading documents or attending meetings, can easily take up all our work hours and some more too. When this happens, we deprive ourselves of the time we need for thinking. We need to make time in our busy work lives to stop and think about what we're doing.

It is easy to have a *bias for action* if that action involves doing the same as yesterday. We may look busy and we may feel busy, but how do we know that we're doing the right thing? Instead, we may be absorbing ourselves

---

[15] See Wastell (1996).

[16] This discussion is really the tip of an iceberg. The role of emotions in the workplace and during change deserves a book on its own. Daniel Goleman's *Emotional Intelligence* (1996) makes a good starting point for further discussion.

in work action in order to avoid dealing with difficult problems. It can be easy to find pressing work to do when the alternative is doing something we would rather not do. For example, Chapter 11 discusses how project retrospectives can be used to improve teams. But if we're fearful of what the retrospective may find, then it can be all too easy to find work that needs doing now and that prevents a retrospective from taking place.

All work and no reflection is bad. All reflection and no work is bad. We need to find a balance between the two. Most importantly, when our reflection shows us some new insights, we need to act on those insights and not hide behind work.

5.5.4 Micro-projects and Solo Developers

Anyone who has worked in software development for more than a few years will have come across individuals who are technically brilliant but are less gifted at working in teams. Such individuals may well possess excellent technical skills and even personal mastery, but they may lack other skills. The situation is exacerbated when these individuals start to see their co-workers as technically naive or inexperienced.

These people present managers with a difficult choice. In solving one problem, they risk creating another. It is a little like the man who goes to the doctor with his brother:

Man: Doctor, my brother thinks he is a chicken.
Doctor: Here are some tablets. Give him two a day. If he's not better in a week, come back.
Man: But doctor, we need the eggs.

Often, managers respond by finding, or creating, some little project where an individual developer might work alone. I call these *micro-projects*. Here, a developer can work on his own code, at his own pace, without the interference of team members. Other developers won't bother him and equally he won't bother them.

This is one example of what Thomas Davenport has called HSPALTA:[17] 'hire smart people and leave them alone'. Assigning developers to micro-projects allows them to work in isolation. Micro-projects have an additional benefit for the manager responsible. They can legitimately claim 'we're working on it' whenever asked how the project is going.

In fact, micro-projects are an example of 'shifting the burden', because while they solve some immediate problems, they create additional problems in the longer term.

---

[17] See Davenport (2005).

Financially, it is more worthwhile to have many developers work on one project at a time. Companies realize a higher rate of return when multiple projects are run in series rather than in parallel. A team rapidly delivering one project and moving on to the next is worth more than solo developers working on multiple projects.

Imagine that we have five projects to carry out, and suppose that each project will take 12 man–months. We could set five solo developers to work. In one year, they will deliver five projects and revenue will start to follow. Alternatively, we could have all the developers work on one project at the same time. A little over two months later, the project would be complete, allowing the company to recognize revenue or savings from the project. Since the money is seen sooner, it's worth more to the company.

Individuals working alone miss out on opportunities for team learning and knowledge sharing. This is reflected in the resulting code base, with different coding styles and different design idioms and patterns in use. Such code lacks consistency and some functionality will be implemented multiple times. In the long run, the lack of knowledge sharing makes the system more difficult to enhance and maintain.

Melvin Conway pointed out as long ago as 1968 that system design will mirror the organization that designed the system. *Conway's Law*,[18] as it became known, states:

"organisations which design systems (...) are constrained to produce designs which are copies of the communication structures of these organisations."

Melvin Conway (1968)

Five systems designed and built by five different individuals will be just that: five very different systems. Without any commonality, the long-term workload will be higher.

While reducing the teamwork and interaction, micro-projects actually increase the amount of management time required. Rather than focusing on one project at a time, managers now need to track and manage multiple projects. From time to time, these projects will come into competition when limited resources (e.g. testers or machines) are needed by several projects at the same time. In these situations, it is quite likely that managers will be called to arbitrate and decide priorities.

Often, micro-projects eventually need to be integrated, perhaps into a common code base. This results in multiple integration events, which themselves consume time. Integration will expose conflicts in the different ways that developers have tackled issues. Inevitably, developers will have made assumptions about how other code works and some of these may be exposed as false.

---

[18] Conway's Law has been the subject of much debate over the years: see Coplien and Harrison (2004), Hvatum and Kelly (2005) and Raymond (1996).

Multiple projects delivering at about the same time will have knock-on effects on the next group in the chain. Operations departments may find that they have multiple updates to roll out, or marketing groups may find that they have a flood of products to advertise.

So, while setting up a series of micro-projects may look like a solution, a little systems thinking shows that such an approach is storing up problems for the future.

Thinking Point: Micro-projects

Look for micro-projects in your organization. What caused them to be set up as small projects? What problems are they storing up? How else might you organize the work?

5.5.5   Resource Pools

There is one particularly nasty block to learning and effective team working that is unfortunately all too common in software development organizations. This is the management of developers as a common resource pool.

Under this model, teams are short-lived entities that exist for one project or one section of a project. At the end of an assignment, developers are returned to a common pool, from where they may be assigned to another project. Usually, the pool is a concept rather than a physical reality. Developers are unlikely to sit around doing nothing. More likely, they will be moved between different projects that are in process.

The aim of the arrangement is to maximize the use of developers and ensure that high-priority projects have all the resources they need. While this model sounds reasonable, it has a number of failings when examined from a learning perspective.

The switching of people between projects makes it difficult for teams to build a shared vision or engage in any team learning. Alignment is unlikely to occur when teams are only together for short periods of time. This is especially true when people join the team after it has started and leave before it has ended.

Developers who know that they're likely to be assigned to another project before the conclusion of their work are less likely to take pride in their work. The knowledge that they won't have to live with the problems can reduce the care taken in the work.

For managers, the pool model is especially dangerous for several reasons. By providing a seeming solution to a troublesome project – *add more staff*! – it can prevent them from looking deeper and examining the real reasons why projects encounter problems. Even if they are so inclined, the constant movement of staff makes it more difficult to actually diagnose problems, let alone fix them.

By moving staff frequently, management set the expectation that staff can be moved. Therefore, when a project encounters problems, they're likely to increase the staffing level even at the expense of other projects. Consequently, management spend a lot of time discussing who should be assigned where and the relative priorities of projects. This in turn creates a fertile ground for office politics and division, rather than consensus and unity.

While it appears to maximize the use of resources, much time and energy is wasted. The movements have hindered learning, promoted naive solutions and encouraged office politics. Management control is more of an illusion than a reality.

The pool model makes two assumptions about the work environment. Firstly, it is assumed that the organization is resource constrained. Therefore it is necessary to ensure that staff are fully utilized every minute. Secondly, the model assumes that it is easy for workers themselves to switch from project to project, and that neither project loses anything except the time of the developer who moves.

Both of these assumptions are wrong. People take time to come up to speed on a new project. When they leave a project they take knowledge with them, and when they join a new project they need time from fellow team members to acquire knowledge of the new project. Consequently, the switching costs for both projects are high.

Development teams are often short of staff and it is sometimes necessary to move people between teams. But making these assumptions turns them into self-fulfilling prophecies.

5.5.6   Failure to Act

One of the biggest reasons why learning gets blocked is simply failure to act on what we learn, or what we think is a good idea. We've already discussed failure to act in Section 3.2, but it's worth mentioning again.

Having warned against partial solutions and 'shifting the burden' type solutions, it might seem that we should extensively analyse each problem that comes our way before acting. Unfortunately, this can lead to the search for the perfect solution, or 'paralysis by analysis'. This happens when the need for further analysis, discussion and thought leads to no action taking place.

Sometimes it is right to hold back on action until more information is available and more people have been consulted. However, this can be a recipe for inaction. The alternative is to try something, see if it works and modify the action in light of the results. If necessary, this may mean reverting to the original state.

This might seem obvious, but it is hard to do. We may be blocked by the need for consensus for any change – even a change on top of a change. Or we may be blocked by fear of looking foolish or admitting that we got it wrong.

It can sometimes seem that, as individuals, our default setting is 'no action' – or to use Tom Peters' expression, discussed in Section 3.2, *a bias for inaction*.

Instead, we need to move to *a bias for action*, to reset our personal default to 'action'. Action means change, and that is where the following chapters of this book take us.

5.6 Conclusion

Together with Chapter 3, I have now laid the foundations of the learning view of software development. At the heart of this is individual learning; team learning builds on individual learning and organizational learning builds on team learning. In describing the theory of the learning view, I have also suggested some actions that you can take to enhance learning.

Agile teams often begin with one individual who discovers the ideas of Agile or Lean development. This is not enough: the whole team needs to learn collectively how to undertake Agile development. Unfortunately, organizations sometimes react to constrain the growth of Agile teams. In the long run, the reverse is true: Agile teams need to live within Agile organizations, so Agile needs to spread if it is to prosper.

There are basically two ways to exploit the learning view for your team or organization. Firstly, take a more active approach to learning for yourself and those around you. Secondly, remove the blocks that inhibit learning. In both cases, learning can't happen without action and that action involves change.

From here on, this book focuses on change and putting learning into action. As it turns out, many of the mechanisms for enhancing learning are also the mechanisms for creating change. As action creates change, more learning will result.

First of all, though, we need to take a slight detour. We need to understand the role of computers, software and all information technology not as *technology*, but as the bringer of change itself.

Information Technology – the Bringer of Change

"Today's problems come from yesterday's "solutions"."
Peter Senge (1990)

Information technology often seems to run on its own change schedule. New CPUs and bigger disks arrive on regular schedule, new languages and operating systems emerge and web sites doing novel things tend to explode into public view. The new and improved technology creates shock waves, resulting in change throughout society and business.

But within business, new technology doesn't just appear. New technology is used by businesses to achieve some objective. Businesses set objectives in order to create change: there's little point in setting an objective that doesn't require change. Technology is simply the means of transmitting and enabling that change. Technology is not the end in itself but, rather, a means to an end.

Technology can be both the instigator of change and the tool of change. It can also be a block to change; and examples aren't hard to find:

- Legacy applications that are hard to modify prevent changes.

- Intra-company cooperation and even company mergers can be blocked by different systems and data formats.

- The cost of supporting and servicing dated systems and software can absorb cash and prevent investment in new IT capabilities for new initiatives.

Changing Software Development: Learning to Become Agile   Allan Kelly
© 2008 John Wiley & Sons, Ltd.

Software development can be a double-edged sword: on the one hand, it can be used to introduce change directly and it can bring about learning. However, it can also hinder change and prevent it from happening.

Consequently, some businesses have come to see IT as a problem instead of an opportunity. Rather than systems supporting business change and allowing the firms to realize new opportunities, IT is too often seen as a block to change and new business.

The Agile software development movement is in part a response to this problem. By allowing businesses to respond to changing environments, Agile practices allow developers to deliver more value. Rather than being a block to change, IT can – and should – be an enabler that helps creates change.

If we want to change software development, we have to change the way in which business relates to and views the development processes. Businesses need to see software development as an opportunity to be grasped – not a problem to be shunned.

Firstly, though, we need to change the way in which software developers see businesses. Developers need to appreciate the role of IT in creating business change and how their own practices hinder businesses.

6.1 Change

It can seem odd when you first think about this, but *change* is a subject in its own right – albeit a slightly abstract one, but then software folks are used to dealing in abstractions. The introduction, management, consequences and failure of change are documented in many books and journals. Sometimes the only thing that all these commentators seem to agree on is that most change initiatives fail.

The hard truth seems to be that most deliberate attempts at change fail. The exact numbers vary, depending on whose work you read, but there's general agreement that most (perhaps as many as 70 %) change initiatives fail.[1] This is a sobering thought to anyone contemplating change.

One of the basic mistakes in creating change is to reduce the change to one of technical implementation. Issuing mandates to order changes overlooks the fact that change is more subtle and multi-facetted than issuing mandates. Mandates have their limits. We may be able to mandate the use of Java, but can we mandate that all programs are bug free – or that all projects will be delivered on time?

Just because we issue a rule doesn't mean it will be followed. There are rules against speeding on the highway in most countries, but people still do it. When we use mandates to bring about change, we ignore the subtleties, risks and realities involved with change.

---

[1] This particular percentage is taken from Beer and Nohria (2000).

Software developers, like many knowledge workers, are often authorities in their own field: frequently, they know more about aspects of the work than those managing them. Just because someone has a higher position on the organogram doesn't give him or her the ability to order change or action. On the whole, managers can't tell a developer what to do as they might a blue-collar worker. A little authority can be useful from time to time, but generally knowledge workers do what they want.

Maybe because we can effortlessly change our screen savers, we believe that changing processes and companies is also effortless. Organizational change is not easy, because it involves people. When people are enthusiastic and embrace change, it is more likely to be a success; when they're fearful of change and – consciously or subconsciously – resist, then it is more likely to fail.

Few IT workers consider change in its own right. What makes this especially odd is that IT itself forces change on others. The act of introducing a new computer system to a company or department forces changes on the people in that department. We, as the developers of these systems, are frequently guilty of ignoring the impact of our systems.

6.2 Benefits of Technology Change

At some point, every successful software project gets deployed. For the developers this might be the end of the project, but for the users it is only the start. The users need to change their working habits to incorporate the new software. Users who have become accustomed to doing things one way can find it difficult to change. They may question why they should do things differently just because the software has changed.

Software is usually designed to change the way in which people work. At a basic level, technology seeks to automate the current process. Businesses benefit because work gets done quicker, possibly to higher quality and possibly more cheaply because fewer people are needed.

Thinking Point: What Changes Will Your Project Introduce?

What changes will your current project introduce? Who will be affected?

However, automation alone won't maximize the benefits from technology. For example, e-mail can deliver a message in seconds: if we keep our old routine of opening all mail at the start of the day, we have lost much of the advantage that e-mail has over traditional letters and memos. Thus, only when technology (e-mail) is combined with changes in the way we work do we maximize the benefit.

So a more ambitious approach is to re-engineer the processes in place to take full advantage of the technology. The need to change processes to maximize the benefits of technology was a major driving force behind the *Business Process Re-engineering* (*BPR*) movement (see the topic box in Chapter 7).

While automation and re-engineering can result in the same goals being achieved more efficiently, a third approach is to change the objective through innovation. For example, at first, iPods and MP3 players were superior versions of the Sony Walkman. However, combined with the Internet, the ability to download music is changing our relationship with the music that we own and the business model of the recording industry.

New technology creates three types of benefit:[2]

- *Automation comes first:* Doing the same thing faster and better is the most obvious benefit.

- *Process change:* Over time – which in some cases is measured in decades – processes are re-engineered and industries change.

- *Innovation:* Technology creates opportunities for innovation (and more technology) that may be more valuable than either automation or process change.

IT and software are not the only technologies to have followed this pattern: many technologies followed the same route before and more will follow it in the future.

Box Technology

Thirty-five foot long steel shipping containers may not look like cutting edge technology, but in 1956 that is exactly what they were. A look at the rise of containerization as the dominant form of shipping graphically demonstrates all the aspect of technology change: the need for change, the opportunity for change, resistance to change; and improvements through automation, process change and innovation.

The cargo shipping industry ended the Second World War in bad shape and by the mid-1950s things were not improving. Sending cargo by sea was time-consuming and unreliable, ships arrived late, and cargo went missing or was left behind on the dock. Ships crossing the Atlantic spent more time loading and unloading cargo than sailing. This meant that ship owners' major assets spent more time tied up at the wharf than at sea earning money. Fortunately, ships were cheap; war surplus ships could be bought from the US government for $300 000. Unfortunately, these ships were small, slow and, as they aged, increasingly unreliable.

---

[2] For more on this, see Messerschmidt and Szyperski (2003).

Things weren't any better at the ports. Loading and unloading ships was a manual task requiring backbreaking work. The ports were old and in need of modernization, the labour force was inflexible and productivity was declining.

Something had to change, but change cost money and few companies in the industry were making enough to re-invest. One solution was well known: several reports had suggested the use of standard containers to load and unload ships. However, this required changes by the shipping companies, the dock companies and the labour unions.

The change was finally initiated by someone from outside the industry. Malcolm McLean had made his money in the US trucking industry. Spotting an opportunity to move freight more cheaply by sea, he got into the shipping industry. McLean's first container ship, the *Ideal-X*, sailed from New Jersey to Houston in April 1958, with just 58 containers on board.

At first, the container was seen as a cheaper way of doing the same thing – it was a form of automation. Containers could be loaded and unloaded from the ship quickly by using cranes. This allowed ships to spend less time in dock and more time at sea earning money. The containers could be packed and unpacked at the dock while the ship was at sea. Fewer men were needed to load and unload the ship, but some were employed loading and unloading the containers.

Process change followed relatively quickly. Rather than sending their goods to the port to be packed in containers for their journey, factories could send a fully loaded container to the port. This eliminated the packing and unpacking of containers and reduced lost goods. In some cases, factories had to increase the size of their production runs.

When the US military adopted containerization to resolve the logistics problems of fighting the Vietnam war, it was process change, not automation, that was the solution. The 'Three Cs' rule mandated one container, one customer, one commodity, and massively simplified the logistics complexity. Processes and procedures changed and the war could go on.

Processes changed in the shipping industry too. Economies of scale meant that it made sense to serve fewer but bigger ports. Rather than collect and deliver cargo from a multitude of ports, shipping lines changed routes and concentrated on the biggest ports. So more containers needed to be transported by train or truck to large ports.

It is tempting to see the benefits of technology unfolding over time: first the benefits from automation, next the benefits from process change and finally the benefits from innovation. However, this hierarchy is based on the magnitude of the benefits, not the passage of time. Automation is usually the most visible benefit and so occurs first. The benefits of innovation may start to appear long before the automation or process changes have completed. So it was with containers.

The *Ideal-X* had hardly completed her first voyage as a container ship before innovations started to occur. Initially, innovation came with new ports and ships. Ports that invested in cranes and container-handling equipment won business from those that did not. Ships got bigger, ships got faster, ships got bigger again, ships got slower, ships got even bigger and some ships started to endlessly circumnavigate the globe. Such innovations contributed far more than automation to the massive price reductions that followed.

Innovation in container handling reshaped the world transport markets and routes. Containers shipped from Tokyo to New York might travel entirely by sea, through the Panama Canal, or via Cape Horn on ships too big to pass through the canal. Alternatively, the containers might travel from Tokyo to Oakland in California by sea and then on trains to New York.

Change also came with the actual containers being shipped. By adopting standard sizes, the containers of one company could be carried on the ships or trains of another. Standardization of containers allowed the economies of scale to be recognized throughout the industry and created a new industry of container leasing.

Hidden within the story there's a warning against incremental change and viewing automation as the only benefit. The first container ships carried their containers on deck only and carried traditional cargo below desk. While this meant that the containers could be loaded and unloaded faster, the ship still needed to stay in port, for the traditional cargo to be loaded and unloaded.

Initially, shipping companies were unsure that containers would succeed. They hedged their risk by using the same ships for containers and traditional cargo – as on the *Ideal-X*, containers were only carried on deck. By not embracing the new system completely, they lost a good deal of the benefits. It wasn't until shipping lines took a risk and broke with the past by operating container-only ships that they could realize the true benefits of the change.
Source: Levinson (2006)

6.3   Change is What IT People Do to Other People

IT departments and projects often bring change to other people whether they want it or not. This may be the result of a direct management decision ('Introduce a new accounts system'), it may be the result of IT policies ('Dump Windows, go Linux') or it may be part of a policy to identify and spread incremental improvements.

Whatever the reason for the change, when the IT systems change, users have to change too. For technical people, whether they are business analysts, developers or operations staff, this is a technical change and often the end of their work. However, for the users it is the start of the change. Unfortunately, on the whole IT people don't think about the changes that they introduce to others. This is partly a result of our training, which focuses on technology rather than change management.[3]

The need for change may come from an external force facing the organization or from an internal decision to exploit some opportunity. Either way, those on the receiving end see little of these forces until they're confronted with the new technology. Such technology is the means by which change is forced upon people.

All too often, software developers and other IT professionals fail to recognize that they're involved in creating change. Consequently, IT staff introducing changes can look like shock troops forcing change on unwilling employees.

Successful software developments may still fail upon deployment if the change programme has failed to involve and prepare the users. By recognizing the role IT plays in change, and the importance of embedding it in a wider change programme, we can improve the success rate of software projects.

For an IT project to be a success, it is no longer enough to deliver on time, on budget and on specification. To be successful, IT project developers must look at how they fit into an organizational change programme and consider how the changes affect the end-users.

IT people tend to get involved only once the decision to use technology to create change has been made. To ordinary programmers, it may be irrelevant why a customer wants a new system: it is enough that someone wants a new system, so that they must implement one. (This is particularly true when short-term or contract staff are used to develop the system.) However, the motivations behind the change affect those designing the system and those evaluating the success, or failure, of the system.

If we want a system that will make things happen more quickly, we can simply model existing working practices and automate them. The success criterion will be how fast things move through the system. In effect, this is an exercise in single-loop learning – 'Now we know how to do it, make it faster.'

However, if we want to obtain the greater benefits of process change and innovation, we need a deeper understanding of processes and objectives. We need to know why things are done the way they are and how technology can help meet these objectives through new processes. A new IT system is just one piece of a larger jigsaw.

As we get more ambitious and try for greater change, the potential rewards increase, but so too do the risks. Different approaches and objectives lead to different attitudes from the staff who will be affected. As system designers, this will have an effect on what we learn and the systems that we create.

---

[3] See Cameron and Green (2005).

6.4 Software Projects Fail: Why Are We Surprised?

IT projects fail. Most IT projects now use commodity hardware, so it is usually the software side that fails. This may be bespoke development, the configuration or customization of complex packages such as SAP or the roll-out to end-users. Examples are easy to find – just read the newspaper or news web sites.

Depending on whose statistics you look at, you can find that 30 % of projects are cancelled before completion, 40 % fail to achieve their objectives and 50 % see implementation as unsuccessful – perhaps 70 % are seen in some way as unsuccessful. The figure could be higher, since many companies don't like to discuss their internal developments. Failures are common in the public sector too, but since these organizations can't hide their failures they tend to get more publicity.

Software development programmes are not alone in experiencing high failure rates. According to some reports, 70 % of all change programmes fail too. Since bespoke software development is just one part of a wider change programme, it is subject to the same 70 % failure rate.

Why, then, is anybody surprised that so many IT projects fail? It isn't necessarily the software that is failing, but the wider change programme. We should expect 70 % of projects to fail even before we consider the technical issues.

However, separating cause and effect in these failures is difficult. Probably the majority of corporate change programmes today involve an element of IT. Whether the change programme fails because the IT fails, or the IT fails because the change programme fails, has to be considered on a case-by-case basis. However, it could be that if IT projects were more successful, the figures for change programmes would be better.

Certainly it seems that some software development failures are actually failures of bigger change programmes. Consequently, it is worrying when we choose to describe failure in terms of 'too many bugs', 'incorrect feature set', 'late delivery' or 'developers didn't understand'. There's every chance that describing a failure in these terms misses the real reason – the technical details mask the real cause of failure.

This is not to say that all failures occur in the development area. Deployment can fail if communications networks or connections to external systems are not in place. Users may not use a new system if they aren't given adequate training. And whole systems can be rendered pointless if the company changes strategy.

Thinking Point: Ways in which Software Can Fail

As software developers, we tend to know a few of the ways in which software can fail, but there are many more. Also, all too often, we start without a clear understanding of what's required for success. Without an understanding of how a development can fail, and what's needed to succeed, attempts to prioritize effort or manage risk are conducted blindfold:

- Make a list of ways in which your current project can fail, and a list of what's required for success.

Here are some technical reasons for failure:

- Late delivery.
- Over budget.
- Too many defects/bugs.
- Lack of functionality.
- Too many features.
- Too slow.
- Doesn't match the competitor's product.
- Poor usability.

As we have said, some of the reasons for failure may be non-technical too:

- Too difficult to use, so employees try to avoid using it.
- Doesn't meet the business needs; for example, fails to address the core problem.
- Represents marginal improvement; for example, only automates existing practices.
- Doesn't justify the expenditure.
- Too costly to support.
- The competitor was first to the market.
- It limits future changes.
- The company has changed direction, been taken over or exited the business.

6.5 Change Starts with Business Requirements

"Stable requirements are the Holy Grail of software development."
Steve McConnell (1993)

Once upon a time, stable requirements were seen as a prerequisite for starting a software development project. There may be a few people who still believe this, but many in the IT world have given up looking for the Holy Grail of stable requirements.[4] In reality, changing requirements have become an accepted fact of life for software developers. Requirements change for good reasons: businesses don't stand still and neither should software projects, so to expect the business to freeze for months on end isn't realistic.

The failure to accurately capture requirements is a regular problem with traditional, waterfall, approaches to development. Consequently, traditional development methodologies impose potentially lengthy requirements for capture and analysis phases before any design or coding begins. The longer the requirements phase, the greater is the gap between the start of requirements capture and the first working delivery. The greater the elapsed time between the start of a project and delivery, the greater are the chances that things will change. Increasing the time spent in the requirements and analysis phases comes at a substantial cost.

Project teams that believe that requirements have been successfully captured will resist changes to those requirements because they think that they're complete. Such projects tend to grow a bureaucracy to handle change requests. Increased bureaucracy, time and resistance to change contribute to the image of IT as a block to change rather than an aid.

Fortunately, Agile development approaches go a long way to making IT more flexible and accommodating to change. Agile approaches reduce these problems in three ways:

- Not producing requirements for work that won't be done.
- Reducing the time gap between requirement generation and software implementation.
- Having those creating the requirements – whether customers, product managers or business analysts – work more closely with the developer.

Requirements gathering is itself a learning activity that unfolds during the course of the project. Even on Agile projects, requirements capture can go wrong. Examining why requirements capture can go wrong is useful in understanding how to improve learning on projects.

When we address changing requirements, we see our organizations become more flexible, better at learning and changing. This allows the company to outcompete competitors, because we can adapt to our environment more quickly. Over time, the ability to adapt and change becomes fundamental to the organization and the basis for competitive advantage.

When we see changing requirements as a problem and not as an opportunity, two things happen. Firstly, our organizations cease to change – this isn't good in a dynamic business environment. Secondly, anyone can implement our requirements, because they're fixed and known. That anyone could be a competitor company or an outsource organization with low costs.

---

[4] The other Holy Grail, 'reusable software', is also finding fewer devotees since the emergence of Agile development.

> ## Thinking Point: Changing Requirements
>
> Think about how the requirements changed on a recent project:
>
> - What requirements arose late in the project?
> - Why were these requirements not requested earlier?
> - What advantage did your company gain from the late arriving requirements?

6.5.1 Mistakes

Perhaps the most obvious reason why requirements change is that we fail to capture them to begin with. Someone writes down 'black' when they should have written 'blue'. Everyone makes mistakes from time to time, and a small mistake by a business analyst can easily go unnoticed for months. Document reviews catch some errors, but mistakes are easily missed in a hundred-page tome.

There are lots of opportunities for mistakes in the requirements capture phase, and not all of them are because some people are better than others. At first, we need to comprehend the requirements; then we need to capture them and communicate them: usually this is done with a text document. Mistakes can arise at any point: comprehension, recording or communication.

6.5.2 Lack of Skills

Capturing and defining requirements is skilled work in its own right. Typically, this work is undertaken by business analysts for bespoke applications and product managers for vendor applications. These people need to understand what's expected of the product: they need to have a vision of what the product will become and they need to ensure that the product develops in line with business need and strategy.

Doing this takes not just skill but also information: about what the product is designed to do, about what the customers and/or business want and about what is actually possible. Unfortunately, even when we have skilled-people in the role, they often lack the information that they need to do the job.

On other occasions, the task of requirements capture falls to people who are neither skilled nor experienced in the role. Having a customer fill the role is very good for the small details, but customers don't automatically take a strategic view of what the product needs to achieve.

6.5.3   Gold Plating and Information Overload

In traditional development, the requirements would often be completed and fixed before any code was written. Those writing the requirements had often experienced previous projects that failed to deliver the specified requirements. Consequently, in a classic example of single-loop learning, the business analysts and product manager writing the requirements documents would include more requirements and detail. By 'gold plating' the requirements documents, they hoped to ensure that every requirement was implemented exactly as they wanted.

However, more detail can be counter-productive. More pages of document mean that there's more to forget. Just because a document is longer doesn't mean that more of it will be retained. More pages means that there are more pages to proof read and argue over. More detail reduces opportunities for new and innovative solutions.

Loading a document with every requirement that the writer can think of doesn't guarantee that all these features will be implemented. Indeed, it may simply provide more scope to cut if and when the project hits difficulty.

In the meantime, extra detail and requirements make it more difficult to see exactly what are the important requirements and features. Those reading the document may actually suffer from information overload. When writers assume that the reader knows very little about the problem domain, they may compensate by writing a lengthy document that discusses lots of details. Readers will be overwhelmed with detail and miss points.

6.5.4   Communication

Any form of communication involves at least two parties: the sender and the receiver. Typically, the business analyst will need to send his or her understanding of the problem to the developer (the receiver). The content of the message is decided by the receiver, who interprets the communication and decides what it means. No matter how much effort the sender puts into his or her message, there's no means of guaranteeing that it will be interpreted as intended.

6.5.5   Mental Models

Alternatively, we could assume that our developer knows quite a bit about the problem domain already and just communicates the bare essentials. The trouble now is that we're reliant on the knowledge that the developer already holds: any omissions or errors in that person's knowledge will actually introduce mistakes that need to be corrected later on.

More subtly, the developer may have good knowledge about the problem domain with few omissions or errors, but this may lead him or her to use assumptions and mental short cuts that may have worked well in the past but aren't appropriate in this case.

To compound things, if a developer knows how things operate now and hasn't fully grasped the changes that are being planned, his or her existing mental models and assumptions will be out of date. Consequently, we end up with a system that entrenches the current situation rather than changing it.

Developers are not the only ones who may hold hidden assumptions: the same may be true of the business analyst, end-users or managers who commission the system. Few businesses have a written operating procedure: often, the arrival of business analysts will be the first time that someone has ever tried to codify what these people are doing.

6.5.6 Tacit Knowledge

In any environment, there's normally a lot of tacit knowledge that helps people go about their business. Not only is this information rarely codified, but it can be difficult to recognize and extract: it is often embedded in the culture and 'the way we do things here'.

As Chapter 2 suggested, tacit knowledge is difficult to capture and document. Putting the tacit knowledge inside our heads into a form accessible by others can be incredibly difficult. As we delve into the process, either through writing a specification or developing code, we'll uncover more and more of this knowledge, which in turn leads us to change our understanding.

On occasions, people may choose to withhold information that is needed to develop software. More often, we simply fail to recognize that information is present or to recognize its relevance. For example, it may seem unimportant that every new recruit is told the comical story of how Old Joe managed to flood the basement one day, but in fact they're being warned about the basement and the water supply.

It is inevitable that we'll fail to capture important tacit knowledge when we draw up our system requirements. Successive iterations may expose more and more, but some of it will only emerge when we reach testing and system deployment.

6.5.7 Time Passes, Things Change

Events in the market or action by rivals can radically change what we require from a new system. Imagine a bookselling firm that commissioned a new stock control and retail system in the mid-1990s. They may have had the perfect specification for internal requirements, but external events will have forced all sorts of changes, from Internet retailing to new revenue generation models.

Requirements documents are at best a snapshot of the way things stand at the time they are written. However things change, if we start the project at the beginning of January, spend a month writing documents then head back to our office to develop the system for ten months, things will have changed by the time we return in December with the completed system. Requirements documents need to be living documents: we may not want to accept every change that is asked for, but by setting them in stone we'll miss important changes.

Few computer systems introduced today merely automate existing practice. Instead, systems are implemented as part of an attempt to change practices. This means that to some degree the specifications are attempts to describe how things will be. Since none of us – not even management consultants – is blessed with perfect future vision, it is inevitable that over time we'll find that changes are needed in the proposed system.

While we have good knowledge about our internal environment and we can make plans for internal changes, we have no such knowledge or control of the future external environment. Things that happen outside our environment can have as much, or even more, influence on what is required of a new computer system as internal events.

The requirements for the requirements document are contradictory. Documents need to be forward looking, but including all possibilities will result in long documents full of unnecessary features. Documents need to be short and easily remembered, but they also need to be comprehensive and contain sufficient detail.

6.5.8   Learning Occurs

One research study[5] looked at the motivations behind software change requests at a variety of organizations during the software maintenance phase. Corrective maintenance (i.e. bug fixing) accounted for only 10–15 % of work, while functional enhancements accounted for over 60 % of changes. This 60 % was broken down into four categories:

- *External changes* – Changes required to meet some need from outside the organization: say, a changed legal requirement.

- *Internal changes* – Changes required because of company changes such as new products, or restructuring.

- *Technical changes* – Changes required to meet new technical demands.

- *Learning* – Changes resulting from learning by individuals or groups.

The study suggested that 40 % of these changes (nearly a quarter in total) were primarily the result of learning. By changing software, an organization can pass

[5] See Edberg and Olfman (2001).

on the benefits of one group's learning to the whole company – potentially saving money and/or time and improving efficiency.

Interestingly though, users who requested changes often didn't attribute their request to learning: they preferred to cite other internal or external factors as the motivation. It seemed that requesting a change that would save them time, and eventually make the whole company more competitive, wasn't seen as a good enough reason to ask for a change.

Not only did users believe that the IT department had little interest in enhancing the software, but people in the IT department had little interest in doing so and made their dislike clear. They saw users' requests as 'superfluous' and believed that users could do their work with the software as it was. The two groups disagreed on what was necessary. Consequently, users tried to explain their request for change in other ways.

6.5.9 Looking for the Problem Changes the Problem

The role of IT systems in learning and change may start before any code is ever written or software installed. Before we write a software system, we need to understand what it needs to do both in the high-level sense ('Put a man on the moon') and the functional sense ('Moderate fuel to the engines'). In order to answer this question, we need to investigate the problem and this itself is an opportunity for learning. Consequently, system development itself can act as a catalyst for people and organizations to learn about their activities. The very act of analysing and specifying a computer system can change the problem.

How often does someone sit down with a manager or other office worker and enquire into what they do? How often do we attempt to map the processes that occur in our work environment? And how often does someone write a document describing what goes on?

Actions such as these are perfectly normal activities for business analysts and product managers writing requirements and specifications. This process can trigger learning by both those asking and answering the questions. Those answering will reflect on what they're doing, why they're doing it and whether things can be done better, and encourage people to improve their processes.

As we investigate the proposed system more and more, we create triggers for learning and change even before the system is written or deployed. There are at least four ways[6] in which software designers and implementers can facilitate learning within the organization:

- Developers have a legitimate reason to study and enquire into the operation of the business.

---

[6] Taken from Ang, Thong and Yap (1997).

- Through technology, the developers engage in the discovery of assumptions and mental models, and (because of their legitimacy) can question these assumptions.
- Involving end-users in the design process provides an opportunity to enrol users in the change and commit them to the changed environment.
- Introducing the new system freezes the change process in the new model.

So not only are IT systems a means of creating change: they're also a means of initiating learning. Here the change and learning centres on the users of the system rather than the developers.

Learning also occurs for the developers tasked with creating the new system, as they gain insights into the business and the application of technology. This will cause them to change their interpretation of the specification and force out any ambiguities in the requirements. When it comes to executable code, issues can no longer be fudged and ignored.

The process of constructing a solution may force a change in the specification. These can be among the most difficult changes to bring about, since such changes may not be what people want to hear about. So it is important that those developing the system, those who will use the system and those who will pay for the system continue to talk as development proceeds.

The completion of software and the deployment of a new system doesn't stop the learning and change, although it may help freeze the process.[7] Consequently, the idea that once a system is delivered we should cease further development work is wrong. Software delivery is merely the end of the beginning: failure to continue delivery and support the incremental change we have started will limit the benefits of the system and risk alienating users.

6.5.10   Late Requests are More Valuable

Software engineering books are full of suggestions on how to manage changing requirements. Unfortunately, many books look at Barry Boehm's economic model[8] of software development and note that the later changes occur in the process, the more they cost. They therefore conclude that change is bad and needs to be resisted.

Resisting change makes IT people unpopular and creates an image of IT departments and systems as inflexible and change resistant. Each time a request is refused, this image is reinforced. Software developers and their managers come to be seen as people who say *No*.

Freezing requirements might be the best way to economize within a software project, but it detracts from the overall business value. When we freeze requirements, we're assuming that change requests made after some cut-off

---

[7] Also described in Ang, Thong and Yap (1997).

[8] See Boehm and Pappacio (1988).

point are worth less than those that came along before the cut-off point. Changes that come along later may be more disruptive, but this doesn't imply that they're valueless. Judging requests by complexity and disruption alone is not enough: they have to be judged by value too.

Imposing a cut-off for requests and changes assumes that the most valuable requirements are all known by that date. We assume that before that date we'll be able to capture all the requirements and assign them a value and thus a priority. This assumption implies that any requests after that date are therefore less valuable.

There are two reasons why this assumption is wrong. Firstly, as discussed in Section 6.5, requirements are not always captured. Therefore we can't accurately assign value and priority.

Secondly, the ability to delay a decision is itself valuable. Options theory, and specifically real options, assigns value to possible future decisions. Making an early decision reduces the value of a project, while delaying a decision and keeping our options open increases the value. Therefore fixed requirements are less valuable than flexible requirements.

Delaying decisions about requirements makes software development more difficult and increases the cost of development. But, postponing decisions increases the value of the project. If we act to reduce costs we also reduce value, while increasing value increases costs.

Early requirements documents tend to document the most obvious requirements – the so-called *low-hanging fruit*. As development proceeds, especially when prototypes are produced, everyone concerned with a project will increase their understanding of the system. This understanding will lead to new requirements. These requirements are potentially more valuable than those that were initially foreseen, because such requirements are the result of a deeper under-standing.

Consequently, ceasing development with a set of features defined early on in the project, on a date decided before anything was developed, may result in the loss of the most valuable benefits of the system.

6.6 Conclusion

Agile software development is about making our software development more responsive: shorter development cycles, iterative development, rapid-application development and so on. Underpinning all of these ideas is the concept of improving the feedback cycle by making it both faster and clearer. In order to help our companies change, we must first change ourselves.

We need to recognize the role that IT plays in enabling and creating change for companies. Because the benefits of this change can be difficult to see before we start work, we need to adapt to changing environments and requirements.

Many IT people have adopted a mindset that resists change. This is paradoxical, given the role that IT plays in creating change elsewhere. When IT ceases to enable and support change, it quickly becomes a block to change.

We actively want to reach a position where new system development is generating new ideas for the business: creating changes and ideas for innovation. Changing requirements are a sign of success rather than of failure, because such changes show that change is happening.

Understanding Change

"In a progressive country change is constant; ... change ... is inevitable."
Benjamin Disraeli, 1804–81, British Prime Minister

The IT industry suffers from more change than most. Some of this is of the industry's own making: new technologies are introduced while older ones are slowly retired. Change also comes from the businesses that use IT: because modern businesses depend on IT, any change to the business can create change in IT departments and vice versa. Entering a new market or leaving an old one, changing processes or responding to competitors can all require IT changes.

Many of the changes in IT itself and in the business demands on IT are the result of learning. New technologies emerge as the result of learning and problem solving. The same is true in business: companies learn how markets are changing, they learn of business opportunities and they learn how to do things better. Today's constant cycle of change means business and IT are at the cutting edge of learning.

7.1 Defining Change

Change means bringing about some form of transformation: making one thing into another thing. A steel mill changes iron ore into steel. The software development process changes requirements first into program code and then into executable software. These types of change are routine: we create factories and processes to bring about these transformations.

Changing Software Development: Learning to Become Agile   Allan Kelly
© 2008 John Wiley & Sons, Ltd.

Such routine changes are frequently referred to as *transactional change*, or just *transactions*. In these cases we understand what needs to be done and how to do it. On the whole, each transaction is performed in the same way as the previous one: variation tends to be regarded as a bad thing, because it disrupts predictable processes and can lead to quality defects. Reducing variability can improve quality and efficiency.

Arguably, if all you do is transactions, then you don't need any managers or any change. The role of managers is often to improve transaction handling. Competition and market forces mean that those organizations that can perform similar transactions more quickly or more cheaply will succeed over those who cannot. Therefore management seeks to create a second kind of change to improve transactional change.

This second form of change is by definition non-routine: it occurs occasionally. Radical change, also sometimes called transformational change, seeks to improve the processes, practices and people involved with transactional change in order to gain competitive advantage. Technology has played an important role in transformational change – although, as described in Chapter 6, the improvements produced by technology aren't always those that we expect. Technology, specifically IT, can also hinder change and even block change outright.

7.2 The Change Spectrum

By nature, routine change should not be disruptive – if it is, then something is wrong. Because it is routine and we all understand what's happening, it contains no fear and we just get on with it. The opposite extreme is radical change, which doesn't happen very often. Only occasionally do you show up at the office and hand in your resignation. When you undertake radical change, it's worrying – *Will I get another job? Will it be as good?* There's far more uncertainty associated with radical change than with routine change.

We can think of both kinds of change as different ends of a spectrum. Between routine change and radical change there is a middle ground where we find incremental change – also called piecemeal change. This is non-routine because it doesn't happen routinely, but it isn't massively disruptive. In part, this is because people are used to change happening.

The severity or disruption of change is one criterion that distinguishes the two ends of the change spectrum. Transactional change isn't disruptive: it's part of our everyday work. At the other extreme, radical change is highly disruptive and may change the very nature of our work.

The second criterion that distinguishes the two ends of the change spectrum is frequency. Transactional change happens every day, or even multiple times in one day. It isn't disruptive; we accept this frequency. Radical change, on the other hand, happens only occasionally.

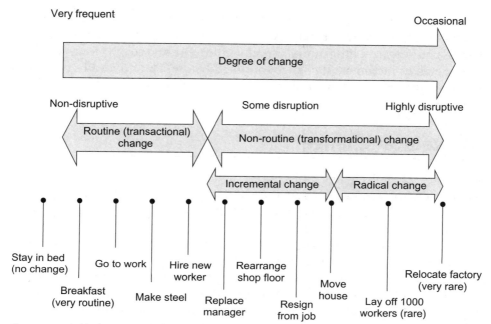

Figure 7.1 Classifying change.

Figure 7.1 shows how these two criteria are correlated with events that happen in our daily lives and work environment. Because of the disruptive nature of radical change, there is a limit to how much individuals and organizations can tolerate. This limit will vary from person to person and organization to organization. When radical change happens frequently, then too much uncertainty and risk is injected into a system for the routine to function normally.

Somewhere in the middle of these two extremes is the idea of incremental change. This happens occasionally and may be mildly disruptive, but not so disruptive as to create problems. Some incremental change happens continually as people learn: such change may represent a change for the better or for the worse.

The challenge for those of us wishing to improve our organizations is to turn *ad hoc* incremental change into an ongoing process of *continuous improvement*. In order to achieve this, we need to speed up changes so they happen more frequently and ensure that they deliver improvement. One way to do this is through increased learning.

The phrase 'continuous improvement' has itself been over-used in process improvement initiatives within and outside IT. Quality movements such as Total Quality Management (TQM), Six Sigma and Lean (where it is called *Kaizen*) all advocate their own form of continuous improvement. As a result, 'continuous improvement' has become a cliché and has been devalued.

Incremental change practised as continuous improvement aims to deliver the benefits of change without the risks and disruption. Ideally we learn a little, change a little, learn a little more, change a little more and so on. However, there are dangers to incremental change (outlined below) and advocates of radical change suggest that incremental change cannot, and does not, address difficult issues or happen fast enough.

7.3 Radical Change

Sometimes radical change is required: sometimes things are so bad – the competition so far ahead – that the company must react. Business process re-engineering is one response, but it isn't the only response. There are many other forms of radical change.

The former head of Intel, Andy Grove, talks about 'strategic inflection points' – the points at which you realize things have changed.[1] Unfortunately, many organizations never recognize that their environment has changed and consequently never take the action needed. Even those that do recognize the need to change may not actually take the action until some crisis occurs to force it.

Radical change is the change model that underpins much of traditional software engineering literature. We start by analysing the application domain, our designers and engineers build the product and after testing it is handed over to customers. The traditional literature usually ends where the software development teams end their work. For customers, this isn't the end, but merely the beginning of change.

Superficially, radical change is easy: it is only necessary that a few senior managers become convinced that change is required. These 'big brains' can then devise a plan of action, announce it to the company as a whole and watch it happen. This is classic top-down type management and change.

Unfortunately, this kind of change can be difficult to implement. It requires that the managers correctly understand the changes needed, create a suitable plan, communicate the plan to the wider workforce and deliver the plan on schedule. This parallels traditional software development approaches and suffers from the same problems.

Ultimately, all change programmes depend on changing the way in which individuals conduct their work. Simply announcing a change programme can create fear and uncertainty in employees, who create their own defences to protect themselves. These defences make change even harder to achieve. Announcing change but withholding the details and actions only increases the fear and uncertainty felt by employees. During this time, productivity is likely to decline as some employees leave, and the remainder spend their time talking and thinking about the coming changes rather than the business of the company. If radical change is needed, then it's best to act fast.

[1] See Grove (1997).

Few change plans will move from concept to implementation without the need to change detail. During implementation, unforeseen problems emerge, which the change program must accommodate. However, openly building flexibility into the change plan can be a double-edged sword, because it increases the uncertainty and doubt that people feel. The prospect of changing the plan and avoiding change may lead some people to resist the changes.

Thinking Point: Radical Changes that You've Known

Think about the change initiatives and programmes that you're been involved in, either as the creator of change or as the receiver of change. These may not have gone by the grand title of *change initiative* – something more mundane, such as *project*, may be used. Consider what the projects were aiming to achieve:

- Who or what was the subject of the change?
- How was the change to be accomplished?
- What were the successes of the project?
- What were the failures of the project?

Radical Change through Business Process Re-engineering

Business Process Re-engineering (BPR) is the poster child for radical technology-based change. BPR appeared on the management agenda in the early 1990s and was evangelized in the 1994 book *Reengineering the Corporation*,[2] although there are many more books on the subject.

The originators of BPR observed that many of the steps and activities performed by employees don't add value to the customer. With the advent of technology, these processes could be redesigned to focus on only the value-adding activities. The same idea lies behind Lean production and product development. However, Lean and BPR differ in one very important aspect. While the advocates of Lean look to incremental improvement and organizational learning to eliminate waste, the advocates of BPR reject incremental solutions. Instead, BPR calls for a programme of systematic process redesign and radical change to achieve the new process.

In order to design the new process, BPR seeks to start with a blank sheet of paper. It assumes that nothing has gone before and looks to align corporate strategy, people, organizational structure and technology to produce highly efficient processes. Most BPR programmes rely on the technology to implement the radical changes that result. This allows

[2] See Hammer and Champy (1994).

organizations to rapidly take advantages of technology-enabled process changes rather than wait for these to emerge after automation.

In the 1990s this combination of clean sheet design, new technology and alignment made for massive amounts of complexity. Not only did the process design need to be right, but the technology needed to deliver support for untried processes. Companies frequently needed to bring in management consultants to run the programmes and deliver the technology. For a time BPR was very popular with corporations, but while there are examples of successful BPR projects, there are also many more examples of failed ones. As projects hit difficulties, the costs of consultants and technology mounted up and employees saw 'BPR' as code for 'lay-offs' – it became a more difficult sell.

Correctly or incorrectly, BPR became associated with corporate downsizing, massive lay-off programmes and expensive consultants. By the late 1990s, BPR had fallen out of fashion. Where BPR is still practised, it goes by names such as *Business Process Design* (BPD) in an attempt to avoid employee hostility and distance itself from some of the previous mistakes.

The sheer complexity of the programmes was one reason why so many failed. Another was the amount of tacit knowledge involved in the original processes. Capturing and re-applying the tacit knowledge in an existing process is an incredibly difficult problem.

There is still logic to the underlying premises of eliminating non-value-adding activities and redesigning processes to capture the return from technology. Sometimes radical change is needed: incremental change may not happen fast enough or may not go far enough. Still, even when the BPR – or BPD – approach is appropriate, it is difficult to carry out.

7.4 Routine Change in Software Development

Transactional change is where the actual production work gets done. Most of our efforts at transformational change are aimed at changing the routine of workers. So it seems reasonable to look more closely at the routine changes that occur during software development.

On the face of it, routine change isn't particularly interesting: after all, this is what we do every day. Figure 7.2 shows a stereotypical view of the daily work of a software developer. It isn't very interesting and we don't need to write books about this kind of routine.

But this very routine provides the raw material that we need to learn and improve. By looking at the action and practices we engage in each day, we can seek to improve our working day. Our very routines can be a major source of

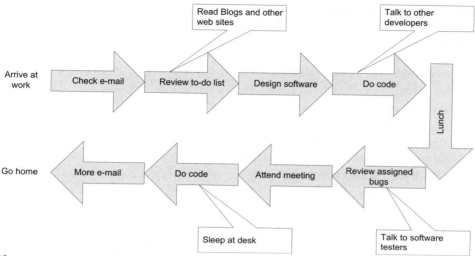

Figure 7.2 A day in the life of a software developer.

learning. The reality of our work is very different to how others might perceive it (Figure 7.2), and again these exceptions to the routine can be the source of learning.

There is some evidence that there's significantly less routine work involved in software development than there is in other types of work. A study by two Indian academics looked to see whether 'software work is routinized'. The study[3] failed to find any support for the hypothesis that software development was a routine activity. It went on to conclude that not only was software development work not routine, but that it was unlikely to become a routine activity in the near future.

Having routines does confer advantages. By making activities routine, we reduce the randomness. This makes activities more predictable and generally leads to improved quality. Routines also make it easier to compare two activities and the results. We actively want routines in the way we work: it just happens to be very difficult to achieve.

Thinking Point: Routine in Your Day

Map out your typical day:

- What events and variations occur?
- How often do you have a normal day?

Repeat this exercise for your working team.

---

[3] See Ilavarasan and Sharma (2003).

7.4.1   Lack of Routine

Those who have worked as developers will know that while there are elements of routine, there are also many things that can disrupt this routine. For example, daily routines are easily disrupted by:

- Any number of technical factors, such as bugs that suddenly appear, changes that have unexpected side effects, hardware that fails, software upgrades that fail or introduce problems and so on. Bugs found in live systems or user testing can usurp any scheduled work at a moment's notice and take days to resolve.

- Various managerial or administration factors, such as unexpected meetings, changed requirements, schedule changes, changing priorities or the need to travel to a customer or other site.

- Lack of knowledge – sometimes we have to pause to learn something new, perhaps about the technology that we're using or the business domain in which we're working.

- Conversely, new knowledge and insights can cause us to stop what we were doing, and even throw away work, as we see new ways of tackling requirements. We can't schedule these insights or innovations: they happen in their own time. We may choose to ignore such insights, but in doing so we lose the benefits of the insight.

These are the day-to-day variables that make software development so unpredictable. Even where these variables are controlled, other variables change the environment from week to week and month to month.

Software development tends to be organized as projects. By their very nature, projects have start and end dates. Projects end and new projects begin. Even when a project establishes its own routine, there will come a day when the project ends and the routines finish.

The way in which software project teams are staffed also works against the establishment of long-lasting routines. Some teams move from one project to another as an entire team, while others are broken up at the end of a project – consequently, routines are lost. High staff turnover rates in the IT industry generally and the use of contract staff mean that it isn't uncommon for teams to see people leaving a project and new people joining. Each time someone leaves, the routines need to change, and each new joiner needs to learn the routines and potentially changes them.

When routine does appear, developers are often able to create tools that change the nature of the work. When a piece of work becomes well enough understood and predictable, then software can be written to automate the work. As discussed in Chapter 1, developers have the ability to change the way in which many people work.

For example, as software has grown, tracking source files that create an executable product has become more difficult. Much of this work is routine: therefore, software developers have created source code control tools to do much of the routine work. And since extracting these files and compiling them is a routine process, we create automatic build systems to ensure that they are compiled in the right order. The more we understand source code control and build systems, the more we automate the routine processes. Tools such as Cruise Control will now monitor source control and automatically run build systems.

Each time developers find routine, they can automate it (as shown in Figure 7.3). With a task automated, new opportunities emerge for further automation. Over time more and more tasks are automated, leaving the remainder – the less well-understood and less routine tasks – for people to do. This approach is perfectly logical, because computers are good at well-understood repetitive processes, while humans (who are bored by repetition) are good at problems requiring inventiveness.

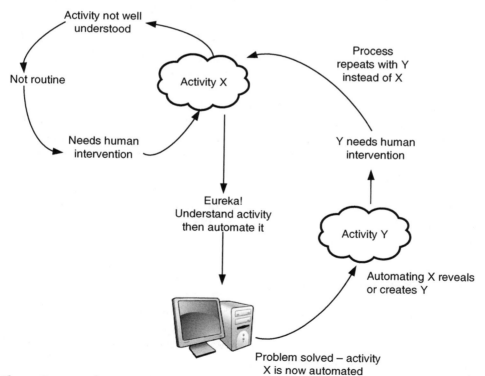

Figure 7.3   Routine activities become understood and automated.

7.4.2   Consequences

For those wishing to make software development a routine process, these findings are bad news. However, for those who can live with uncertainty and a slight lack of routine, these findings are positive. Changes in requirements are a sign that more valuable requirements are replacing the less valuable ones. The increasing automation of routine tasks represents a specialization of labour, allowing humans and machines to do what they do best. This increases the total value produced.

The lack of routine also means that the re-occurring idea of a software factory is unlikely to be realized. Factories are good at producing large quantities of products using a uniform process. In software development, neither the end products nor the process of creating them is routine or likely to become routine. Therefore factory processes are inappropriate for software development.

Not only are software factories unlikely to work; nor are attempts to inject a high degree of routine into the development process. Any process or methodology that attempts to do so is unlikely to succeed. In the short run, such a process might succeed by limiting some variables – say, by freezing requirements or preventing the creation of tools to automate activities. In the longer term, such a process would limit the value that arises from the development activities by limiting changes.

Traditional software development methodologies seek to bring about routine in order to make the process more manageable and predictable. However, imposing a routine on an inherently non-routine activity will bring about conflict.

If software development is largely devoid of routine, then there would seem to be little point in spending time and energy seeking to improve the routine. Rather than putting our energy into devising better, more complete and predictable processes and methodologies, we would be better devoting our time and energy to those things that do make a significant difference – namely learning, change and knowledge creation and sharing.

Developers are likely to continue confronting many new opportunities and problems that have not been seen before. This in turn means that developers need to keep learning and innovating.

7.4.3   Finding Routine

Routine may be difficult to find, but that doesn't mean that it isn't valuable. The very rarity of routine actually makes the routines we have more valuable. We should seek out and value routines when we find them, but we should not rush to create routines when work is poorly understood and highly variable.

Rather than create routines about actual development, we can instead create routines around our learning and action activities. By making learning activities routine, we embed learning and change into our teams and organizations. Examples of such activities include:

- *Daily stand-up meetings:* Primarily, these are exercises in communication aimed at focusing the action of the team.
- *Project and iterations retrospectives:* These promote team learning and improvement.
- *Personal reflection:* This promotes individual learning and focus.

Making such activities regular and routine increases their value. One retrospective is useful; one every month is many more times more useful. Many of the tools presented in this book become more effective when performed regularly.

In a complex environment, it helps to keep routines simple. Simple routines are more flexible and can adapt as the environment changes. Complex routines work against flexibility because they add their own complexities; they're more difficult to learn and more difficult to change.

Finally, we still need to seek out opportunities to automate whatever routines we can. We can't automate a team retrospective, but we can automate build systems, tests and similar activities. Automation creates opportunities for further process improvement and innovation.

7.5 Continuous Improvement

Agile development is built on a different change model from that underpinning the traditional software engineering literature. Both in the development and deployment processes, Agile development assumes incremental change and continuous improvement – neither of which is a panacea. They present significant challenges to the teams and team leaders, and entail their own risks.

When incremental change is ongoing and when these changes are for the better, then change becomes continuous improvement. Changes may be large or they may be small; the important thing is that teams continue to look for ways to change what they're doing for the better. The challenge to team leaders is to ensure that change is sustained. Change and improvement must be guided, so these produce benefits in line with the organization's objectives and strategy.

In seeking to both do their work and improve their working environment, processes and practices teams need to play both the finite and infinite games described in Section 5.2. In order to do this, teams need some slack (see Section 5.3.2) – both in terms of time and resources.

Ideas for improvement in a continuous system may come from anywhere. There's no monopoly on good ideas held by managers and consultants. Confining our expectations to managers ignores the ideas and experience of the workers.

Ideas from users are as valid as managers' ideas, which are as valid as ideas from secretaries and ideas from customers. Sometimes good ideas come from people who have been with the company for years and have been observing; sometimes they come from people who have just joined and see things afresh. If the team boundaries are drawn too tightly, we will lose the insights of those who work closely with the team but aren't formal members.

In order to harvest these ideas, we need to create an environment in which it is acceptable to have ideas and make suggestions – in other words, a learning organization. Unfortunately, IT people don't always see things this way. As suggested in Chapter 6, requests from users aren't always looked on positively. All too often, the mental model of change in the IT department is diametrically opposed to that needed for continuous improvement.

Thinking Point: Experiences of Continuous Improvement

Think about the continuous improvement programmes or initiatives that you're been involved with. If you haven't been involved with one before, try to imagine what one would look like:

- What improvements did the programme make?
- What obstacles did the programme encounter?

7.5.1   Failings of Incremental Change

Incremental change isn't free from problems. Some issues are shared with other change approaches, while some are specific to incremental change and continuous improvement. Such change tends to start small and grow. Creating the force to start the change can be difficult: maintaining the force can be even harder. Failure to maintain momentum means that the change initiative is likely to stall and wither.

Self-deception can be a problem with incremental change. This occurs when we convince ourselves that we're changing but in fact we're largely maintaining the current position. Rather than actually changing, we have stopped change from happening, but publicly claim that it is. Not only does this mean that we aren't changing, but we can block others from changing and reduce the trust that others have in us.

Perspective can be a factor here. What looks like change to one person may not look like change to another. In order to avoid falling into this trap, it can be worth keeping a record of all the changes that have been made over time. This can help to bring a degree of objectivity to the question and form the basis for discussion with others.

Maintaining incremental change can also be problematic. Inevitable blocks arise (see Chapters 5 and 8) and must be overcome. These blocks may be as much personal as they are organizational. Inevitably, we invest a lot of our own energy, drive and personality in a change initiative, and it's too easy to get demoralized when things don't turn out the way we hope they will.

7.5.2 Failure to Go Fast Enough

Change always takes time and usually longer than expected. When attempting change, we need to keep up some pressure for change. We need to keep forward momentum and a sense of urgency. Allowing a 'change is slow' mindset to develop only makes it more difficult to maintain momentum.

By its nature, incremental change is slow. It means making one change, seeing what the result is, learning about our new system and then repeating the process. From time to time, a change won't be as positive as we expected, and we'll want to revert to the original way of doing things.

In some environments, the pace of incremental change may be unacceptably slow. This in turn can create pressure for more radical change and increased risk taking. This can be a good thing if it helps us increase the pace of change and allows more risks. However, it can be counterproductive if the pressure is excessive.

Organizations need to change at an appropriate rate and one that is compatible with their wider culture. So, for example, you wouldn't expect a pension fund to rapidly adopt new and risky practices and processes. Institutions whose customers look 50 years ahead and value security are likely to shy away from rapid change. Conversely, hedge funds, which exist to take high short-term risks, may well have a culture in which rapid change is embraced.

In order to introduce any change at all, we need to move faster than the generally accepted rate of change. Therefore we should aim to push the boundaries of what's acceptable.

Sometimes external forces create a rapid pace of change. A company faced with collapsing sales may need to rapidly change the organization or revenue model. Incremental change may not be able to deliver the changes quickly enough. Faced with such problems, there may be little choice but to act quickly and make radical changes.

Thinking Point: the Need for Speed

Try to think of an occasion where the pace of change in your organization has been too slow:

- What would have been the advantage of moving faster?
- What would the extra risks have been?

7.5.3 Failure to Go Far Enough

Changing incrementally means changing pieces individually. Yet sometimes changing one piece alone won't result in any benefit. In these cases, isolated changes aren't effective: they may even look like backward steps. Consequently, we sometimes need to expand the scope of our changes to have any real effect.

The *Box Technology* topic box in Chapter 6 detailed how shipping companies that carried containers as part of a traditional cargo didn't recognize the benefits of containerization. In order to obtain the benefits, it was necessary to make a broader change and move to a cargo made up entirely of containers. All incremental change risks missing benefits because the change doesn't go far enough.

Similarly, a software development group that adopts some Agile practices may succeed in producing better-quality software faster, but if the test group fails to make corresponding changes, only limited benefits will result. As a result, limited success may actually deter further changes, because the problem has become less severe.

Unlearning

Changing the way in which we work means two things. Firstly, it means doing something differently: probably undertaking a task in a new way. For example, changing to *Test-driven Development* (*TDD*) means that we write our software tests before we write the code. There has to be a first time for doing anything.

Secondly, the flip side of doing something differently is that we aren't doing something else. If we adopt TDD, we cease to undertake unit testing in the way we did before; whether this was by writing tests after we had written the code, manually putting test data into the system or stepping through the code with a debugger. Once we start doing TDD, we stop doing what we did before.

In some cases, the 'not doing something' part of the change means 'not doing nothing'. For some developers, adopting TDD means that they stop *not testing* their code.

Changes such as this typically affect more people than is immediately obvious. We expect developers who start using TDD to produce better-quality code with fewer defects. This in turn has an effect on the software testers who test the code. Here, change for the testers mirrors that of the developers. At first, the testers will notice their tests run more smoothly because there are fewer faults, and in time they may stop running some tests and concentrate their efforts elsewhere.

When we accept that learning is change and change is learning, then such changes in behaviour constitute an *unlearning* process. With unlearning, previous understandings need to be discarded and actions need to be stopped in order to do new things.

Unlearning can be difficult, because we need to give up something we think we know in order to advance our knowledge. It's like walking backwards so that we can change direction and move further forwards. Before we can start to walk backwards, we first need to recognize the need to change direction. After the recognition of the need comes the decision, and then the action.

In practice, this can be difficult. We need to stop acting in a particular way. It may be that we're giving up something that has brought us success in the past. This can entail an element of personal risk as we move from what we know well to something we know less well. Where knowledge has served us well in the past, it can be difficult to put aside. Unlearning isn't something that we need to do every day. Most days, we can work with the knowledge and experience that we have to hand – like the single-loop learning we discussed (Chapter 4). However, when we need to go deeper and engage in double-loop learning, we may need to re-examine what we think we know. In this way, the exercise of unlearning is the exercise of exposing and changing mental models as proposed by Senge (Chapter 5).

7.6 Charting a Course

Given the 70 % failure rate for change programmes, it may seem illogical for anyone to embark on such a programme. Radical change seems the most risky, but the alternatives aren't risk free either. Faced with such odds, it's hardly surprising that many managers choose to do nothing. Yet not changing also involves risks; these risks are just less obvious.

Undoubtedly, radical change is sometimes necessary. Sometimes things are just so bad that something has to be done. Companies sometimes get themselves into a position where the only option is to lay off thousands of workers, to restructure divisions, axe departments and so on.

The bad news seems to be: if you face the need to change radically, you're most likely going to fail in your attempts. No wonder so many people put off changing and try to avoid it. Given the statistics, sticking your head in the sand and ignoring the need to change is almost the rational thing to do.

The answer to this problem is not to get in this position in the first place. Faced with the question 'How do I save my organization from impending doom?' no wonder the answer is so often 'You don't want to start from here.'

Individuals and organizations need to take proactive action to avoid getting into situations in which risky radical change is required. The consistent application of continual change and learning can help avoid the need for radical change, and help reduce the disruption when radical change is needed. This means taking action now to avoid radical action later. Taking some risk now should result in less risk overall.

Even with continuous change and improvement, there's no guarantee that the need for radical change can be avoided, but we can reduce the chances of needing it. On the other hand, if we don't practise regular change and improvement, we'll eventually encounter the need for radical change. If we don't take matters into our own hands, then eventually we'll lose control.

Continuous improvement is no easy option. We need to proactively promote learning and engage in change. This means creating a culture that encourages learning and accepts change, and it means allowing slack in the workplace so that people have the time and resources to learn and change.

7.6.1   Make It Continuous

In order to avoid stagnation, we need to take note of the *continuous* element of *continuous improvement*. Activities to encourage learning and change need to be ongoing. It isn't enough to have a learning initiative for a month or two. Activities must be ongoing and must form part of the normal pattern within organizations.

This doesn't mean that we repeat the same activities again and again; there needs to be continuity, but this needn't imply 'boring' or 'repetitive'. Activities such as book study groups (Section 4.7.6) can change formats, or people can be rotated in and out of activity leadership positions to keep them fresh and open to new ideas.

Ideas can come from within or from outside (see Section 4.7). Simply examining what your organization is doing can prove a fertile ground for ideas. Analysing the position of the company, the development team, and processes and practices within the company can bring forth new ideas and the sharing of existing ones.

7.6.2   Going Further

Emphasizing the *continuous* aspect of continuous improvement can help ensure that change doesn't stall. Next, we need to ensure that our changes and thinking are broad enough to avoid dead-end solutions and changes that benefit one group at the expense of another. Tools such as systems thinking and unlearning can help here.

Boundaries can be difficult to recognize: some are real and need to be observed – particularly where they exist for legal reasons. Other boundaries only exist in our minds or the minds of others in the organization. Some boundaries come from our own fears: we may be concerned about how others will view us, our role within the company or our own legitimacy.

In order to go further, we need to regularly push the boundaries of what we can do and what we can change. Other people can help us find and recognize barriers in the organization and in our own thinking. Explaining our ideas to someone else may help us see boundaries and problems ourselves.[4]

We need to aim to push the boundaries of what we can achieve and the problems that we can affect. However, we need to be aware of what our own limitations are and when we might be out of our depth.

Warning! – Removing Camouflage Reveals Problems

Most organizations will have experienced some negative learning in the past. Individuals, teams and even whole departments will have adopted practices and processes that look as though they work, but in fact contribute to the problems that an organization is facing. The deeper problems are camouflaged by partial solutions.

Consequently, once you start to change, things may start to look worse at first. Problems that were hidden previously come into the open. People now struggle with processes that used to work, and may blame your change process for breaking things. It may be tempting to reverse the change and put things back to how they were. The real solution is to continue changing and address the problems rather than hiding them.

7.6.3   Little Bits of Radical Change

Exposing ourselves to others from outside our own silo is one way of ensuring that we consider the effects of our changes on other groups. Another way is to purposefully engage in systems thinking exercises to make us consider others. Individuals and small groups can use systems thinking casually to think beyond their immediate boundaries. It can also be used in a more structured fashion.

Exercises such as *retrospectives* and *workouts* (Chapter 11) are occasions when we actively engage in systems thinking. Outside facilitators (Chapter 11) can be brought in to run specific sessions using the tools of systems thinking to examine specific problems.

Specific events such as these – sometimes called *interventions* or *change events* – have some similarities to radical change programmes. These events don't form part of the normal work pattern, although they may be held on a semi-regular basis. Because they are special events, they can be more challenging and more focused than general ongoing activities.

---

[4] The *Cardboard Consultant* pattern describes how even explaining your ideas to your dog can help (Weir and Noble, 1999).

7.6.4   Hard Choices

None of the above techniques can avoid the need to make tough decisions from time to time. Even with a continuous improvement culture in place, there will be times when non-continuous actions need to be taken for the greater good of the team or organization.

For example, from time to time it may become necessary to dismiss a member of staff who is under-performing and disrupting teams. In situations such as this, avoiding a decision can be more damaging than not taking a decision. When such decisions need to be taken, there's a need to take action without disrupting the overall culture. Failure to take a decision and act on it can be more damaging and disruptive the longer you leave it. Often, team members will be aware of the problem and will recognize the need to do something.

7.7   Internal and External Forces for Change

So far we have considered how change manifests itself, as a gradual process or as a sudden process. We also need to consider the root of the change: *Where does the force for change come from? Is it internal or external?*

Change may be brought about by external forces that impact on you; for example, a new competitor enters your market and sales fall, or a celebrity is seen using your product (unexpectedly) and sales rocket overnight. External forces are beyond your control; however, you still need to react. Changes in the external forces and environment can be ignored for a while. You can pretend that they don't exist. Sticking your head in the sand is an option; granted, not a good option, but an option all the same.

If you're lucky, then the situation will resolve itself. Your new competitor might have even more problems then you do and might pull out of the market. Or maybe your product is just so good that customers never consider alternatives. A more likely scenario is that eventually you'll have to respond. At this point, you start to encounter internal change. Ignoring external forces may allow pressure to grow, so that when you eventually do respond you need to act more radically.

Forces for change can also arise within your organization. This may come about because the company restructures, a new manager is appointed or assets reach the end of their life. Given the right perspective, most internal forces can be traced to external events.

7.7.1   Combining Internal/External and Radical/Incremental

We have seen how the force for change can come from inside or outside the organization, and we have described how change can be incremental or radical in nature. These two variables are independent of one another. Figure 7.4

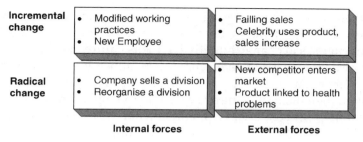

Figure 7.4   Four types of change.

combines these ideas to show four types of change. In Chapter 8 we will look at some models that try to better explain change.

The central theme of this book is learning. The learning model works best when change is internal and incremental. In essence: *you learn a bit; you change a bit.* Your change is internal, so you run at your own pace. External change may force you to pick up the pace a bit – it may give you some new experiences to learn from – but the model stays essentially the same.

Radical change tends to place the learning after the change. Somebody, somewhere in the organization, decides on a change and then imposes it on others. In this case we're changed, and then we have to learn how to cope. So we change and then we learn. The danger is that because the change didn't originate from ourselves (i.e. the individual or the team), we don't understand it entirely, we limit our learning and, more dangerously, we look to someone else for the next change.

Thinking Point: Four Types of Change

Consider the matrix in Figure 7.4 and think of examples of when you've encountered each of the four types of change:

■ Which quadrant looks the most advantageous?

7.7.2   Choosing between Radical and Incremental Change

Some of us will be in the fortunate position of choosing between radical or incremental change. Faced with an organizational problem, we may choose to undertake radical change – perhaps selling a division or launching a BPR initiative. Or we may choose to create a learning culture inside the organization and gradually resolve the problem.

In reality, few people will have the luxury of this choice. Radical changes such as structural reorganizations and BPR initiatives are likely to occur in response to some internal crisis or external events. Incremental change may not be acceptable to our stakeholders, because it isn't fast or radical enough.

Launching a radical change initiative is, by its nature, not a trivial undertaking. Most of us, even senior managers, can't launch such initiatives without consulting others and getting approval from colleagues and superiors.

While incremental change may not be able to respond rapidly enough to a crisis, it can help prevent crises from arising and it can help us to cope better when they do arise. You can launch your own improvement initiative, on our own. You can start with yourself – say, by taking time to reflect in a diary – and grow over time by adding other people and activities.

How you go about creating a learning culture will differ depending on your level of seniority and authority in an organization. In some ways, it is harder for managers at the top of an organization to have a direct influence on learning, because they are so far removed from what actually happens. Conversely, those of us who are actively involved in the day-to-day routine of an organization are well placed to seed learning and promote change.

7.8 Conclusion

Although it is tempting to think of radical change and incremental change as alternatives that we can rationally choose between at any time, this is not the case. Often, our decision to use one form of change instead of the other is dictated by forces outside our control. These include our position within the organization, the speed at which change is needed and the level of risk that we can accept.

Traditional software development methodologies have assumed radical change. To this end, the development team delivers software and the users are forced to change overnight. As we saw in Chapter 6, this limits opportunities for organizational learning and change by our customers. This approach has helped foster the image that IT is inflexible, difficult to work with and a barrier to change.

Agile software development is built on the idea of incremental change – quite different from traditional development. This reduces risk from development projects and opens opportunities for organizational learning by our users and development teams. However, this model still involves risks, most specifically that change won't happen fast enough or go far enough.

Agile also extends the incremental improvement model into the development team itself. As we have said before, the best Agile teams are themselves learning teams that are constantly improving the way in which they work and adapting to their environment. The same dangers hold within the team. Having achieved a form of 'Agility', teams may be tempted to stop changing or to freeze the change in a process document. Therefore, we need to change the culture of our development teams just as much as the practices and processes that we follow.

CHAPTER 8

Change Models

"My personal law of management, if not of life, is that everything can look like a failure in the middle."

(Moss Kanter, 1999)

Why discuss change theory? After all, this book is aimed at practitioners who want practical ideas and suggestions. Actually, there are several reasons, some of which were covered in the introduction.

Change is an abstract idea: by looking at models of change we can discuss different aspects of change and common themes in the hope of preparing ourselves for the process. In doing so, the models help set our personal frame of reference. Good theories and models allow us to see the world in a different way. By placing a different lens over our view, we can see things that we couldn't see before.

Examining models allows us to look at new ideas and theories. In doing so, we may come to understand other people better and can think about what we would do in these scenarios. This allows our plans and the planning process to be better informed.

The models given here look at change from different angles and at different depths. They aren't necessarily incompatible: indeed, at different times it can help to view your organization and change progress through the lens of different models.

Changing Software Development: Learning to Become Agile   Allan Kelly
© 2008 John Wiley & Sons, Ltd.

8.1 Learning and Change

Learning and change are closely related: indeed, we have argued that they are the same thing. We can learn facts such as that the 'First World War started with the assassination of Archduke Ferdinand on 28 June 1914'. However, what difference does this make? It's a simple fact, it happened, there's nothing I can do to change that fact, and it's very unlikely to change me.

Once we move beyond simple facts, learning occurs with change. Suppose that I learn of a new bus route that I can use for my morning journey to work. I may choose to ignore this learning, in which case have I really learnt anything? It has about as much effect on me as knowing when the Archduke was assassinated. But, if as a result of hearing about the route I take the new bus to work, then the learning has created a change. I have changed my route to work.

As a result of this change, I'm going to learn more. I'm going to learn the type of bus, the frequency of the buses and the reliability of the route. Over time, all this information builds up in my brain and I make an informed choice based on my learning.

If I choose to ignore this information, if every day I go to the bus stop and find it takes me an hour to get a bus, then I'm not changing and I'm not learning. If I ignore the information that I'm receiving, then I'm no better than a simple machine (Figure 8.1).

Learning of the new bus route and not acting, like learning the date on which the Archduke was assassinated, is simple single-loop learning; no change occurs. Only when we act on this information and change our behaviour do we reach up to double-loop.

This theory is basically a description of single- and double-loop learning as set out in Chapter 4. Problems occur when someone engages in the single loop, but either refuses to act on it or feels unable to do so.

Scott Adam's anti hero-Dilbert is an example of a single-loop learner. Dilbert constantly learns of failures and craziness in his organization, but can never act on the information. Sometimes he makes a personal decision not to act, perhaps because he feels unable to, but on other occasions action is restricted by the people around him.

Too often, developers in software organizations learn information about their project but fail to act. Many times, I have been told that some code needs

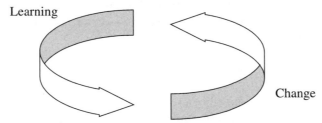

Figure 8.1 Learning and change are the same thing.

refactoring, but the developers shy away from doing it. Occasionally, this is because they're actively told not to, but more often it's because they feel unable to act and refactor.

At one level, good developers are always learning. Good developers invest in their own skills, they read books on programming and design, and they may learn a new programming language, API or operating system. Often, this learning causes a direct change in behaviour: developers program differently, they program something that they haven't programmed before or they design software differently. Learning and change are happening; even double-loop learning is occurring. However, this change is at the level of the individual, not the team – it's micro-change.

Sometimes, change precedes learning: we learn as the result of change. At other times, learning comes first: we change when we act on learning. When trying to introduce change, it can be easier to start with learning and let change follow. Learning can motivate change. So if we start by seed learning and encourage people to engage in more learning, they will eventually see the opportunity for change.

When we initiate change through learning, we need to avoid the Dilbert trap. If those who are learning feel unable to act and change, then we'll be restricted to single-loop learning and change won't follow. In order to avoid this trap and allow learning to create change, we need to empower people to take action themselves. (For more on empowerment, see Chapter 11.)

If we restrict people's ability to change while enhancing their learning, we'll create frustration and discontent. Individuals who know that the organization is doing 'the wrong thing' and not taking advantage of learning will become cynical and unhappy.

8.2 Lewin's Change Theory

One of the simplest and older models of the change process comes from psychologist Kurt Lewin.[1] This simple model (Figure 8.2) starts from the assumption that things are in a steady state. Things might be getting better or worse, but they're doing so in a predictable way.

Into this steady state we introduce the need to change. The model doesn't explain why we introduce change. The first thing that needs to happen in order to facilitate change is to unfreeze the current status quo. The need for change needs to be explained and people need to be prepared for change. For whatever reason, it needs to be explained that the status quo is no longer an option. Consequently, some *unlearning* is required: people need to be prepared to give up some existing behaviours and understandings.

---

[1] Originally from Lewin (1951), this model has been expanded upon elsewhere by Edgar Schein.

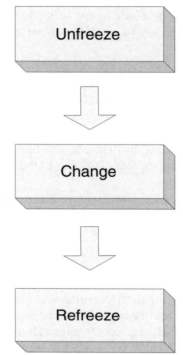

Figure 8.2   Lewin's basic change model.

The second step is for the change to take place. At a high level, the model doesn't explain the details of how the change happens. Once the change is complete the model enters the final stage, where the changed system is frozen in the new form.

At a high level, this model serves to outline a simple change process. The need to move from 'what we do now' to an environment in which things are different is clear. Moving from one position to another clearly requires change.

What is less clear is whether we actually wish to freeze the resulting changes. In an environment in which external change is happening constantly, do we really want to freeze ourselves? And, if we accept the *learning is change* argument from earlier, do we ever want learning to stop? Indeed, *can* we stop learning?

There are times when we want change to happen quickly and there are times when we want it to happen slowly. Rather than refreezing after change, we may simply want to slow things down and ensure that change continues at a sustainable pace.

Lewin's model is a useful starting place to understand change, but it says very little about what we actually do. For that, we need other models to understand the process further.

8.3 Satir's Theory of Change

Satir's change model[2] derives from work on family theory. Like the Lewin model, it starts with the status quo, although in this model the current position is shown as the first stage in the model. Gerry Weinberg[3] has done much to map Satir's model into the software development domain.

Figure 8.3 shows Satir's model graphically and is almost self-explanatory. In this model we start in a stable state; things are better on some days and worse on others, but on the whole we continue just as we always have done.

Then something happens. Satir calls this a 'foreign element', but it could be something, someone or some event. This could be a relatively minor change, or it could be major change such as switching to a new programming language. At first, we try to resist the change and carry on as before, but performance declines as nothing that we do any longer produces the same result.

Now we're no longer in our old state, but we don't know how to act in the new state. For the individual, chaos ensues: dread, panic, despair and apathy. To the rest of the world this may look like normality, but to the individual things are unclear.

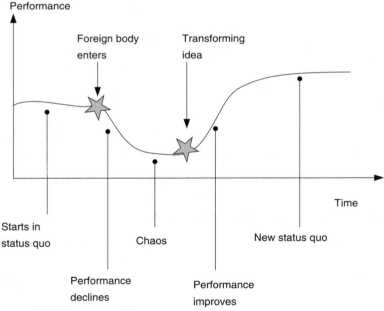

Figure 8.3 Satir's change model.

[2] See Satir (1991).
[3] See Weinberg (1997).

Eventually, we have a 'transforming idea' that enables us to understand what's happening and start to make sense of the changed world. Things don't get better instantly: over time, as we integrate this idea into our thinking and the way in which we act, our performance starts to return to our initial state. For a therapist it may be enough that our performance returns to 'normal', but for the organization and those attempting change there's little point in the change if it doesn't lead to improved performance.

For example, with a new programming language, at first we use the syntax of the new language but continue to think and design in the idioms of the old one. Our performance suffers as we try to make sense of the new language in the terms of the old one. During this phase we may blame the language and we may feel inadequate. Eventually, we come to understand the new language and our performance starts to improve. After a while we're thinking in the new language and taking full advantage of the capabilities. At this point we have reached a new, hopefully improved, status quo.

Lewin's model is hidden inside Satir's model. Both start with the status quo, then something happens to change it – unfreezing for Lewin and a foreign element for Satir. In the Lewin model change follows, but Satir recognizes that we don't move seamlessly from one state to another. For the individual, things may get worse before they get better; there may be confusion and the benefits of the change may take time to be recognized. Finally, both models end up at a new status quo.

Satir's model is useful for those introducing change, because it explains what's happening. When we introduce change, we're acting as the foreign element. We're suggesting that things should be different. For a while, people don't know how to act and may be worried by our new ideas. Even when people embrace new ideas and ways of working, it takes time to fully appreciate how to use them. During this time we mistake this reaction for resistance or a failure to *get it*. Eventually things do improve, but it takes time for the full benefits to be recognized. During this time we may suffer setbacks, but the overall trend is upwards.

Thinking Point: Observing Satir's Model

The *Thinking Points* in Chapter 7 asked you to identify some radical and some incremental changes that you had experienced or seen. Try to map these changes on to Satir's model:

- What was the foreign element?
- What was the chaos period like?
- What was the transforming idea?

8.4 Kotter's Model of Change

Kotter's model[4] differs from the previous models in that it describes an action plan for bringing about change. Essentially, Kotter has enlarged Lewin's three-part model into eight distinct actions and phases to be undertaken to bring about change (Figure 8.4).

As with Satir's model, the diagram effectively describes what the model is about.

Kotter starts by suggesting that change won't happen unless there's some sense of urgency. Without this, he suggests that change will happen too slowly

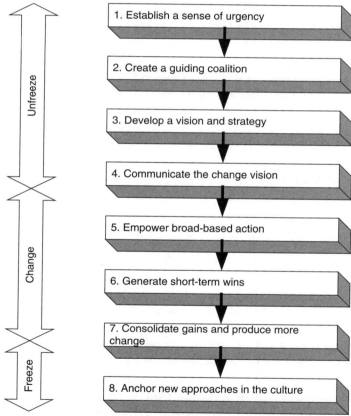

Figure 8.4   Kotter's eight-stage model for creating major change.
Reprinted by permission of Harvard Business School Press. From *Leading Change* by John P. Kotter. Boston, MA, 1996, p. 21. Copyright © 1996 by the Harvard Business School Publishing Corporation; all rights reserved.

---

[4] See Kotter (1996) .

to be effective, nor will there be any real drive to action the change programme. While creating the urgency itself may be done by a single person (assumed to be a senior manager) or a small team, the change programme need to be managed by a coalition.

Only when the urgency has been established and the coalition formed does the model actually consider what changes should be made. The implication is that the sense of urgency and coalition is built around the problem rather than the solution.

In practical terms, this means that software teams should not start their change with a solution in mind. Instead, teams need to first ask: 'What problems do we face?' rather than starting with a solution such as 'Write in Java' or 'Adopt eXtreme Programming'. Java and XP are solutions, not problems.

Although we needed a problem in order to start the process, this isn't necessarily the same as the trigger to create the sense of urgency. The trigger could be a problem, but it could equally be a failure or some new demand made of the team.

For example, losing a big customer account might be the trigger to start the change process. The loss creates the urgency, but it isn't the problem that you need to solve. Losing the customer is a problem, but in order to fix that problem you need to delve deeper to find the root problem: *Why did we lose the customer? Was our service shoddy? Is our quality too low? Did we miss delivery schedules?*

Only when the problem is established should we proceed to solution. So, if the problem is 'Our software only runs on Solaris', then the solution might be 'We should write in Java'; or if the problem is 'We missed the completion date and our quality is low', then the solution might be 'We should adopt eXtreme Programming'.

Once the problem is known and the coalition has a solution, the team moves into communication mode. The need for change and the proposed solution are communicated out from the coalition. To do so, the coalition needs to find channels and opportunities to communicate its message.

Next, the organization moves to empower individuals to change, and to change in line with the strategy. Kotter doesn't consider individual empowerment as optional. For him, all change programmes involve individuals bringing about change themselves. This implies that authoritarian action is ruled out, because such action would be dis-empowering.

Kotter suggests that change will take a long time. *How long is long?* Let's say that it's: (a) longer than you expect; and (b) longer than you think you have. This is consistent with other authors. In order that momentum isn't lost, it's necessary to take short-term wins when and where possible. And this implies building short-term wins into the change programme.

However, celebrating short-term wins isn't an occasion to stop the change. At the very moment that wins are celebrated, the change leaders must guard against creating complacency. In celebrating a win, there's a risk of allowing a 'Now we have changed we can relax' mentality to arise. Instead, an attitude of

'Much done, more to do' is needed. Thus, we move to consolidate the wins that we have achieved and use these to motivate further change. In celebrating one win, we set the task for the next.

Finally, Kotter sees the need to refreeze the organization around the new structures and mechanisms. However, this doesn't mean that we can stop changing: even while we're anchoring the changes, we look for more changes and improvements. In short, we need a culture of continual change.

In describing his model, Kotter explains where change fails. At each step there are mistakes that can be made that will undermine the change programme. Indeed, he believes that if any steps in the model are missed, or the steps are reordered, then the chances of success are significantly reduced.

Thinking Point: Applying Kotter's Change Model

Think of some problem that you'd like to tackle. Draw up a plan of action based on Kotter's model. Consider what problems you would encounter and how you might overcome them.

8.5 Theories E and O of Change

Theories of change abound: not content with offering one theory, the academics Beer and Nohria actually suggest two.[5] Rather than claiming supremacy for one theory or another, these writers identify two broad categories of change, one rooted in economics and one in organizational capabilities:

- *Theory E, the economic approach:* This is a hard approach to change that emphasizes economic value and shareholder value. This type of change encompasses corporate restructuring, worker lay-offs, mergers, acquisitions and divestments.

- *Theory O, the organizational approach:* This is a softer, slower, approach to change that focuses on building organization and personnel capabilities. This type of change encompasses team and personal development.

Broadly speaking, *theory E* corresponds to the discussion on radical change in Chapter 7, while *theory O* corresponds to the incremental change model outlined and running throughout this book. On the face of it, it appears that theory E can result in quick returns, while using O is a slow, gradual process that builds over time.

Managers who alternate between applying theories E and O will confuse employees, because there are conflicts between the two theories. Employees may not trust managers who talk about developing people but then lay off

---

[5] See Beer and Nohria (2000).

workers. Alternatively, managers who don't lay workers off when necessary may cause more damage to the company by delaying necessary decisions.

Both theories describe recognizable actions. The challenge therefore, is to know how to apply the appropriate theory without conflict or confusing others. One option is to apply theory E and then, once all the pain is out of the way, switch to a theory O approach. Persuading employees that management have put their hard-nosed approach behind them will be difficult, so it might be necessary to switch management teams.

The second answer is to openly recognize the conflict: while senior managers take hard economic decisions, they spend time working with people. In doing so, they connect with the workers to explain themselves, understand problems and encourage theory O type change. By showing honesty and a willingness to listen and learn, managers aim to carry employees with them through E type actions.

This second answer is more complicated and difficult to implement than either the first or straight E or O options. It requires leaders who can take hard decisions and then engage with people, rather than isolating themselves from criticism and employees' pain.

One more difficulty that readers of this book might face in applying theory E is one of authority. Only those with authority in an organization can engage in theory E type actions. Conversely, anyone can see to improve the organization from within.

Thinking Point: Identifying Theories E and O in Action

Think about your own experience of change. Can you identify any theory E and theory O programmes that you've experienced? Which were most successful?

8.6 Appreciative Inquiry

Many of the change theories that we have looked at so far start from an assumption: *There's a problem and we need to fix it.* This isn't really surprising: it's the way many of us have been taught to think. However, this does have some negative consequences. If you come looking for a problem, you'll find one. In fact, you'll find more than one, and in the process you risk creating a negative mindset and invoking personal defences.

Fortunately, there is an alternative approach and it's compatible with the change through learning approach taken in this book. The technique is called *Appreciative Inquiry (AI)*[6] and it starts from the positive: *Let's look at what's good here and see how we can make it even better.*

---

[6] See Cooperrider and Srivastva (1987).

8.6.1   The Change Trap

When faced with a failure, or a failing situation, people naturally get protective and try to avoid problems. Failure can breed fear and uncertainty. Some people will react by sticking their heads in the sand to avoid the problems, while others will redouble their efforts at what they know.

Neither reaction is good for creating change. Those with their heads in the sand won't see the need for change, while those who are working harder will be too busy to hear the message or take part in attempts to improve anything. Either way, people will seek security in what they know and fear what they don't know.

Once we embark on a 'find a problem, fix a problem' type approach, we change our mindset and language. We're looking for problems, we're talking about problems and we're thinking in the negative, seeking out what's wrong. After a while, we see problems everywhere we look. This becomes draining and saps our energy: we go home at night burdened with problems for which we need solutions. Naturally, we start to create defence mechanisms to protect ourselves from the problems that we see.

Taken together, these forces make change more difficult. People not only fear change, but they don't have the energy or time to learn new things and try them out. Fear of further failure creates an aversion to risk. There's no space or time for learning or change.

8.6.2   A Different Approach

Appreciative Inquiry starts from a different perspective. Instead of focusing on what the problems are, we seek to focus on what's good – and there's plenty of good in any organization. It could be a new company with all the excitement and wide-open horizons that start-ups have. Or it could be an organization that has been around for a while, in which case the success of simply surviving is worth celebrating.

Once we start to look at what's good in an organization, people become positive and our energy levels rise. Rather than taking problems home, we take home enthusiasm. When people have a positive outlook they learn more, and in such an environment it is easier for learning to flourish. In a safe, successful environment, people are more likely to try new ideas.

However, success can bread complacency and can sometimes block change: *If we did it right last time, then why change?* So we need to make sure that we drive learning to produce change. We can do this by looking for opportunities to learn more and put our learning into action. Opportunities come in many shapes and forms: just because you're doing well doesn't mean that you can't do better.

We might start by having teams identify their strengths. Perhaps these strengths allow them to ride over their problems, or perhaps having recognized their strengths they see opportunities to do even better, or maybe they can help other teams copy their strengths while they copy another team's strengths. By unleashing positive energy, we enthuse people to go further.

8.6.3   Appreciative Inquiry in Use

At a personal level, AI is about having the correct mindset: *Look for the good, not the problems*. Sometimes you'll need to switch between AI's 'seek out the good' and 'problem-seeking' modes of operation, but if you are to maintain your energy levels and positive approach, it's necessary to use the AI mode more than the problem-seeking mode.

Most software developers are by nature problem solvers. Every working day, they solve problems by creating software. There's a positive feedback loop here: *problem–solution–success!* It is when this chain of events gets broken that negativity steps in: when we can see the problem but can't solve it, or when we solve the problem and nobody notices the success.

AI can be used as part of a structured process; for example, during a project retrospective (see Chapter 11). Some writers have reported good results using AI with teams for the purpose of team formation and to create shared vision,[7] and elsewhere it has helped organizations dream of creating new products and better companies.[8]

Thinking Point: Good Things

Make a list of as many positive things in your work environment and process as you can: How do you feel once you've made the list?

8.6.4   Aspirational Change

Appreciative Inquiry leads aspirational change. As humans, we want tomorrow to be better: no matter how good today is, tomorrow could be better – we could earn more money, meet an old friend, meet a new friend, win a prize or any number of other good things. The aspiration of a better tomorrow can motivate us to change today – fear of an unknown tomorrow can stop us from changing.

It is the aspiration to solve a problem that leads us to try to fix it. The same aspirations can be harnessed to find and exploit opportunities. We may run out of problems, but we'll never run out of opportunities. The continual urge to do

[7] See Busche (1998) .

[8] See Kinni (2003) .

better can drive us onwards, to bigger and better change. Change can create change and success can breed success.

Conversely, when those aspirations are blocked – when there's no hope of a better tomorrow – things go into reverse. Fear of losing what we already have leads us to focus on maintaining the status quo. When we're confident of a better tomorrow, we have less to protect today.

This means that our work is never done: there are always more opportunities to seize and improvements to make. The challenge is to constantly look for opportunities to make things better, and not to fall into complacency or allow ourselves to tire.

8.7 Models, Models, Models

We could go on listing further models of change: if you would like to know more, there are plenty of books on change that can give you an overview of more models. Then there are countless journal and magazine articles on change. Magazines such as the *Harvard Business Review* regularly carry studies of organization change and authors proposing new models to understand change.

In Chapter 7 we looked at a simple grid (Figure 7.4) that categorized change as incremental or radical, and internal or external. The models that we have looked at above can be mapped on to this – as shown in Figure 8.5.

Appreciative Inquiry fits best in the incremental/internal quadrant, but could find application elsewhere. It may be used to radically redesign an organization or combat an external threat. Used regularly, it represents a form of continuous improvement, by helping an organization to appreciate what it does well and use this as a force for change.

One quadrant, *incremental change from external forces*, lacks a model. Yet this might be the most common form of change: no matter how stable our internal environment, things are always changing outside. There's no model because this quadrant represents no control. Change is happening, but there's no coordinated response. Eventually, something will change to move us to one of the other quadrants.

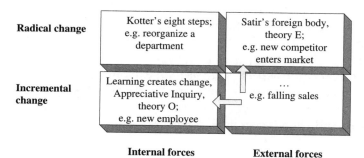

Figure 8.5 Which change model?

The forces outside the company may become felt within the company. People inside will start to notice what's happening and the external force will manifest itself as an internal forces. When this happens, the company will move from the bottom right box to the left, as a more structured form of change takes hold. This allows the organization to start learning and adapting.

Alternatively, we reach a point at which the external changes can no longer be ignored and they cumulatively have the effect of a foreign body entering the system. We may choose to understand this event as a *tipping point*,[9] when the gradual progression of one or more forces becomes so great that it triggers a reaction. In this case, we move vertically up a quadrant, as the incremental forces have the combined effect of a foreign body in the system.

8.8 Motivating Change

Each of the models that we have looked at in this chapter starts with a steady state. Yet something happens to move the organization or individual from the status quo to another state. Something has to happen to cause change: this might be an internal force, some external event or someone aspiring to do better.

By its nature, external change happens outside of the system considered in the models. Within an organization, there needs to be a mechanism for signalling external events. This mechanism could be money, as when cash flow declines people start to look for things that have changed. Or this mechanism could be someone who sees the change and signals it within the organization. In either case, there's an external reason to create a change. When the motivating force is internal, it can be more difficult to motivate people to change.

For any change to happen, a number of people must want it to happen and they must be prepared to act to do things differently. They must motivate others to change. Actually motivating people to change is one of the first problems that anyone trying to introduce change is going to face.

8.8.1 Push-and-pull Motivators

There are many reasons why we might want to change, and there are many reasons that we might give to other people to encourage them to change. Broadly speaking, these break down into two types: push motivators and pull motivators.

Push factors include aspects such as fear, existing problems and competitor actions. Push factors can be very powerful motivators, because they appeal to our survival instinct. However, such push factors can also create a negative environment and trigger personal defences.

[9] See Gladwell (2000) .

In the short run, it might be easier to motivate change through the push factors. If you need rapid change, you might be tempted to order people around, talk up the problems facing the organization and even threaten a few people. Even if this kind of push works in the short run – which is doubtful – it isn't sustainable.

Over time, people will respond with their own defences and camouflage problems. People may simply tune out those who constantly talk about problems, or they may comply with instructions without enthusiasm and with limited efficiency. As people erect defences, less learning will occur. People who live in fear won't take the risks necessary for experimentation and innovation to occur. Consequently, people will feel less empowered and less able to act on their own initiative. Given the opportunity, people will vote with their feet and take their skills and knowledge elsewhere.

Alternatively, factors such as success, recognition, aspirations and the idea of a better life represent the pull motivators to change. At first sight, these can seem soft compared to push factors, but in the long run they're more sustainable for an organization. If the pull factors are absent from your environment, they can take time to establish.

The trouble with pull factors is that they can also lead to complacency and a resistance to anything that might risk success. When this happens, people may not see the need to change anything: *It worked last time, so why do it differently?* Fear of success slipping away can increase the perception of risk.

This is not to say that we should sit down and cold-bloodedly select a set of motivating factors. More likely, anyone wanting change will already have some understanding of why the change needs to happen, and these reasons will translate into push and/or pull factors. At some point, these reasons will be translated and communicated to others to motivate the change (Figure 8.6).

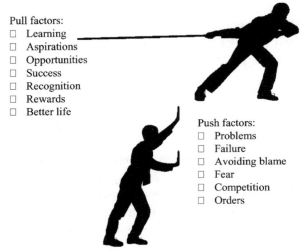

Pull factors:
- ☐ Learning
- ☐ Aspirations
- ☐ Opportunities
- ☐ Success
- ☐ Recognition
- ☐ Rewards
- ☐ Better life

Push factors:
- ☐ Problems
- ☐ Failure
- ☐ Avoiding blame
- ☐ Fear
- ☐ Competition
- ☐ Orders

Figure 8.6   Push-and-pull motivators for change.

Failure and Success are Constructed

When we talk about success and failure, we seldom stop to think about the definitions of success and failure. *What constitutes success? What is a failure?*

Some development projects have criteria that allow a clear judgement to be made: delivery by a given date, delivery within a certain budget or a set of specific features. But even these can lead to different understandings: *Is a project a success if it's on time but over budget?*

Different people on projects can have different impressions. In one study,[10] developers considered the project a success – technically it worked, the team was good – while management saw a failure – late and over budget. My own discussions with software developers show that this case isn't unique.

One developer I interviewed told me about a successful project that he had worked on: how it was a good design, with good code and high quality. He had already told me that it was scheduled to take three months, so when I asked how long it actually took, I was surprised to be told that it had taken 12 months. I said, 'Some people would consider a project that overran by nine months on a three-month schedule to be a failure', to which he responded, 'I never thought of that.'

Even where a project does have objective criteria, people may not want to recognize the result. One project that I worked with was considered a success by the development team: it was late, but so were most other projects in the company. Nobody from management came and said 'this was a success' or 'this was a failure', but the company never paid the team the success bonuses to which they were accustomed.

Whether a project is a success or failure is defined by the stories that we tell about the project. We construct and tell those stories in order to understand the project and learn from them. These stories help us keep the better practices from the project and avoid the ones that didn't work.

When different project stakeholders come to different understandings about the project's success, then they will draw different conclusions. This in turn makes it more difficult for both groups to make the changes that they wish to make in future.

In order to avoid this, it is essential that everyone involved with the project comes to a common understanding and shares common stories. This can only happen when these disparate groups talk to one another and help each other understand their points of view.

[10] See Linberg (1999) .

8.8.2   Shared Understanding

In order to motivate anyone to change, it is necessary to explain why a change is necessary. Simply ordering someone to 'do it' won't yield the best performance. Indeed, in general, knowledge workers – and IT staff in particular – don't respond well to authority. Being told 'You don't need to know the reason – just do it' may be acceptable in Hollywood films, but it isn't going to bring out the best in your co-workers.

At the very least, you need to be able to explain why things need to change. In some cases, simply communicating your message often and powerfully enough may create the change that you desire.

Frequently, however, simple communication isn't enough. By helping more people see the present opportunity or problem, we can harness their knowledge and action to tackle the issue. To do this, it is necessary to create a shared understanding both of the status quo and how the future may look after some changes.

People are more likely to engage with change if they can see the issue for themselves. Being told 'we never meet our deadlines', and seeing it visually for themselves are very different things. Once individuals recognize the need for change, they're more likely both to suggest a solution and to act on the proposed resolution. Frequently, the failure to change doesn't come about because some individual is resisting change; rather, it's simply that their perception of the situation is different from the way we see it.

Problems can be hidden, or camouflaged, by partial solutions that hide a bigger problem. For example, a friend of mine assumed responsibility for a development team in London. The team was worn out and not working efficiently, so she saw the need to change. However, the team's customers in Edinburgh didn't see any problems. They saw that the team always managed to deliver its software by the scheduled time, and any Saturday working was simply a sign of commitment.

In the context of motivating change, a shared understanding helps people to feel part of the change process. Rather than it being something that is happening to them, they're part of a team making the change happen. Without a shared understanding, team members can feel isolated, left out or undervalued. In a world in which business change so often leads to job losses, it's important to make as many people as possible part of the change.

8.8.3   Blocks to Change

Often, the motivation to change already exists within people. Good people naturally want to do a good job, and if something needs changing they will change it. As we noted earlier, good software developers are by their nature problem solvers and learners. The IT industry is one in which new technologies are always appearing and which need learning. Writing software is the process

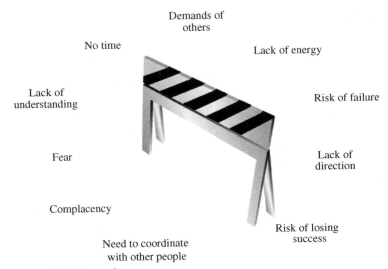

Figure 8.7 Roadblocks to change.

of solving problems. Such people should welcome change and be quite willing to try new ideas. So, what stops change?

Blockages – such as the blocks to learning that we noted in Chapter 5 – can get in the way and stop action. When blocks persist, people become demoralized and uninterested in improvement. In such cases, creating change is less about motivating people to change and more about removing the blocks that prevent change, and showing that change is possible.

Unfortunately, it's all too easy to stop or hinder the progress of change and learning – Figure 8.7 illustrates a few of these blocks. Blockages are frequently interrelated, so a lack of direction makes it hard to coordinate with others, and the demands of others reduce the amount of time available to try something new and increase the risk of failure. Some blocks may be very real, while others are imagined, assumed or carried over from previous projects.

For example, one developer I worked with regularly asserted that project management wouldn't allow him time to undertake test-first unit testing and refactoring. Other developers answering to the same manager were equally clear that they'd adopted Test-driven Development (TDD) practices and had been successful with them. Whether the block existed in the developer's imagination or – to some extent at least – really did come from the manager is hard to say.

A large part of creating change and learning is the identification and removal of blocks. Blocks may take many shapes and forms. For example:

- Physical blocks, such as the lack of suitable desks to do pair programming.
- Organizational blocks, such as teams split across geographical areas.
- Personnel blocks, such as two individuals who don't see eye-to-eye.
- Mental blocks, such as obstacles in our own minds: 'I've never done that before.'

Unfortunately, our own prejudices and assumptions impede our own change and can mislead us into seeing problems and blocks where none exist. Thus, we need to constantly be on the lookout for blocks, whether they are real, in the minds of others or in our own minds. Once we have identified these blocks, we need to remove them. This can be easier said than done.

Fear can be both a push motivator for change and an inhibitor blocking change. Unfortunately, some managers rely on fear to create change, which builds resentment and reduces performance. People living in fear will be less likely to feel empowered, to take risks and to apply their learning and judgement. It was with good reason that Edwards Deming included 'drive out fear' in his 14 points for quality improvement.

The approach of failure can motivate one person to change things, but equally it can make another person more resistant to change. Using fear of failure to motivate change has a simplistic rationale to it, but it's a risky strategy and one that will show diminishing returns if used repeatedly.

8.9 When Not to Change

Of course every project is important – if it were not, we probably wouldn't bother doing it, and if we did we wouldn't be motivated. But if we're going to make changes, we have to allow some slack to take some risks.

Some projects are more risk averse than others. For example, critical-safety projects, such as the software for a nuclear reactor, need to avoid risk. Such projects will take a lower-risk approach than projects for less critical systems. Alistair Cockburn[11] calls this aspect *system criticality*. System criticality distinguishes between systems where failure cause discomfort, loss of discretionary money, loss of irreplaceable money and loss of life. Cockburn proposes a scale of escalating criticality, where failure becomes progressively more consequential (shown in Figure 8.8).

When deciding how much risk you can accept, it's important to consider the consequences of failure. All change involves an element of change, but so too does inaction. Not changing may make the current project safer, but may endanger the longer-term survival of the organization. When deciding how much change to accept, these risks need to be balanced.

If you can't accept any risk in the current project, then you'll have to find ways of learning and practising outside of the project. For example, airlines are highly risk averse and so they use flight simulators to train pilots and update them on airports and planes. This approach is expensive, since people undergoing training aren't productive and training equipment is needed.

[11] See Cockburn (2002) .

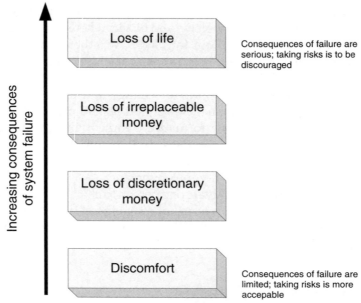

Figure 8.8   Cockburn's scale of escalating criticality.
Source: Based on a diagram from Cockburn (2002)

8.10 Conclusion

There are different types of change. Frequently, we find that external conditions impose change upon us, but sometimes we need to make change happen within. Some organizations adopt a continual change ethos but even here, from time to time, there's a need for radical change.

There's no shortage of change models that attempt to explain change or guide us through the process. Which one is 'right' depends on a number of factors – not least the type of change that we're facing. By looking at these models, we can change our own outlook and the way in which we think about change.

Initiating change requires some motivating force. Some forces try to push people into change, while others pull people towards the promise of a better world. The push factors may bring rapid results, but they are high risk. The pull factors of aspirational change represent a more sustainable model for continual change, but aren't without their own risks.

Common to all change is the need to learn, because, as this book argues, change and learning are the same thing. In order to produce change, one motivates the learning process and removes obstacles to learning and change. Humans are by their nature creatures who learn, and good software developers have an appetite for learning. If we work on the learning side of the equation, change will follow.

Making Change Happen

"learning is better, because it is more intensive, than teaching; the more that is taught the less can be learned"
Josef Albers,[1] 1888–1976, artist

The underlying idea for most of this book is that learning leads to change. By learning something, we create a force for change because we want to use our learning, so we change because we have learnt.

In the last few chapters we have discussed types of change and models for understanding them. This chapter focuses on what you can do to bring about change in a more practical way and expands on things you can do to bring about change. Some are simple and low cost, such as listening to people.

This isn't the last word on what you can do to create change. Quite the opposite. This is an introduction to what you can do – indeed, this chapter may contain too many ideas to take in one go. Other authors have covered this subject in much more depth and offer more advice (see the Further Reading section).

Still, no matter how many books you read and techniques you hear about, you still have to do it. You have to move from learning about change to acting on it. Only you can do this.

Every individual is unique and every organization is unique. The advice given by this book and others isn't tailor made for you or your organization.

---

[1] Quoted in Borchardt-Hume (2006).

Only you can decide what applies and what's useful. You must find your own route to change for you and your organization.

9.1   Build a Case for Change

Learning-induced change can happen without a specific case for change being made. This is typically incremental improvement and it occurs when someone sees an opportunity to improve the current product, processes or practices. It also happens when experimentation leads people to try something different.

This kind of change is good, because it leads to continual improvement and feeds the learning cycle: failure to change would stall the learning cycle. Sometimes it becomes necessary to focus on change itself rather than learning. This can happen when a more radical change is required, or when learning requires help from others. When this happens, it is necessary to persuade others of the need to change, and in order to persuade others you need to make a case for change.

As we saw in Chapters 7 and 8, you need to understand why change is necessary. You, yourself, need to understand why change should come about. Then you need to explain this to other people.

It is never enough for you alone to understand the need for change. At some point, you'll need to explain it to others. If you aren't clear in your own mind why change is needed, then it will be difficult to explain to others why they should change.

9.1.1   Find the Problems and Forces

At the start of any change initiative, we should ask: *Why do we need to change?* And we should look behind the answers to this question to find the forces at work creating the need to change. By understanding the forces creating the need for change, we acquire a deeper understanding of the need for change.

Sometimes, we start not with the problem or opportunity, but with a solution. An idea for change appears in our minds without any clear understanding of why it is necessary or what forces are driving it. For example: Agile software development could shorten your delivery cycles, but *why would you want to do this*? And what benefit would this create?

It isn't wrong to start with a solution, but we need to validate the solution. We do this by working backwards from the solution to the problem that the solution is solving, and understanding the forces that make the solution a good solution.

By working back to the problem, we're validating the solution and the need to change. It is entirely possible that there's no problem. If this is true, then maybe you don't actually need to change. Alternatively, it may mean that you haven't dug deeply enough into the issues, or it may indicate that other people don't perceive the problem.

While it may be difficult to understand the problems and forces, knowing them is more useful than knowing the solution alone. Not only is it easier to make a case for change when you understand the problem, but it also helps you show that you have the right solution for the problem.

Thinking Point: Finding Problems and Opportunities

Finding the problems in your organization requires observation:

- Look at what the company is doing: What's the objective of these actions?
- Is it to compensate for some other problem?

9.1.2 Finding Problems

Coming up with new ideas, finding problems and creating solutions is something of a chaotic process. You'll find problems that you can't solve and need to leave alone for now, and you'll think up ideas and find that there's no application for them.

Problems abound in all organizations, so ask people about their work and their problems. Talking to people can be a good source of problems:

- *Talk to the developers: What problems do they face meeting manager's expectations?*
- *Talk to the managers: What problems are they facing? What changes do they see coming?*
- *Talk to the customers: What problems do they see?*

Problems, forces and opportunities are all ammunition for your change initiative. Knowing the problems that you face helps direct your learning and persuade people of the need for change. Addressing real problems means that you can produce real improvement.

Another rich source of problems and opportunities is the company's stated strategy, vision or objectives. From the outside, company strategy can be hard to see, but when you're on the inside it should just be a case of asking the right person. Of course, there's no guarantee that your company actually has a strategy, but that is a different problem. Look at the company strategy:

- What is it that the company is trying to do?
- Is it trying to cut costs?

- Is the company trying to grow organically from within?
- Is the company trying to innovate with new products and services?
- Once you know the strategy, work backwards again: *What is needed for the strategy?*

A company that is trying to grow from within will emphasize different things compared to a company that is trying to cut costs. Growth involves acquiring more customers, offering more products, reaching new markets and hiring new people. Cost cutting may mean leaving markets, turning customers down, refining processes and cutting staff.

Armed with this information, try to work out what it means to you and your team.

- Will your team need to expand or contract?
- Will you do the same things more cheaply or will you do different things completely?
- How will you operate when you have ten customers instead of one?
- Will the *ad hoc* development practices work when you have more products?

The answers to these questions could be reasons for change or they may suggest areas to improve your learning. Either way, the answers will help you explain the need for change to the organization.

Despite what these questions suggest, there's no systematic way of finding problems. Sometimes you see the problem first and then find the solution; at other times you see a solution and have to work backwards to find a problem and validate the solution. It may be that you see an opportunity for improvement and when you work backwards you find a different problem.

Be careful to avoid talking yourself into problems. As Section 8.6 on Appreciative Inquiry noted, once you start looking for problems you might see them everywhere, and you might find it demoralizing. Always try to validate the problems that you see with other people. If they don't see something as a problem, then it might not actually be a problem.

9.1.3   Communicate the Problem

Once you understand the problems and forces driving the need for change, you can start to communicate these to others. In an ideal world, we would just schedule a meeting with a few key players, present our findings – possibly via PowerPoint – and listen while they accept our recommendations. Unfortunately, the real world doesn't work this way.

Communicating the need for change, and the opportunities available if we change, is going to be hard work. It means talking to those who have the power to sanction the change, those who will be affected, both in managing it and in implementing it, and everyone in between.

Some communication can be planned: we can send e-mail, issue memos, arrange meetings or schedule presentations. Other communication is opportune: bumping into a senior manager in an elevator, finding somebody useful in the kitchen or at the coffee machine. On occasions, you might want to arrange an accidental meeting: know who you want to talk to and make sure you get a coffee at the same time they do.

One way of explaining the change can be through telling stories.[2] People can associate more directly with a story than they can with a raw fact or statistic. Stories have the power to involve people with the change idea. Understanding a story is easier than understanding formal documents or statistics. A story tells about the problem and a solution, and lets listeners fill in enough detail to imagine it happening in their own environment. Sometimes, what is left out of the story is more important than what's included.

As change happens, it is easier to find success stories within the organization. These stories can be repeated to others to expand on the need for change and opportunities. Collect your own set of stories of problems, solutions and changes that have occurred. You don't need long essays or novels: good stories may only be a sentence or two long. Having stories prepared means that you have them ready when an opportunity arises to enthuse people about your ideas or discuss a problem that you've identified.

9.2 Slack in Action: Make Time and Space for Learning and Change

For change to happen, people need to have both time and space to actually change. As we observed in Chapter 5, organizations need to provide *slack*. Without time, resources and physical space, people won't be able to reflect on what they're doing, try new ideas, experiment and fail.

Giving time and space to discussions, change and experiments has a direct effect: it allows people to make sense of change and internalize the change. It also has a second, equally important, function: it sends a message that such discussion and changes are valued, that we aren't in a constant break-neck environment.

Doing something differently means not doing it the way you've been doing it, which means that it's going to be more difficult to know how long something will take – and it probably means that the first time you do it differently will take longer than when you were doing it in the old way.

For example, a team adopting *Test-driven Development* (*TDD*) practices will undoubtedly find that it can't give an accurate estimate of how long it will take.

---

[2] For more details and a fuller description of how and why stories work, see Denning (2001).

It may, or may not, be able to give an accurate estimate based on the old way, but certainly using a new approach will take a different amount of time.

At first, everything may take longer, but as the team becomes more familiar with the techniques, as it learns the new way of working, things will speed up and the time taken will reduce.

However, if the team is to improve, it needs time to learn the new way of working and internalize the practices, it needs time to try different techniques and compare the results, and it needs time to talk about its experiments with team members and reflect on its own experiences.

Sometimes things will go wrong: new techniques and practices won't work the way you thought they would and you'll need to change your approach, maybe even writing off the time spent on trying a new way. In other words, you need to allow time to fail. If you can't afford the time to have a failure once in a while, you won't recognize the learning opportunities that come from trying something different.

Change isn't going to happen if you don't allow time for it. When people are under pressure to make a deadline and deliver as fast as possible, they're far more likely to stick to what they know; they will avoid trying things that take longer (even in the short run) and they will avoid taking risks with new techniques and ideas. Without some slack, change can't enter the system.

Taking time to change often comes down to priorities. People often postpone change until 'I have finished this task' – whether the task is a one-off code change or a three-month project. Creating change often comes down to persuading people that they do have time to change now, and that change is a high priority rather than something to be put off.

You also need to allow time for the change to happen – things won't happen overnight. When agreed changes don't happen instantly, don't condemn the team. Change takes time. This isn't an excuse for letting things slide: don't let people put changes off indefinitely, but don't expect things to happen instantly.

Time isn't the only requirement for change. People need space as well: physical space to rearrange desks, put up charts, pair-program and create a different environment. People need space for thinking: perhaps a quiet room where they can reflect on events, and space where they can gather in groups to discuss and argue about what has happened and what they do next. A crowded office with no meeting rooms doesn't present a safe environment in which new ideas can be discussed, results compared and new techniques devised. Knowledge and learning can only be spread when people have the time and space to actually do it.

9.3 Leading the Change

Leadership is a tricky subject: it can be difficult to define, but most people will recognize it when they see it. Some would claim that leadership is a personality trait, and that some people have it while others don't; others claim that leadership can be taught and learned.

Whatever the truth about the nature of leadership, someone has to lead change. Somebody has to care enough to do something. Someone who really cares, and the more passionately the better, is the natural change leader. If you're passionate about these things, don't be put off by your lack of experience; on the other hand, if you've done this a thousand times before and aren't interested in going through the motions again, then let it drop.

There's a difference between *managing* and *leading*. Just because you're a manager doesn't make you a leader, and just because you're not a manager doesn't mean you can't lead. If you have some position of authority leadership may be easier, but it might also lull you into a false sense of security if you make the mistake of thinking that you can tell people to learn.

Legitimacy is more important than authority. When you have legitimacy, you have the right to involve yourself in issues and others respect your right to be there. Without legitimacy, others may question your role and question your right to intervene.

Creating change isn't about mandating people to do something different. Instead, creating change is a process of helping people who want to change. Some people will be more receptive to change and learning than others.

The key thing in making change happen is just that: *making things happen*. Somebody has to care, somebody has take action and somebody has to make the things discussed above happen.

9.3.1 Create Awareness of the Problem

Sometimes other people don't see the problems that we see. There are various reasons why this might be: it's entirely possible that what looks problematic to us isn't actually broken: if we take the time to watch and listen, we may find that there's a good reason why it's the way it is, and that nothing is wrong.

At other times our observation is correct, but others haven't seen the problem. And if other people haven't seen the problem, then it's hardly surprising that they haven't tried to fix it.

So before we try to fix anything, it's pretty important to help others to see the problem. You could try the direct approach: 'What do you think of . . .' Or you could try a less direct approach: 'What do you think the problems facing us at the moment are?' or 'What do you think of X?'

Once people become aware of a problem, several things start to happen. Firstly, they might just fix it themselves: if something is entirely within their control, then this is quite possible. Secondly, they may be willing to accept your help in fixing the problem.

This becomes particularly important when you're dealing with a group of people who are all affected by the problem and who all need to change to produce a fix. Without a shared awareness of the problem, the group isn't going to attempt any change. Only when those concerned see a problem can we move to the fixing stage.

Sometimes it isn't a team that is missing the problem but an individual; in particular, someone who is more senior in the management structure. Such people hear of problems every day, but they prioritize what they hear and decide what they will act on depending on their own agendas. Just because you see something as an urgent problem doesn't mean that they do.

Faced with such a scenario, there are broadly two options. Firstly, you may choose to pass over the problem that you see. Instead, find out what this person sees as high-priority problems and then try to address these problems.

Alternatively, you may choose to pursue the problem that you've identified and try to progress a solution. Since the senior person doesn't regard this problem as a high priority, it's unlikely that you'll get much support; but on the other hand, it's quite likely that you'll be able to address the problem that you see with your chosen solution.

9.3.2   Create Awareness of Opportunities

The word 'problem' deserves a few caveats. Not everything we want to address is a problem; that is, not everything we want to improve or change is necessarily causing us pain. Sometimes when we say 'problem' we're really talking about an 'opportunity'. Almost by definition, every problem we face is an opportunity to make things better, but the reverse isn't always true. There are always opportunities to make things better, but these things aren't always problems.

For example, suppose that we have a software development team that is working well. It delivers its software at the scheduled time, it achieves good, or at least acceptable, quality and it stays within the budget. Why would we change anything? Is there really a problem here? Maybe not.

But this doesn't mean that there isn't an opportunity to do better. Even this team may be able to reduce the time it takes to make a delivery, it may be able to improve quality still further or it may be able to deliver a higher proportion of functionality. Indeed, if we believe in the principles of Lean, then this team certainly can improve.

In such cases, the issue isn't about making people aware of a 'problem', but making them aware of an opportunity. Again, we return to the definitions of success and failure: what might look like a problem to us isn't necessarily a problem for our manager, and what looks like a problem to the manager may not look like a problem to us.

Before you rush to re-label every opportunity as a problem, or vice versa, remember our discussion of the definitions of *success* and *failure*. It might be easier to motivate people to fix a problem, but having too many problems can be overwhelming and create a defensive, siege-like, mentality. Ideally, you want to prioritize your efforts and balance your approach between solving problems and embracing opportunities.

9.3.3 Beware Unsolvable Problems

The second caveat about the word 'problem' is that it implies that there isn't only a problem to solve, but a solution to the problem. To put it another way, *the difficulty with the word 'problem' is that it can be deceptive*, because 'problem' implies that there is a solution; sometimes we face problems for which there are no solutions. In such cases, we might want to settle for a palliative approach: rather than fixing the potentially unfixable problem, we treat the symptoms and lessen the pain.

The danger here is that by limiting our ambitions, we never get to fix a problem; and when our problem is part of a bigger problem, we may be making everything worse. Therefore, palliative care should only be viewed as a temporary solution.

9.3.4 Communicate a Failure

As the topic box in Chapter 8 noted, the definitions of success and failure aren't clean cut, but where one group regards a development as a failure, it's important that this is communicated to a wider audience. Keeping failure to yourself, or to a select few, makes it harder to learn and to address the issues.

Firstly, if it's only you who sees the failure, is it really a failure? When others don't share your view of a situation, you should attempt to understand the difference in views. It could be that their understanding of the issue is better than your own.

Secondly, if you limit knowledge of the problem, then you'll increase the mental gap between yourself and others. The bigger this gap, the harder it is to fix problems.

Finally, if you don't communicate failure, then it has no value as a motivator for change or as a source of learning. You end up with all the down sides of failure without recognizing any of the up sides.

Unfortunately, some people just don't like talking about failure, while others are scared of creating defensive reactions by discussing failure. True, constantly telling someone that they have failed isn't good, but then nor is shielding them from reality.

The Problem with My Cooking

One of my hobbies is cooking: some people even think I'm a good cook. My problem (which might not actually be a problem) is that I can find fault with every dish I cook – the meat is overcooked, the vegetables were ready too early, the sauce has too much cream . . . and so it goes on. Most people don't see these faults – they just enjoy my food – but for me they're a reason to improve next time.

9.3.5   Focus the Team on What Needs To Be Done

Once the team is aware of the problem or failure, it's time to do something. This means drawing a line under the 'why' and 'who' questions of understanding what went wrong and focusing on asking what's to be done. The smaller the team dealing with the issue, the easier it is to get it to focus. If there are just two of you, then a good conversation will probably suffice. If the team has eight, ten or more members, then you need some more structure.

Visual aids are good for this. Left to conversation, either verbal or electronic, people will get distracted, return to the 'why' questions and come up with a variety of solutions that aren't necessarily remembered or agreed on. It's far better to put everyone in a room with a white board or set of cards, so that they can work out what needs to be done, agree the items and prioritize them.

Sometimes, there's one large overreaching thing that needs to be done. This is quickly agreed, but by its nature it's hard to see how the team is going to tackle it. Left as a single big entity, each team member could cherry pick his or her preferred piece. Left as a big entity, it's hard to tell how much work there really is to do. Faced with a single large problem, the team needs to find some way of breaking the problem down into smaller chunks – classic decomposition.

Once the problem is clearly defined, the team needs to work together to address the problem together. This starts with an exchange of views and opinions. Next the team needs to generate options for action – it's better to generate several options before selecting one. Taking time to consider the issues as a team means that when action starts, the team acts together.

Why Can't We Ship Tomorrow?

I once joined a team porting a product from Windows to Unix. This process had been going on for over a year, and after a few months on the team I couldn't see it getting any nearer. As someone who had ported large applications in days rather than months, this frustrated me – but nobody saw it as a problem, so I watched and waited.

Then the trouble started. A new CEO arrived: he didn't talk to the team much, but we all knew that the company's sales had been poor lately. When the CEO started laying people off, the team felt the pressure – we all agreed that we had to ship something.

At first, we were like rabbits caught in headlights, paralysed by the sense of what was going to happen. It felt like watching an accident play out in slow motion, with no sense that we could do anything. Eventually, we convened and focused our thoughts. I asked one of my favourite questions:

'Why can't we ship tomorrow?'

> This was the question that focused the team. We took stock of our position, looked at what we wanted done in order to ship and then threw out everything that wasn't absolutely necessary. We got ruthless: we only needed minimal functionality, so we could compromise in some areas, just as long as we could make show success quickly. Shipping the most basic, cut-down, stripped-back product on Unix was far more likely to save our jobs than anything else. Decisions and compromises that we were previously not willing to make became possible.

9.3.6 Explain the Change

We have already discussed talking about *the need for change*: once the change starts happening you have to keep explaining the *need*, but you also have to supplement it with explanation of what the change is. Don't get too far ahead of the team: you want it to discover its own route to change, but you need to keep it moving and focused on what it does now.

People need to know how things will work after change is implemented. This is for two reasons; firstly, because people fear change and worry about the consequences. The more people understand the change, the less they have to fear and worry about. Secondly, people need to know what's expected of them and what they need to do after the change is implemented.

When change is imposed on a team, it's essential that the team is fully briefed on what the change will bring. When the team decides on a change itself, it still needs to understand the change in depth, but it is itself the best source of information. Therefore the team needs to be given the opportunity to collectively imagine and rehearse how the change will work.

Unfortunately, it's possible to spend too much time and energy briefing people about changes. When teams are overburdened with too much detail, people will start to forget some bits. Worse, they will recognize that this is happening and get worried. Don't expect people to take it all in at once: you may need to repeat the stories again and again. In fact, people may never actually take it all in and understand what's happening until they've actually done it and have experienced success. Chapter 11 describes process miniatures that can be used to help communicate what happens after the change.

9.3.7 Model the Changes Yourself

As the leader of the change, you need to live the change. It's no use telling the team that there will be a stand-up meeting at 9.30 a.m. every day if you continue to roll in at 9.45 a.m. As a leader, you need to play by your own rules.

Your actions and behaviours are examples of the change that you want to see in the team. If you don't ask for your code to be reviewed, then why should anyone else? If you don't write your unit tests, then what makes you think others will?

There are two sides here. The first is negative: *If you can't follow the changes that you've suggested, then why should anyone else?* Don't be guilty of *do as I say, not as I do*. If you really can't follow your own suggestions, then you can't expect anyone else to either.

Secondly, and more important, is the positive side: by modelling the changes yourself, you can help alleviate fears – people can just copy you. Your actions provide an example of what people should do.

It helps here if you're actually engaged in the same tasks as the people around you. So this technique is more applicable to those who are trying to introduce change among their immediate work colleagues. Managers trying to introduce change amongst their staff may find it difficult to model some changes simply because they don't do the same work. In this case, you need to find other ways of showing your support, or maybe you can find a champion who can help lead the change in the team.

9.3.8 Ask for Volunteers (Self-selecting Teams)

When you need people to try something new, you get better results when you ask them first. For example, before deciding to adopt SCRUM, ask your team members: *What do you think? Would you be willing to give it a try?*

This is another example of listening to people, but it goes further: by actually consulting with people beforehand, you're more likely to get motivated and involved. When it comes to forming teams, it's always better to ask for volunteers.[3] Asking people if they want to join a team is always a good move, and when the team is trying something new it's an even better one.

Self-selecting teams work best when people have a selection of teams to choose from, but more often it's only possible to ask whether someone would like to join a team or not join a team. When someone doesn't want to join a team, it should be treated as an opportunity to learn why not. It might be a personal preference or they may have some useful insight into the workings of that team.

Self-selected teams aren't without problems. There's a danger of creating a team of enthusiasts, while leaving behind those who don't want to change. You could see this as one of those *nice to have* problems: at least you have one team that is enthusiastic, and in the process people have probably separated themselves into their preferred working groups.

A self-selected team isn't necessarily a cross-functional team or a multi-skilled team. For example, all your Java programmers may opt to be in one team and all the Cobol programmers in another. This might not produce the right mix for the work that needs to be done.

---

[3] For more information, see the pattern *Self-selecting Teams* (Coplien and Harrison, 2004), which describes the advantages of teams that have chosen to work together.

When it comes to staffing a team, there's also the small matter of practicality. If you only have five people in your technical organization, then these are going to be the five people on your team. If you absolutely must have specialist knowledge and Fred is the only person with the knowledge, then Fred must be on your team.

Even given all these limitations, it's still important to give people a choice of where they work. Few things are as demoralizing as telling someone to work in a team or on a project when they don't want to.

9.4 Create Feedback Loops

Whether you're working up to a change or starting one off, it pays to build feedback loops. At the most basic level, a feedback loop allows people to see the effects of their actions, thus creating awareness of problems and possible improvements. Without feedback, it can be difficult to know how well you're doing.

Short feedback loops are more effective than long ones, because there's a closer connection between cause and effect. For example, program code may be written today but not tested for a month. It might not be integrated for another month. Consequently, by the time we know the effect of our actions, we've forgotten what we did. Even if we do know the full cause and effect, two months have elapsed, during which time the same faults may have been replicated.

It isn't enough to create feedback loops. We need to speed them up, reducing the gap between cause, effect, observation and further action. Identifying existing feedback loops and creating new ones is all part of systems thinking, as discussed in Chapter 5.

Feedback loops deliver the messages of failure that motivate us to change and improve. Feedback loops also deliver the messages of success that tell us that we're doing the right thing. As such, feedback loops can play a key role in creating learning and change.

Feedback can occur in any number of forms. These include:

- *Personal communication* – actually talking to people about their performance.
- *Statistical* – counting some criteria.
- *Systematic* – like the kanban cards used in Lean manufacturing.
- *Financial* – bonus payments for successful projects.

One of the most powerful forms of feedback is: money. Money isn't only expenditure and income: it's also information. Money flows tell us where we're putting our efforts and resources, and they show how successful our product is in the marketplace. Because the exchange of money entails sacrifice by one party, it's a particularly powerful form of feedback.

If people don't want your product, you'll know because your income will fall. When someone is willing to part with hard-earned cash for your product, this shows that they value your product above others, and that your product has some advantage over the competition.

Thinking Point: Identify and Invent Feedback Loops

Identify the feedback loops in your team and organization. Are the feedback loops effective? Could they be made shorter and faster?

Also try to identify places where new feedback loops would be useful or where existing feedback loops are broken.

Check-in

Some people are happier sitting in meetings and listening to others without saying much themselves. There is nothing necessarily wrong with this: it's simply what some people prefer to do. Still, there are times when we want to involve everyone in the meeting and hear as many points of view as possible.

One way of encouraging people to say more and put people in the right frame of mind is to start with a *check-in* round. To do this, ask everyone in the room to briefly say a few words. When groups haven't met before or don't know one another, this is often a personal introduction.

For groups that meet regularly, a check-in can still be useful to get the meeting off to a good start; but since people know each other, some different formula is required. The meeting host or organizer may pose a question and ask each person present to answer it as they please. Suitable questions are:

- Can you tell the group some good news?
- What have you learned recently?
- Tell me something positive.
- In a single word, describe how you're feeling.

In some groups, the answer is less important than the action of involving everyone. In other groups, the question can trigger reflection on the part of individuals and the group as a whole.

In one book study group I organized, the question became a useful mechanism for people to apply ideas from the book to their team. The discussions that followed the check-in were often more interesting than the book itself.

At first, groups might find it odd to be expected to say something at the start of the meeting. I have heard engineers in England describe it as a 'crazy West Coast idea', so you may need to be brave to introduce a check-in to your organization.

Holding a check-in at the start of every meeting is probably overkill and people would probably tire of it very quickly. Similarly, asking the same question every time can get boring, so you may like to vary the question from time to time.

9.5 Remove Barriers

One of the reasons why change fails to happen is simply that there's some barrier that stops it. We have already discussed barriers to learning and motivational blocks (Chapters 5 and 8, respectively). Many of these barriers are the same ones that stop change from happening. Therefore, it follows that if we remove barriers to change, then change will happen.

Some of the actions already covered in this chapter are aimed at removing blocks to individual change. By providing time and space, and by empowering people and resolving conflict, barriers that prevent change are removed.

Other blocks may be organizational; for example, research and development teams that don't communicate with the production group. Or they may be financial, such as budgets that don't allow books to be bought. These barriers can be more difficult to remove, because they do require authority and the involvement of managers.

The hardest blocks to remove are those that we don't see. Before you can remove a barrier you need to see it, and before you can see it you have to be looking for it. Many of these problems only exist inside our own heads or in the accepted practices of our teams and organization. Therefore we need to learn to recognize blocks that stop us from changing. Over time, as we learn to recognize the barriers and become practised at removing them, then it will become easier.

9.6 Conclusion

Almost by definition, creating and leading change isn't easy. If either were easy, then there would be little need for a book on the subject. Any change that is easy will certainly have been carried out already, so what's left is most probably the difficult part.

Start by understanding the need for change and what could be achieved. At this stage think about what advantages changes might bring, rather than specifics of what could be done or what ideas might be applied. Such specifics are the means to the end, not the end itself.

Once you know what you're trying to achieve, communication becomes the dominant activity in leading change. Communicate the need for change, the options for change, the agreed solution and the actions required to implement the solution. This communication is a two-way process: listen to other people, and collect their thoughts and ideas – help other people to communicate their own thoughts.

The other key tool for change is focus. You need to focus yourself on the issues in hand and help others to focus on opportunities, problems and solutions. Once focus is brought to bear on a problem, it quickly becomes clear which barriers need to be removed, what information is missing, where there are disconnects and what needs to be done to bring about change.

Individuals and Empowerment

"Everyone is talented. Every healthy man has a deep capacity for bringing to development the creative energies found in his nature."

Josef Albers,[1] 1888–1976, artist

All change involves people, so every attempt at creating change differs because it never involves the same individuals twice. Different organizations employ different people. Even if, by chance, you get the same individuals in your team as once before, they are still different people – they're older, wiser and have been through it once before.

When you start to introduce change, people will react in different and perhaps unpredictable ways. None of the ideas presented here can be guaranteed to work for your change initiative in your organization. That said, people share common characteristics, and over time common patterns, themes and reactions can be observed. While no technique can be guaranteed to work, there are many that may help.

It's essential to remember that each person is an individual. Their fears, passions and experience will all be different. We can generalize about people and teams, but each individual will be different. Each person has potential and brings his or her own talents; everyone deserves respect as an individual.

[1] Quoted in Borchardt-Hume (2006).

Changing Software Development: Learning to Become Agile   Allan Kelly
© 2008 John Wiley & Sons, Ltd.

10.1 Involve People

Ultimately, any change initiative needs to change the processes and practices followed by individuals. Since these individuals are people, not machines, we can't simply reprogram them as we would a computer. Nor can we rely on authority and orders. Even if we have the authority, business organizations aren't the army or navy, so we can't expect people to jump when we order them to do something.

It's surprisingly easy to fall into the trap of seeing people as obstructing change. Once we start to see people as a block to change, this view can become a self-fulfilling prophecy, because we interpret their actions as resistance and change our approach to them.

We need to see our people not as blocks but as part of the solution to our problems. Individual people bring their knowledge and experience, which can be used to address our problems and exploit the opportunities that we face.

10.1.1 Motivation

People are far more effective and productive when they undertake tasks that they actively want to be doing. Traditional approaches to software development tend to ignore this aspect and substitute processes, rules and controls in order to ensure that people do what their managers want them to do. This is an artificial approach that tries to force through a set of defined actions rather than harnessing people's enthusiasm.

Agile development depends on individual and team commitment and enthusiasm. The challenge for leaders is to harness individuals' passions and motivate them to want to tackle the task in hand. Good developers are motivated by at least three things:

- *Doing a good job:* Good developers take pride in their work and actively want to deliver good-quality program code and useful programs. It can actually be demotivating to developers to deliver poor-quality code and programs that users don't like.

- *Completing work:* Part of doing a good job is seeing a task through to completion. Allowing developers to follow tasks all the way to the end increases their sense of ownership and pride in building something. While many developers have come to accept they may not see the completed project, it can still be frustrating for them when they're taken off a piece of work before it's finished.

- *Learning and problem solving:* As we have already argued, creating software involves continual learning and problem solving. The best developers revel in this task, and seek out opportunities to tackle new domains and learn new technologies.

Motivating developers is relatively easy: let them complete work to a high quality and allow them to learn new things along the way. While this agenda sometimes conflicts with business priorities, it doesn't conflict as much as is commonly believed.

Thinking Point: Motivations

Think about your own motivators. Make a list of the things that motivate you.

Then think about the individuals in your team and make a list of things you think motivate them. If you're feeling confident, ask them to complete this exercise too and compare the lists.

10.1.2   Time for Listening

Actively involving individuals in your project and your change initiatives is less about telling them what to do and more about listening to their views and opinions. Only by listening to what people have to say can you harness their experience and knowledge.

On a busy day, it can be hard to find time to just listen to people. There are meetings to attend, e-mails and telephones to answer and lots of people wanting your opinion and decisions. It's easy to spend your time talking to people and expecting them to listen to you, but harder to find the time to listen to others.

Listening takes two people – one to talk and one to listen. Less obviously, the meaning of the message is decided not by the one doing the talking, but by the person doing the listening. The person doing the talking may think that their information has been communicated clearly, but if the person receiving the message isn't listening or has assumed the meaning of the message, then the message won't be received. Listening therefore requires time, an open mind and concentration.

By listening, we're able to receive the feedback of others. We can learn about our shared environment, their problems and the opportunities that they see. In doing so, we demonstrate fairness and build mutual trust.

10.1.3   Ask People Their Opinions

Asking the opinion of the individuals in your team is one of the most powerful techniques you have at your disposal. The people who actually do the work are the ones who know the issues involved better than anyone else. Not only does asking bring their experience, intellect and learning to bear on a problem, but it also helps motivate them to join the initiative and shows that you value them.

Some people find it easier to speak their minds in a one-on-one situation, so it may be better to ask someone's opinion behind closed doors. In private, it's easier for people to ask their own questions – especially difficult ones: you can address individual concerns and talk in more depth, without interruption or fear of what others may think. A one-to-one meeting may be time-consuming for you, but it does ensure that you really hear everyone's voice.

When you're new to a team or an organization, it's particularly worth asking what people think. When you're new, you don't know the problems of the team or its history, so asking and listening can help you to quickly understand the current position.

As a new team member, there's also a more subtle advantage to asking what people think. When you're new, you're an outsider: asking, and listening, can help you integrate with the team.

One-to-many group meetings don't give you the privacy or opportunities present in a one-to-one meeting, but do have other advantages. Obviously, it's quicker to hold a group meeting, so you may be able to do it more often.

Group meetings allow people to share experience with many others and help build a consensus of opinion. Such meetings can promote team bonding and thinking: they can help individuals adopt a team position and reduce fear of change, because everyone is committing to the same thing.

10.1.4   Find and Remove Mental Blocks

Many blocks to change and learning don't exist in the organizational structure. Nor do they exist in the rules and regulations of the company or government – or in the company management. Many blocks to change exist only within the minds of individuals. These blocks are the mental models, assumptions and personal defences described in Chapter 5.

For whatever reason, people can come to believe that 'It won't work here', 'Nobody will let me', 'We have a deadline' or some other similar block. Part of our work as change leaders is to help remove these blocks. Leading change is largely a case of removing individual people's blocks.

Individuals set up their own blocks for a number of reasons: past experience, second-guessing the future, misunderstanding the situation, not believing that change is possible and many more. Some of these are simply acts of self-defence to prevent them from getting hurt.

The way to remove the blocks is through asking questions:

- *What's stopping you?* – Listen to the answer and work on the component parts.

- *What assumptions are you making?* – Identify the assumptions and question them. When there's a genuine problem, look behind it.

- *What caused that problem?* – Systems thinking (Chapter 5) can help us drill down into a problem and find the underlying cause. In doing this, we're helping people to remove their mental blocks and allowing them to see the problem more clearly.

Pay special attention to the initial problem statement, which is often packed with assumptions or camouflage. Some words deserve particular attention:

- *They and Them* – Who are these people? Are they actual people or are these words hiding an assumption?

- *Management* – Similar to *they* and *them*, this word can hide an assumption about a cadre of people without actually identifying anyone who holds the assumed view.

- *Should* – This word actually says very little. It implies that something ought to be a particular way, but isn't. Both sides of the equation need to be questioned: *Why should it be that way?* and *In what way isn't it like that?*

- *Why* – Is the speaker asking 'What caused it to be this way?' or are they asking 'What's the objective?'

10.2 Coaching

During the past few years, it has become increasingly common to find a coach attached to a software development team. In eXtreme Programming (and other Agile methods), the coach's role is to help the team follow the process and improve. The practise of professional coaching within business has been established for some years and there are many good books on the subject.

Yet there are differences between business coaching and the Agile development coaching. Agile coaching tends to focus more on the project in hand and the team. Business coaches tend to focus more on the individual and on improving his or her performance. Agile coaches are often involved with a team daily or weekly, while business coaches may work with an individual far less regularly.

There is much that Agile development coaching can learn from the field of business coaching. Because business coaching is more established, there's simply more written and taught about the field. Much of this can be used to inform and improve development coaching.

For someone attempting to introduce Agile development and improve the learning within their organization, there are two uses of coaching. The first is for yourself. Actually being coached by someone else can help clarify your own thoughts and help you move towards your objectives. For this, you might like to engage a professional to actually coach you through the process, or you may have a manager, mentor or confidant in your organization who can take on the role.

The second use of coaching is to employ it as a tool yourself. This is the model that is more often discussed in books on Agile development. By coaching your team and your team members, you can help them with the change to Agile development and help to direct and improve their learning. While you don't have to be fully qualified to coach people, there's much that can be learned from professional coaches. Coaching in general can be a valuable management tool for someone who is introducing change and seeking to help teams improve their performance.

There are two distinct approaches to coaching: *directive* and *non-directive* coaching. With directive coaching, the coach is an expert in the subject under discussion. The coach is able to draw on his or her own knowledge and experience to advise the coachee on the available options and the best course of action.

Directive coaching can be used to introduce Agile practices and help people work in new ways. Therefore the coach needs to be an experienced Agile practitioner. You may be able to hire someone for the team or employ a consultant to help out.

For example, a team adopting Test-driven Development (TDD) might employ a coach who is experienced in the practice. The coach would work with individual team members, perhaps making use of pair programming, to help individuals learn the test-driven approach. The coach would impart his or her own knowledge and experience to the coachee.

Non-directive coaching takes a different approach. Here, the coach isn't necessarily an expert in the subject and, if he or she is, will seldom draw on personal experience. Instead, the coach seeks to help coachees focus on their own goals and work to achieve them. This form of coaching starts from the assumption that the coachees know the answer or are capable of working out the answer for themselves. The aim of *non-directive* coaching isn't only to help the coachees solve the problem in hand; it's also to enhance their ability to tackle problems in future. Therefore it isn't necessary for the coach to be an expert in the subject under discussion, but only to be practised in the art of coaching.

This type of coaching requires a coach who is practised in coaching rather than a particular technique. It's best used with experienced teams that are looking to find better practices and individuals who need to develop specific skills or achieve specific goals. In both cases, the coach needs to use questions to open up the subject and help people think through their own problems and solutions.

One four-stage model of non-directive coaching is known as GROW.[2] Firstly, the coach starts by asking the coachee about his or her *goals*; the two might spend some time refining and quantifying the goals to be achieved. Next, the coach asks about the current *reality* and how this compares with the goal.

Having established what the coachee wants to achieve and what the gap is between here and there, the coach turns his or her attention to future actions. The coach asks what *options* are available to the coachee. Importantly, the coach avoids making direct suggestions; instead, the idea is to help the coachee to find

[2] For more on GROW, see Whitmore (2002) or, alternatively, Downey (2003).

his or her own options. Finally, the coachee is asked *what* he or she will do now, and possibly *when* it will happen.

10.3   Empowerment

Empowerment means giving authority or power to other people so that they can act independently. It's important because it puts the power to act into the hands of the people who need it, the people who face problems every day, who know what the problems are and who know the most about them. The people who are working most closely on the development of software need to be able to incorporate their knowledge and experience into that development.

Empowerment gives people trust and allows them to learn and to change. Not to empower them means that you want to limit them and perhaps control them in some way. In empowering someone, you're delegating some of your authority; that is, you are giving something up. And you give it up in the belief that those who you're empowering will become more powerful, and will make more effective use of the power than you would have done.

Empowerment has become something of a cliché in modern business: it sometimes seems that everyone is empowered. Unfortunately, it's too easy to claim that people are empowered without actually giving them power. As the above definition says, empowering people means giving them authority. There's more to empowering individuals and teams than just saying 'You are empowered'. Really empowering people requires more than just talk.

In simply talking about empowerment but not actively empowering people, you run the risk of apportioning responsibility without providing the power to take action. Not only is responsibility without power a depressing state of affairs for individuals, but it also prevents real action taking place, because those with the power fail to take responsibility.

Thinking Point: Empowerment

Think back over your career and try to identify companies or teams where you've been highly effective. *Were you empowered? Did you consciously know you were empowered? What made it possible for you to act?*

Now think about your present situation. *Are you effective? Are you empowered? What's blocking you from doing things?*

10.3.1   Why Empower People?

Essentially, there are two good reasons why you want to give away authority. Firstly, by doing so you can set more brains to work on the problem. Rather than wrestling with a problem by yourself, you can engage a variety of other people.

After all, you can't be everywhere and you can't solve every problem. Bringing more brains to bear on the problem helps to solve it more quickly: different people have different perspectives, experience and understanding of the problem, and so are likely to think of different solutions. Additionally, there are now more people to work on actually implementing the solution.

This brings us to the second reason for empowering people. When people are involved with creating a solution, or coming up with a new idea, they're more likely to act on the idea – and when they do act, they will do so with more energy and enthusiasm. Even if it takes longer to reach a decision, you'll save time in turning the decision into action, because everyone is involved and in some way owns the decision.

So, it's in your own interest to give away your power and authority.

10.3.2   How Do You Empower Individuals?

Empowerment should snowball: people should come up with more and more ideas, and more people should contribute ideas. Some won't work, but at least people are thinking.

Your reaction will be noted by the individuals who come up with the ideas and by everyone else. React negatively ('I told you it wouldn't work') and you'll deter others from trying. Conversely, react positively and not only will you encourage the same person to try again, but others will take note and feel more empowered.

If you really want to empower someone, you really have to mean it. Giving people authority has more to do with how you act than with what you say. In most work environments, the more senior people are, the more authority they have. This authority might not mean that they have their every utterance acted on, but it does mean that colleagues assume that they have authority and act accordingly. If you want the people who work for you to believe that they have their own authority, you have to start acting as though they have authority.

The first thing you have to do is to make time for these people. If your boss asks for a 20 minute chat, you'll find the time. What if your someone who works for you asks for a chat? Will you have time today – or tomorrow, or next week? To repeat Section 1.1, giving people time is an important sign that you respect them and value their opinion.

Taking time to listen to employees is the start of empowerment. Simply giving others time to discuss their ideas will help them feel that their ideas are valued and important. In your mind, your employees might already be empowered and may not need your permission to try an idea, but this might not be the case in their minds. Although a simple *Yes* might not be required, they may feel more confident if you say so. Having your explicit agreement may also help them overcome objections that they meet in trying to implement their idea, because they can say that you support the idea.

Even if people don't feel the need to get your permission, they may value your opinion and insights. Giving them time to discuss ideas can help them improve the ideas and it lets you know what's happening.

When you empower people, you agree to trust them. When you listen and talk through other people's ideas and plans, it's important not to hijack them. You should not steal ideas for yourself, or try to substitute your own ideas for theirs. Instead, try to coach people through their ideas, to identify the opportunities, the problems and the risks involved.

Letting people follow through on their own ideas means that you have to be prepared to let them fail. Some ideas aren't going to work, but if you constantly try to weed out those that you think will fail, then you'll come to be seen as a block. In doing so, you'll take power away from people, and over time they'll offer fewer ideas. Rather than dissuading people, help them to see the difficulties and improve their ideas to reduce the risk of failure.

This doesn't mean that you should deliberately let people fail. If there are points that they haven't thought about, then ask them to think about them. If similar ideas have failed in the past, then ask them how their idea is different, or ask them to investigate the differences before proceeding.

Ultimately, empowering people means that you have to let them fail once in a while. Sometimes you have to suppress your own scepticism and caution and let them just do it – you may be surprised!

Thinking Point: When To Sit Tight

Next time you feel the urge to tell someone how to do something: *stop!* Before you say anything, ask yourself: *Do you really have a good reason for intervening? Or is it just your personal preference?*

The end result is more important than how we achieve it. Sometimes our personal preferences, and experiences, suggest that we should tackle something one way, but really there's no reason why it can't be done in another way. By trying to rationalize and understand our own reasoning, we may find that really it's just down to personal preference.

Doing something in a different way isn't always a problem. Ask yourself whether there's money or time or anything else at risk, and whether you can afford the consequences if things don't work out. It might be that a different approach fails at first, but provides valuable learning and eventually leads to a better solution.

None of us has a monopoly on the best way to do things: we should let others do things their own way and we should allow experiments. If our way is truly the right way, then over time others will come around to our understanding without our intervention. If, on the other hand, someone else finds a better way, then we have something to learn.

10.3.3 The Leader's Role

In a team that is empowered, you might wonder: *What's the role of the leader?* Delegating authority means that leaders have less need to exercise authority themselves, which removes some workload.

As well as empowering people, leaders need to set a direction and encourage work that will build towards the final product. This means encouraging innovations and projects that fit in with the overall direction. It also means cancelling projects or stopping activities that don't fit with the chosen direction.

One of the leader's responsibilities is to ensure that people get the resources that they need. Some ideas can just be acted on – they don't need much – while others need resources: a meeting room, food, perhaps machines or software tools; or it might be as simple as raw cash. Leaders need to provide the support and resources that your empowered people need.

Leaders also need to ensure that those who take action and implement new ideas are rewarded, either in public or in private, face-to-face or in their pay packet. When people invent new ideas and take risks, they rightly expect to see rewards. Rewards themselves can be useful incentives, but failure to reward can also be demoralizing and can deter people from trying new things.

People who repeatedly generate new ideas, take risks and create change are obvious candidates for future leadership positions themselves. Such people need to be developed professionally and receive promotions and advancement within the organization. These people are potential future leaders.

Finally, leaders also need to be there when things don't work out. They need to be there to help pick up the pieces without being judgemental. They need to help others talk through what happened and see what everyone can learn.

Resources Are the Easy Bit

When I established a company TechTalk programme on Friday afternoons, I needed the biggest room in the company – that bit was easy. I also needed a slot in everyone's calendar, and at first I needed the support of authority figures to say 'Look everyone, keep this hour free.' Then, to get the ball rolling, I needed a guest speaker; I needed hard cash to pay an expert to come in and talk to us for a couple of hours. After that, people saw that the programme had arrived. I was empowered to start the programme, but I still needed support and resources; there's a limit to how much one person can do on his or her own. The hard bit came later on: keeping it going – finding the supply of people to fill the slot I had created. Having created the programme, it was up to me to fix these problems.

> I also had to consider the future. I knew that one day I wouldn't be present to run the programme. For the change to stick and become permanent, it had to continue after I was gone. This meant that I had to seek out a future leader who would take over after me.

10.3.4 How Do You Empower a Team?

Empowering a team shares much in common with empowering individuals. Again, empowering a team is about more than just telling them that they're empowered: authority needs to be delegated to the team; the team needs to be trusted and allowed to make its own mistakes.

First of all, though, the team needs to recognize itself as a team rather than just a work group, or a bunch of people who happen to work in the same office. For this, it needs some unity of purpose – *What is it that the team exists to do?* This can be the source of its empowerment. The team typically exists to take responsibility for something and this is why it has been empowered.

Next, the team needs to know that it owns a problem. The team should be clear about what falls within its area of responsibility. The reverse isn't necessarily true: if a team comes up with an idea outside its area, it shouldn't automatically be dismissed, but it should know where its responsibility and ownership lie.

The team leader also has a role to play in both defining the team and the responsibilities. Some teams may derive their sense of identity from their team leader. On occasions, team leads need to be imposed, but – in keeping with the spirit of empowerment – it's better to avoid this if possible. One solution is to let a leader emerge, but this can take time and isn't always straightforward. Another solution is to select the leader and let the team assemble around this leader.[3]

Leaders should be able to command technical respect from their team, but being brilliant technically doesn't necessarily translate to being a good leader. In the software development world, all too many team leaders get to be team leader by virtue of their technical skills. People who don't take an active role in coming up with ideas and acting on their empowerment don't make for good team leaders.

For a team to be empowered, it needs to know who is in the team and who is not. The team needs to know who is involved in decisions and actions and who is not. People who wander into the team for short periods won't necessarily be attuned to the team's approach and beliefs. This can be a problem when some people try to work part-time on multiple projects.

A team will interact with many stakeholders during a project, but the team members need to know that they alone are responsible for completing the project. When non-team members play a role, it obscures the lines of

[3] This is described in the pattern *Self-selecting Teams* in Coplien and Harrison (2004).

responsibility. Once the team ceases to feel responsible for some aspect of a project, it will cease to feel empowered about that aspect of the project.

10.3.5   Empowerment Takes Time

The need for time and space applies to empowerment too. You have to give people the time to take their own action. This may mean that they need more time to think about a problem and come to a conclusion, or it may mean that you don't simply present them with a solution. They need time to see the consequences of their actions and decisions.

People work at different speeds, so you should not expect everybody to work at the same pace as you. Sometimes you need to be patient while other people work through a problem, so resist the urge to jump in with a ready-made solution. Letting people think and act for themselves may take longer in the short run, but the payback comes in the long run.

In a corporate culture where empowerment hasn't been the norm, it will take time for people to see that you mean what you say about empowering them. It will take longer in environments where management have spoken of empowerment but not allowed people to act with empowerment.

At the start, people may not respond when you tell them that they're empowered. You'll need to prove that you really mean it and find ways of giving them the chance to take their own action. This takes time – it doesn't happen overnight.

10.3.6   Empowerment Conflicts

In any organization, some people will come up with more ideas than others, and some people will be quiet and have few, if any, ideas. These people will be happy to just carry on as they were, or to agree with the majority view.

If you've genuinely empowered your people, then *have you empowered them to be quiet*? By empowering people, you give them choice: if they choose to not do anything, they're acting within their rights. You might even be glad of a few quiet people, because if everyone were constantly coming up with new ideas your workload would increase.

The problem comes when lack of action is itself a block to change. This might not be intentional: there may be no plan to block a change. Still, inaction can block change and create conflict.

Individual rights and empowerment can come into conflict with other individuals' empowerment and the empowerment of the team. Consider, for example, a team that holds a daily stand-up meeting at 9.30 a.m. Does empowerment mean that people can arrive late? If the team postpones its meeting, for how long should they postpone it? An individual exercising one

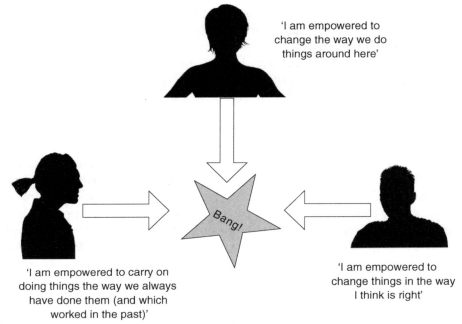

'I am empowered to change the way we do things around here'

'I am empowered to carry on doing things the way we always have done them (and which worked in the past)'

Bang!

'I am empowered to change things in the way I think is right'

Figure 10.1   Empowerment can cause conflicts.

right – say, the right to arrive late – may block the right of others to hold a morning meeting (Figure 10.1).

Nor is empowerment to do nothing the only block that can arise. There may well be multiple ways to address a problem and different people will suggest different solutions. Each solution may have its advantages and disadvantages, but acting on one solution may block the other.

The problem is that sometimes the block to one person's empowerment is actually somebody else's empowerment. When one of those people is actually choosing to do nothing, then the conflict can be much worse. On such occasions, it's useful to have an arbiter, who can intervene and help the two sides reach an agreement or compromise. It may help if this person is a higher authority, or it may help if the arbiter is neutral. If such situations aren't proactively managed, they can escalate and cause bigger problems.

10.4 That Difficult Individual

From time to time, someone disagrees with the change programme or actively doesn't want to change. You may come to see such a person as 'that difficult individual', but this is an over-simplification.

Start by asking yourself if the person really is *a difficult individual*, or whether you're just labelling them as such? Once you label someone and start thinking of that person in a particular way, it can become a self-fulfilling prophecy. You come to see that person's actions and comments as being difficult, no matter what they say or do. Perhaps the problem isn't with the individual but with yourself: maybe if you approach the situation with an open mind, you'll see it differently.

Next, consider what other assumptions you may be making: Is this really an individual? Or is there a wider group of people? Before assuming that this individual is an isolated case, look to see if others feel the same way.

Consider also whether your learning and changing initiatives have reached this individual or group of people. Perhaps it isn't resistance that you're seeing, but simply some people who haven't been included. Maybe their work keeps them away from your initiatives, maybe they're too overworked to change or maybe you've done something to deter them from engaging or changing.

Nor should you overlook the possibility that the person, or people, in question are actually right. They may have seen something that you missed, they may have good reason for not wanting to change, or maybe they're simply saying what others think but don't feel they can say. The *Wise Fool*[4] pattern suggests that organizations should value these people. They are the ones who speak out while others stay silent. By challenging decisions and assumptions, these people fulfil a valuable role, and organizations with such individuals will make fewer wrong decisions.

So it's worth giving these individuals time. Talk to them, listen to their concerns and understand what they're saying. Rather than arguing with them, first seek to appreciate their point of view. The weaknesses that they see in your approach may be valid; you may have overlooked some issues and questions. With this information, you'll be able to improve your initiatives. Giving these people time makes them feel valued and included in change.

Acknowledging and addressing the objections raised by people may be enough to change their attitude to your initiatives. You may want to go further and involve them actively: consider the advice of US President Lyndon B. Johnson, who famously said of the FBI director, J. Edgar Hoover, 'It is probably better to have him inside the tent pissing out, than outside the tent pissing in.'

Bringing the individual inside the tent gives them a chance to be part of the initiative and affect the outcome. This will also bring them up against the problems that you face, so that they can better understand your reasoning. Sometimes these difficult people themselves do want to see change and improvement, but are frustrated by their lack of opportunity: by giving them what they want, you can win them over.

Spending time with these people, either on a formal or informal basis, gives you a chance to engage one-on-one and open their minds to many of the ideas that you're promoting. These individuals too can benefit from learning and change. It may be that they already feel isolated and will welcome a way to engage more widely.

---

[4] See Coplien and Harrison (2004).

When you first start introducing change, it can feel lonely – after all, you're the only one advocating change. You too may be seen as the difficult individual, or the *Wise Fool*. As your initiatives start to meet with success, you'll find support and allies who can help you progress further, and in time your ideas will become the conventional wisdom. As you make the journey from difficult individual to change leader, others will feel isolated. Some may find themselves making the reverse journey.

When you first introduce new ideas and change, people may not want to be associated with your ideas because they're different. By nature, human beings want to belong, so people may avoid associating themselves with changes that place them in a minority group. Over time, as your ideas take root, people will want to join in changes because they want to belong to the group and don't want to be isolated.

If you've labelled and ignored a 'difficult individual', then that person may find it hard to join the new environment. Making differences public, labelling and excluding people all make it more difficult for people to change their positions. Therefore, you need to take care not to erect barriers that make it difficult for people to change their point of view.

It may be that such individuals can't accept your changes and the new environment created. At some level, the changes that you've introduced may disrupt their beliefs or conflict with their value system. In these situations, they may decide of their own accord that it's time to leave the organization.

This is perfectly natural, but once they're gone you may find yourself missing them, because each individual brings skills, talents and experience to a situation. With one individual gone, you may simply find that another fills that 'difficult' slot – possibly because of your own perceptions.

Thinking Point: What Do They Do Better Than Me?

Before you label someone as difficult, ask yourself: *What is it that this individual does better than me?*

In other words, look for the individual's strengths, the things that you'll miss when they're gone.

Losing someone from the organization leads to a loss of knowledge and experience. One option is to find these individuals other roles in the organization, perhaps in a different group, or to give them some new responsibility within the existing group. In this way, their experience is retained and you can still ask them questions, but they're removed from the immediate issues.

At the same time, it's healthy for organizations to have some degree of staff turnover. Without it, we risk sealing ourselves off from new ideas. Without a few vacancies at a senior level, there's no scope for promotion when people are ready for a new challenge.

If after listening to these individuals; if after addressing their concerns, bringing them inside the tent and offering them an opportunity to belong; and if after challenging your own labels and looking for the value of these individuals, and perhaps after offering them other roles – if they still can't be persuaded and they still find it difficult to change, then maybe, just maybe, you might want to consider dispensing with their services. However, this isn't an option to be considered lightly.

Quite possibly by this point, these people are feeling a bit out of line themselves: if everyone else has changed and they're hanging on to the past, or on to a different set of values, then they may themselves have doubts about their future. To start a conversation about this might actually be a relief to them; it may allow everyone to find a route to resolve these problems.

Ultimately, you may decide to let these individuals go. By the time you reach this point, this shouldn't be a surprise to anyone. However, you should never rush to let people go; in all probability you'll need to replace them and you have no way of guaranteeing that their replacements will be any better. The whole process takes time: when new people are hired, they lack knowledge about your organization, your products and your strategy.

You also have to consider the effect on the rest of the team when someone is let go from the company, particularly if this person has publicly failed to grasp the change. If the rest of the team sees this person as being out of step, they may see his or her departure as a good thing – both for the team and the individual. However, if the team has yet to embrace the change, they may see the departure as management getting rid of those who don't accept change. This may be interpreted as an implicit threat to those who are yet to embrace change, and could encourage others to leave of their own accord.

10.5 Developing the Next Leaders

Leading learning and change can be rewarding. In creating change, you'll engage in your own learning and change as you do it. But there's always more than you can do yourself: you can't be everywhere at once; nor can you be there forever. True change needs to survive beyond any one individual.

So, developing the next set of leaders is part of your work to introduce change. You need these people as your lieutenants, to carry on learning and changing in your absence. You need these people because yours must not be the only voice making the case for change and learning: you start the change journey alone, but you need to find your supporters. You need these people because you don't have all the solutions – other people have good ideas and you need to include them.

Put together, these three reasons mean that your lieutenants will carry the change programme into parts of the organization you can never reach and embed the ideas of the programme into the day-to-day functioning of the organization. If you're trying to introduce change to others and won't necessarily be present all the time, you need these *change champions* even more.

But perhaps most of all, you need to develop more leaders because they too will experience the learning and growth from being part of the change programme. This will in turn propel them to continue your programme and go beyond your original ideas.

One method is to delegate wherever possible. Rather than trying to do everything, yourself give away as much as you can. Have other people arrange events and training, send others to conferences and encourage them to talk about their experiences.

10.6 Time to Go

Teams need consistency and people value steady leadership during times of change. However, eventually there will come a time when you'll want to consider whether your initiatives are better continued without your involvement. The true test of a change initiative is whether it survives when the original driving force is no longer present.

When you've successfully led a major change, there may well come a time when you want to look for new challenges yourself. Creating change within an organization won't only change the organization – it will also change you. Achieving your goal and completing the changes that you envisaged may be satisfying, but it might also leave you wanting more. And successfully completing a major change initiative will most likely open up new career options.

You may start a change initiative with a goal in mind. When that goal is achieved, you may be happy with the result and simply want to sit back and enjoy the outcome. However, true change is never done because learning continues – so reaching your goal may simply be a sign that a new wave of change is required. Having piloted the previous change, you might be the ideal person to repeat the process, or it may be better for the new change to be led by a new person.

Even if your goal isn't met, there are times when you may want to consider leaving a project or organization. Sometimes changing leaders can re-invigorate a change initiative and actually create more learning and change. There are several scenarios in which you may like to consider leaving a change initiative in order to enhance it.

Introducing change can be a lonely and difficult endeavour. During the initiative, you'll feel defeated, rejected and isolated at times. Such feelings can drain your energy and demoralize you. As the leader of change, your feelings affect the change programme. Without energy and enthusiasm, you can't seize opportunities and influence people.

Issues such as personal morale and energy can result in you becoming *that difficult individual*. It's possible that rather than being a change leader, you become a block to change. This can happen in other circumstances too. Personal disputes or differences over approach between yourself and others can block forward movement. Rather than debate focusing on change issues, debate centres on personal conflicts and change is blocked.

When you become the block to change, then leaving a project will allow the project to advance. Be careful not to rush to this conclusion: before you make any decisions, look for supporting evidence, talk to people you trust and look for alternatives.

If you do decide to leave a project, there will inevitably be a period of transition. While you'll want to work for an orderly transition, we know from Satir's change model (Chapter 8) that some period of chaos is bound to follow. It may simply be better to make a quick and clean break to avoid apprehension and allow the team to move on.

Hopefully, before this happens you'll have had time to develop some lieutenants to continue your work after you've gone. Your departure should allow these people to step forward, take on responsibility and advance their own learning. As a change leader, people will have come to see you as a source of knowledge and action: your departure may at first leave them short of these resources. By removing yourself, the people who want to continue the change will be forced upon their own resources and this in itself will provide them with learning experiences.

There will never be a perfect time to leave a project or change initiative. Nor can you expect to choose your time of leaving in advance. This is why it's essential to start developing the next leaders early and help people learn of their own accord: doing this will ensure that change continues without you.

10.7 Conclusion

The success or failure of our projects and change initiatives ultimately rests with the individuals we work with. As leaders and managers we're dependent on these people, so it pays to respect them and afford them both time and trust.

Since we can't do everything ourselves, we need to trust others and empower them to do the work that needs to be done. If we don't give people the authority to act on their own initiative, then not only will we make a lot more work for ourselves, but we won't make the most of their experience and skills.

CHAPTER 11

Rehearsing Tomorrow

"In preparing for battle, I have always found that plans are useless,
but planning is indispensable."
Dwight D. Eisenhower, 1890–1969, President of the United States

Most of the time, our actions are defined by what we have done before; change occurs when we put our new learning into effect and take different actions. This book has emphasized the need to move beyond simple learning and the necessity of coupling learning with action to create knowledge. This chapter looks at techniques for learning new actions.

On the whole, we develop software today in the same way that we developed it yesterday. So tomorrow is an extrapolation of today. If we are to improve anything, if we are to change and make tomorrow different, we have to stop extrapolating from today. We have to do things differently tomorrow.

This means that we have to know what to do – and then we must take action and change. Rather than operating on automatic pilot and repeating ourselves, we need to push beyond the comfort zone of things we have done before. We need to try new things, take risks and experiment. In doing so, we'll encounter new problems, things will take longer (at least at first) and sometimes we'll fail. These dangers, risks and fears represent inhibitors to change.

Many of our inhibitors are within ourselves – we place our own blocks, real or imagined, in the way. At other times, these blocks will come from the need to work in groups and the need for the whole group – or even organization – to change rather than one individual.

Changing Software Development: Learning to Become Agile   Allan Kelly
© 2008 John Wiley & Sons, Ltd.

One of the ways of overcoming such blocks, removing fear and reducing the risk is to practise change in advance. In the same way that actors rehearse for a new role and musicians rehearse new scores, we need to rehearse. We rehearse so that we know what to expect and so that the whole team knows how to work together.

The rest of this chapter will look at tools that we can use to help us rehearse our change. These tools complement the learning and change tools presented in earlier chapters. On the whole, these tools focus on organizational events and actions that can help rehearse our future. However, some of our traditional tools may hinder learning rather than enhancing it, and so must be discarded and unlearned.

11.1 Future Memories

In the book *The Living Company*, Arie de Geus[1] suggests that our brains are constantly observing our surroundings, thinking about the future and devising possible courses of action. Imagine that you're reading this on your train home from work: you may be thinking about skipping this section, or returning to re-read an earlier section, or looking for a convenient point to close the book. You may also be watching the train's progress, calculating how much longer you have for reading before you have to get off. You may hear a familiar name mentioned by a fellow passenger and suddenly tune into their conversation.

Your brain is trying to make sense of the world around you and decide what you should do next. Options for the future are considered and evaluated. In doing this, it's processing multiple inputs; and some inputs are ignored – like the conversation before that well-known name was mentioned.

All of this processing is influenced by your past experiences and memories. Your past memories act as filters; your past actions influence the options that have will be considered. Such memories form part of the mental models discussed in Chapter 5 and are a necessary short cut in everyday life. But at the same time they constrain our actions and blind us to information.

As individuals, we do this constantly and quite naturally; it's part of living. When we work in teams, a similar thing happens: initially team members bring their own experiences, past memories and future memories. Over time, the team will build up a memory of the past that will allow it to think about the future as a team.

When we discuss the future, it's usually in terms of *What will happen if . . .?* This leads us to consider how the future will affect us in a passive way, so we consider how potential events might affect us without considering our response. In contrast, de Geus suggests that a more useful question is *What will we do if . . . happens?* because this question asks us to take an active view and

[1] See de Geus (1997).

consider how we would respond. In doing so, we begin the process of building our *future memories* and creating a repertoire of actions that we could take. Such thinking recognizes that we are far from powerless when faced with events. Rather than considering our future from a passive perspective, we actively set out to change our mental models.

The tools described here can help to create future memories. These are tools that will challenge some of our mental models and allow us to rehearse the future and the actions that we can take. The objective isn't necessarily to predict what might happen and have a ready-made reaction ready to hand, but to allow us to consider a world that differs from our previous experience. By stretching our range of responses, we create more options for action.

This is valuable for an individual, but it's perhaps even more valuable for a team. In a team, if one individual starts behaving differently the other team members will be confused; the team may view the individual as irrational or erratic. For a team to act as one coherent unit, it must share the same future memories and share a range of actions – shared knowledge is far more valuable to a team than individual knowledge.

A team can only create a shared understanding and range of actions if it has been given the chance to consider such a world. A team that never stops to create its own future memories will be confined to a small subset of the team members' collective memories upon which everyone implicitly agrees. Over time, this repertoire will grow slowly, and not always positively.

Therefore, the challenge for those leading the team is to help it create a common shared memory of the future and the actions that it may undertake. By actively setting out to create such future memories, we can help the team form positive memories early in its existence.

11.2 Planning

When we talk about planning in a software development project, we usually consider it as an exercise in scheduling. Yet there are many other plans that we make on a software project. *Software design* is both an activity – a verb – and an abstract thing – a noun. We create *software designs* through the process of *software design*.

As an activity, design is a form of planning. The result of design activity might be something formal, such as a set of UML diagrams, or it might be something less tangible, such as a set of mental models[2] shared by the development team. Used in this way, the design process is an exercise in creating future memories of what the software will look like.

Even in the earliest stages of a software project, we're planning, creating plans and building mental models. From the moment we conceive of a

---

[2] See Holt (2001).

software product, through requirements, specification, design and even into coding, we're planning, creating plans and refining the plans that we've made. Successive refinements change requirements into designs and into code.

However, planning isn't without problems. It's far from a benign activity: creating plans can create unintentional problems; and once made, plans can be used to force behaviour on a team. Sometimes we're better off not planning.

Unpopular Estimates

Between developers, stories abound of planners refusing to accept unwelcome estimates. Unfortunately, a number of poor practices have grown up around estimates:

- Estimates are requested with little or no information about the work needed. The less well defined a piece of work, the less accurate is the estimate.
- Estimates are asked for after deadlines have been agreed. When estimates don't fit the deadline, they're questioned and arbitrarily reduced.
- Upon seeing an estimate that they don't like, managers, planners and business analysts pressure developers into reducing estimates.

Developers share some of the blame for inaccurate estimates:

- Rather than lose a particularly interesting piece of work, developers supply artificially low estimates.
- Rather than challenge the lack of requirements, developers make estimates that are little more than guesses.

Time estimates are often the basis for determining the cost of a project, which may in turn influence whether or not a project goes ahead, or whether or not a company wins an order. This introduces incentives to manipulate time estimates.

This is not to say that the estimating process would work if everyone concerned were honest. There needs to be active discussion about how work should be conducted and about whether or not work should be carried out. However, it's far from clear, even when honesty and good debate hold sway, whether anyone can give really accurate time estimates.

Nor should we forget that estimates are still only estimates. An estimate is an educated guess at how long a piece of work might take to do. An estimate is inherently not a commitment. Committing to deliver work in two weeks is very different from estimating that a piece of work will take two weeks.

In short, the whole process of estimating is flawed. Most Agile approaches try to turn the estimating process around. Rather than asking *How long will X take?* the approach is to ask *How long do we have?* and then determine how work could be structured to deliver pieces of X.

Unexpected Consequences

I once sat next to a developer who was working on a project that was running late. On Thursday morning, the project manager paid him a visit and the conversation went something like this:

Boss: 'Will we have this finished by the end of the week?'
Developer: 'I'd like to, but I can't be sure, Tuesday or Wednesday'.
Boss: 'But this project is already two months late and last Friday you said it would be one more week. If it isn't done by tomorrow, we might have to work the weekend'.

This developer was a family man: he had a wife and children and liked to spend the weekend with them. The thought of working the weekend didn't make him happy; and the idea of the project manager working the weekend was odd, since his presence wouldn't actually get the work done. So 'we' really meant 'you'.

Fortunately, the developer in question was able to report the software complete by the end of the next day. Unfortunately, the testing team took less than an hour of work on Monday morning to reject it and send it back to development.

11.2.1 What's the Problem with Traditional Planning?

Schedule planning has long had a bad reputation amongst developers and managers alike. Schedules are hard to predict and manage. Projects routinely overshoot milestones and deadlines.

Sometimes scheduling is used in an attempt to predict the end date for a project and sometimes it's an attempt to make a project finish on a pre-defined date. Either way, scheduling is dependent on estimates given by developers. These estimates are notoriously inaccurate. This is for two reasons:

- Firstly, as stated above, estimates aren't commitments: the very word *estimate* tells us that the answer isn't accurate. Switching our scheduling to work with commitments rather than estimates doesn't work, because learning is continually occurring.

- Secondly, because learning is occurring and our knowledge is in a state of flux, commitments are only valid for a very short period, the period for which are knowledge is accurate. Therefore we can't commit to something beyond our current knowledge. People may be coerced into saying that they commit, but this invalidates the commitment.

Many of the techniques designed to improve estimates just add complexity to inaccuracy. A common technique is to pad estimates to guarantee that work can be completed within the allotted time. However, this approach is wasteful and makes projects uneconomic.

Planning tends towards extrapolation of the past. People tend to implicitly assume that the next project will be like the last one. This leads us to plan for the problems that we encountered last time, and blinds us to new opportunities and problems in the future. In trying to second-guess tomorrow, we assume that it will be like yesterday, so we limit our expectations and create a self-fulfilling prophecy.

Yet schedule inaccuracy isn't the only problem with viewing traditional planning as scheduling. The use of schedule planning can actually make a software development project substantially worse for several reasons:

- *Planning by a few for the many:* Small software project teams often skip project planning altogether and just get on with it. Where teams are larger, we find a project manager who asks developers for estimates and compiles them into some kind of graph with dependencies. This approach restricts the learning to the planners rather than across the team as a whole. The planners may create some future memories for themselves, but few of these will be passed on to the team. The resulting project plan is a limited, low-bandwidth, communication tool and an opportunity for shared learning and vision creation is lost.

- *Illusion of certainty:* Just because a schedule is in place doesn't mean that a team will keep to it. A large number of things can happen to disrupt the schedule. But the appearance of certainty leads others to base their plans on your plans. This creates a cascade effect, and once one schedule slips the effect is magnified.

- *Plan as rigid map:* Once the plan is completed, some managers switch from scheduling to enforcement. The schedule becomes law to be followed, estimates silently become commitments and change becomes more difficult. This in turn reduces flexibility and reduces motivation: the more detailed a plan, the more disruptive any change will be. Consequently, there's greater resistance to any changes in requirements or software design, and to customer requests.

- *Loss of initiative and learning:* Keeping to the plan means that we can't take diversions to learn something new or try a different way of proceeding. Teams are thrown back on their existing memories and actions rather than experimenting.

- *Loss of motivation:* A team executing someone else's plan won't have the same motivation as a team following a plan that it has created. As milestones (and carrots) are missed, punishments such as weekend working are introduced and risk-taking initiatives are discouraged, motivation will fall.

- *Increased bureaucracy:* Enforcing the plan and resisting calls to change some aspects will lead to the creation of a bureaucracy. This takes the form of change request controls, worker time tracking and reports against plan. No value is added by this bureaucracy: indeed, it's both costly and it further undermines motivation.

- *Goal deferment:* As projects drift further from the plan, efforts centre on getting the work back on schedule rather than ensuring delivery.

Over time, adaptive behaviour occurs and creates vicious circles. Developers increase their time estimates for work, while project managers arbitrarily reduce estimates. Customers who have experienced projects that resist change respond by front-loading requirements documents with everything they can think of. Managers often respond by offering completion bonuses, or threatening weekend working. Like any targets, such incentives are prone to create unanticipated side effects.

Targets and incentives may encourage people to 'game the system'. This happens when individuals or groups of people treat the targets as an objective in a game. They work to meet the target at the expense of some other aspect of the system. For example, a team given a target of '80 % test coverage' may meet that target, but the tests may hold little value or even fail.

These problems won't occur in all organizations, but the risk is always present. When problems set in, trust breaks down and eventually nobody believes the plan, but they go through the motions of following it. We have all the disadvantages and none of the claimed benefits. This is why planning can be far from benign.

The Rise and Fall of Strategic Planning

Many of the criticisms of planning listed here draw on the work of Henry Mintzberg, in his book *The Rise and Fall of Strategic Planning*.[3] Mintzberg charts the rise of strategic planning by organizations through the first half of the twentieth century and then the relative decline later in the century. He asks *What is planning?* and *What is strategy?* Business strategy has an important parallel with programming: both are mental exercises that in their own right produce nothing physical. Many of Mintzberg's comments about strategic planning apply to planning in the software world too.

---

[3] See Mintzberg (1994).

Having asked just what we mean by planning and strategy, Mintzberg goes looking for evidence that planning actually works. He finds the evidence somewhat thin on the ground and concludes:

"conventional planning tends to be a conservative process, sometimes encouraging behaviour that undermines both creativity and strategic thinking. It can be inflexible, breeding resistance to major strategic change and discouraging truly novel ideas in favor of extrapolation of the status quo or marginal adaptation"

(Mintzberg, 1994)

This is where we start to see his central argument: planning is a form of analysis, and by itself analysis can't produce anything. In order to produce something – whether it be business strategy or software – we must have synthesis. Since *analysis isn't synthesis*, planning alone can't produce anything.

Analysis does have a useful role to play in codifying existing strategy so that it can be elaborated, communicated and the consequences analysed. However, when taking action day-to-day, managers are informed by their intuition, not analysis.

Planners themselves can play a useful role through the exercise of planning rather than the writing of plans. They can find new strategies, help informed decision-making and act as catalysts to encourage and help others plan.

Again, we see that planning is a useful activity, but that the expected end product of planning – that is, plans – isn't in itself so useful. Thus we return to the Eisenhower quote that opened this chapter.

11.2.2   Planning as Learning

There is worthwhile planning that can be undertaken for a software project, but it isn't scheduling. Considering planning as scheduling means that we miss an opportunity to use planning to advance our projects. Planning and even plans can be valuable learning tools, but we need to treat them as such. We need to involve many people and we should recognize that learning continues after the planning is finished.

Planning can be a learning exercise to help accelerate individual and team learning. By planning together, teams create new mental models and language to describe and map the coming development effort. In other words, *they create future memories.*[4] Once created, these memories help decision-makers to view events differently and consider new outcomes.

[4] The ideas of future memories and planning as learning come from de Geus (1997, 1998).

In a software development environment, planning includes software design and architecture; it includes requirements gathering and specification writing; and it includes test plans and acceptance tests. Planning allows new mental models of the world to be formed. Tackling these elements in isolation can result in mental models that are incomplete.

When the software planning process is carried out by individuals or small groups who don't communicate with one another, our future memories are incomplete. Software architects, project managers and business analysts all see part of the future, but not the whole. Planning needs to be a collective process, one that involves as many team members and roles as possible. Only by involving everyone and allowing them to participate and learn together can the whole team create the necessary shared mental models and future memories.

A planning process should not plan for one case alone, but instead consider several alternative scenarios. These don't need to be full-scale scenario plans (described below), but the team should consider alternatives. By repeating the design planning activity, the team creates more future memories of how the software might look. The design process is more important than the final design itself.

The objective of such an exercise isn't to create a definite software architecture or project schedule. Rather, the exercise creates a set of shared models within the team members' minds and allows a variety of different routes to be considered. In doing so, implicit models and assumptions are exposed and challenged. (Software prototypes often play this role too.)

Most teams will at some point need to synchronize with others: product development teams need to synchronize software release with marketing, documentation needs to be printed and CDs need to be pressed. Such synchronization doesn't just happen and schedule planning can't deliver what is needed. The solution is to include the teams, or at least their representatives, in the earlier planning process. You should allow other teams to help shape the mental models of the development team and vice versa. As the project continues, keep these teams updated and listen to their concerns.

11.2.3   Scenario Planning

One type of *planning as learning* is *scenario planning*. In creating a scenario, the idea isn't so much to forecast the future: rather, it's to think about the challenges and opportunities that you, your team or your business may face as the world changes. Scenario planning allows you to visit a possible future and create future memories of how the world may look.

Scenario planning has its roots in military planning, and has been popularized in business through its use by Royal Dutch/Shell and authors such as Peter

Schwartz.[5] Firstly, we seek out information that may affect the future. Some of this is knowable right now: for example, the world population is growing, X babies were born last year, and so in 12 years time the number of 13-year-old children will be slightly less than X.

Other information is from 'weak signals' and comes from talking to technologists, business people, academics and other thinkers. Such people will have insights and ideas beyond the consensus view of the future. These ideas will help to expose some implicit assumptions and help you imagine a different sort of world.

Shifting through this information reveals the forces and events that shape your scenario. This information allows you to construct a story that explains the facts, highlights the forces and provides insights. You may want to construct several scenarios: each story must be internally consistent, but each should represent a different future.

It is unlikely that any scenarios will come to pass exactly as forecast: they only show what could happen. In creating these scenarios, you consider how the world might be different and you can consider what you'd do in each case. Your future memories contain not just a description of the world, but a new set of actions and options that you could pursue.

Stuart Brand[6] suggests that scenario planning can be used in designing buildings. By thinking about how a building may develop in future, we may consider what features are important, what's irrelevant and what obstacles we may be creating in a new construction. It's a short step from buildings to software.

Software development can benefit from these ideas too. Software designers aim to create flexible products that can absorb change, that can be reused and that are easy to maintain. Each of these attributes comes at a cost and may not be necessary. This has prompted advocates of eXtreme Programming to take the opposite view and do the minimum work required.

Reality is going to be somewhere between these extremes, but how do we know? Scenario planning offers one way of exploring the future of our software and flushing out real requirements.

Scenario planning may also be used to uncover risks entailed in your project, where to expect change requests to arise and what future opportunities may open up as a result of the project.

Large framework scenarios used for company strategy and government policy can take months of work to produce, but it's also possible to run smaller project scenarios to examine specific areas of interest. Even here, though, you probably want to conduct some research and then take several days to analyse what you've gathered, agree the forces and write your stories.

---

[5] See Schwartz (1991, 2003).

[6] See Brand (1994).

11.3 Change Events

Many of the ideas that we've looked at in this book are personal (e.g. listening more) and some work in the background (e.g. creating book groups). Sometimes you want to say very openly 'We're going to try to learn something' or 'We're going to change things around here'.

Such occasions happen when you need to speed things up, when you've become stuck, when a problem really needs to be solved or when you decide to grasp an opportunity. On such occasions, a more direct approach can be useful.

Your first thought might be to call a meeting. You spell out the problem and ask everyone to come up with a solution. And all too often, such meetings end in failure . . . You don't understand the problem well enough and can't agree on the course of action, let alone the solution. Someone will ask 'Is this the problem we really want to solve?' and then a wide-ranging debate follows, on a hundred different problems, and no two people agree on which one you should solve. Or perhaps the opportunity that you see simply isn't seen by others . . . or maybe you agree on what needs to be done, but nobody follows through on it, so the action doesn't take place.

That's if you are lucky. If you're unlucky, the meeting will run around the same old solutions and the fact that 'they've been tried before and they didn't work'. However, meetings don't have to be like this. There are a range of events that don't necessarily conform to the standard meeting for getting people to think about problems and solutions – even where the problems are vaguely defined. Such events require prior planning and they may involve expenditure.

11.3.1 Improvement Meetings

Change events can be as simple as asking people to think about ways to improve their working and holding a meeting to discuss ideas. Team leaders and managers can simply call their teams together and start building a shared vision.

Such events need a focus; otherwise, people are liable to wander from subject to subject without coming to a consensus. To avoid this, decide on a subject beforehand and ask attendees to bring some ideas. Questions such as 'What is good code?' or 'How can we improve our quality?' help focus attendees and help create shared understanding.

There's a danger of biting off more than you can chew, so it's probably better to tackle the shared vision in a series of discrete steps. For example, hold a monthly meeting where you address some of these questions. Start at a high level and work your way down to a lower level. Have the team reach a consensus on the subject and adopt this as the team standard – get someone to write a brief conclusion of what the team decides.

11.3.2 Improvement Worksheet

Improvement efforts can be given more structure by creating a framework or worksheet within which to ask questions. An improvement worksheet can ask a series of basic questions aligned with company goals, such as:

- Did the project deliver on time?
- Was unit testing adequate?
- How much manual testing was needed?

Asking each development team to repeat the exercise every few months serves a number of goals. Firstly, teams are challenged to think about what they have been doing. Filling in the sheet can expose problems and identify improvements that teams can make immediately. Over time, teams can see what issues recurred and how the changes that they made affected their performance.

Secondly, managers have material that allows them to look across teams at what issues are encountered and how teams are reacting. Teams and management can benchmark themselves against other teams and look for opportunities for improvement.

Finally, both groups have a history that they can go back to and examine, to see how changes result in improvement, to find out what problems occur regularly and to spot changes in the issues that they face.

Thinking Point: Create Your Own Worksheet

Create your own process improvement worksheet. What would you like to draw your team's attention to?

Show the worksheet to your team and managers and get their suggestions for additions to the sheet.

What would it take to start using the sheet?

11.3.3 Process Miniatures

In Chapter 10 we discussed the need to communicate changes so that people understood what was happening and what was required of them without being overwhelmed by details and becoming fearful of missing something. One way of answering people's questions and giving them practical experience is to run a *process miniature*.

As software developers, most of the processes that we follow day-to-day are pretty much the same as those of yesterday, last week and even last year. The problem that we're working on, and even the technology we're using, may change, but the actual way in which we go about work often doesn't differ much. We know what to do because we've done it before.

So, when you ask people to do something different, they can be a little lost. *What do I do now? What do I do when X happens?* This is where future memories can help.

Like actors rehearsing a role, we can practise our new processes through play. Having done this, we'll know roughly what to expect; the future is less strange and intimidating, so our fear is reduced. Then, when we actually come to work differently we aren't completely lost; we have an idea, a memory, of what will happen next.

Such miniatures emulate the process that you're aiming for, but on a smaller scale. Well-known process miniatures include *59 Minute SCRUM* and *The Extreme Hour*. Both of these reduce an iteration to a couple of hours. The team get to carry out just about everything they would do in a true iteration, but on a smaller scale and, importantly, in a safe environment.

By running the miniature in a safe environment, people can make mistakes and experiment without risk. They can experience what the future could look like, thus creating future memories, enhancing learning and motivating change for a better tomorrow.

Thinking Point: Your Process Miniature

Search the Internet for examples of process miniatures. Well-known examples include *The Extreme Hour*, *59 Minute SCRUM* and *XP-Game*. Conference presentations can be a good source of new exercises.

Think about how you could construct a miniature to model your process.

11.3.4   Retrospectives

The idea of post-project reviews is widely known. While the IT industry likes to call them *retrospectives* or *post mortems*, others may simply call them project reviews. The US Army and the Marine Corps call such events *After Action Reviews* and this title seems to be gaining some use in other fields.

Well-done project retrospectives are one of the most powerful learning exercises that teams can use to improve their process and practices. Retrospectives require trust and honesty from all participants and they need to be inclusive.

Unfortunately, while such reviews are well known and while many people see value in them, they're performed less often than you might think. Some people avoid such reviews for fear of what they may find out, blame that may be apportioned, mistakes that might be revealed or simply because of the time they take to conduct. Even when retrospectives do take place, they may fail when key people are missing, or if people are scared to discuss the events or agreed actions aren't followed afterwards.

The basic form of a retrospective is to put everyone in the same room and ask *What could we do better?* A slightly more advanced form is to ask three questions: *What do we do right? What could we do better?* and *What still puzzles us?*

An alternative set of questions could be: *What did we set out to achieve? What did we achieve?* and *What can we learn from the difference?*

In either case, the objective is to identify options to improve the way in which the team works. There are a number of exercises that can be used to help people focus on the project and generate ideas for improvement. For example, people tend to focus on the most recent events in a project. To offset this, it can be useful to construct a project timeline to remind people of the longer project history.

Space prohibits a longer discussion of project retrospectives here. Others have written more fully on this subject. Norm Kerth[7] mainly considers retrospectives lasting several days and examining projects lasting several years of elapsed time. Esther Derby and Diana Larsen[8] describe a newer style of retrospective, known as *heartbeat retrospectives*, that have emerged within the Agile community. These occur more regularly in line with the iterative cycle of Agile teams. Again, teams pause to examine how they're doing, what's working and what needs improvement.

Although retrospectives occur at the end of a project, they are in fact the beginning of a change. Assuming that a team stays together, which isn't always the case, the team needs to take on board the outcome of the retrospective and make the changes that have been agreed upon. This is perhaps the biggest challenge facing a retrospective and it's the challenge that this book has discussed at length: *How do we turn our learning into action and thereby knowledge?*

Thinking Point: Projects for Retrospectives

Consider the projects that you are involved with. If you're involved in one large project, consider when the next milestone is. Look for opportunities to hold a project retrospective. Find someone who would make a good facilitator. Is there anyone within your organization who isn't connected with the project and could facilitate a retrospective? Or can you find someone outside the organization you would work with?

11.3.5 Workout

General Electric (GE) have developed a technique known as *workout*[9] that is used throughout the company to improve processes, products and services, and generally to solve problems quickly. The technique is designed to involve

[7] See Kerth (2001).

[8] See Derby and Larsen (2006).

[9] See Welch (2001) and Tichy (1993).

workers at all levels in the company and empower them to create a solution and achieve rapid management approval.

The basic form of workout is well known:

- A manager identifies a problem that needs to be solved. The manager should be of sufficient seniority to be responsible for all aspects of both the problem and the solution.

- A cross-functional team is created, with representatives from all areas of the business that either touch on the problem or are involved with a solution.

- If the team members are new to workout, they're trained in problem solving techniques.

- The team members meet at an off-site location, where the manager presents them with the problem to be solved. The manager then leaves until the final stage.

- The team has several days to analyse the problem and find a solution. The solution must address all aspects of the problem and represent a complete plan of action.

- Outside facilitators are used to run the process and help the team with problem solving techniques. As with retrospectives, it's better to use neutral outsiders to help.

At the end, the manager returns and the team presents the solution. The manager has to make a decision on the solution. He or she has several options:

- To accept the solution and plan as is.

- To reject the solution and provide an explanation.

- One other option is available: to ask for some time before accepting or rejecting the plan. Managers are expected to explain why they need the time and at the end of this time – say, 30 days – they must return to the team and announce their accept/reject decision.

While workout is undoubtedly a powerful technique and has helped GE achieve rapid change, it isn't to be undertaken lightly. Workout is time-consuming and expensive, because it temporarily creates a diverse team of people from different parts, and perhaps locations, in the company.

In order to actively run a workout, the senior manager must be prepared to accept the decisions of the workout and respond accordingly. Failure to accept solutions or give reasons for rejecting plans may undermine both the individual sessions and the wider programme.

One group of researchers[10] tried to copy GE's workout in another organization. They encountered a large number of problems, which aren't necessarily

---

[10] See Schaninger, Harris and Niebuhr (1999).

obvious from a brief description but that highlight how important the GE culture is in allowing workout to succeed.

For example:

- GE places great importance on quick decision-making. Companies that take a more consensual, slower-paced, approach to decisions will have problems accepting that one person can make rapid *Yes/No* decisions.

- Workout utilizes, and enhances, the empowerment of many employees. In an organization without a history of employee empowerment, the participant may hold back on making recommendations and difficult suggestions.

- The flip side of empowerment is that managers welcome employee suggestions and plans. In organizations where managers aren't used to hearing brutal truths and suggestions from employees, they may feel threatened by such a process.

Workout is a tool with great potential, but transplanting it directly from GE to your organization isn't necessarily easy. Workout might work for you, or it might inspire you to devise your own problem solving system.

11.3.6   Kaizen and Kaikaku

Those who implement Lean manufacturing and product development frequently use Kaizen events to drive improvement forward. Kaizen is a version of continuous improvement. Teams refine their working practices and processes to improve their efficiency and the quality of the products. Much of this book describes Kaizen-like activities.

Sometimes, organizations and teams need to go further. In addition to regular Kaizen, Lean teams use occasional Kaikaku events to bring about more far reaching change. Kaikaku, another Japanese word, means *revolutionary reform*. Such an event may be held at the start of the change to Lean production, or by teams that are already practising Lean and want to improve further.

The format of an event will depend on where the team is starting from and what the team is seeking to accomplish. Fault-finding and value stream mapping may be used, as may some of the other techniques outlined in this section. At the same time, Kaikaku lays the foundation for further improvement through Kaizen.

Kaikaku events involve all those concerned with the process. Together, they're responsible for understanding the current process, determining what needs to be done and devising a better process or processes. Once changes are decided, the same team is responsible for implementing the changes.

11.3.7 Frequency

Some of the change events described here, such as workout and process miniatures, are held infrequently. When they are held, they are big events and they can create big changes. Other events benefit from being held much more regularly. Improvement meetings should be held frequently: once a month might be normal. Similarly, the events described in Chapter 4, such as book groups and TechTalks, also benefit from predictable regularity.

By making these events part of the routine work pattern, they become part of the culture and embed themselves within the organization. The learning and change resulting from such events also become embedded. People come to expect the events and the results that follow. Making events regular also helps them outlive any particular person or initiative.

Some teams use retrospectives regularly, perhaps at the end of every iteration or after every second iteration. Typically, these are heartbeat retrospectives. While the first few may take up several hours, subsequent ones will take less time. As issues are dealt with and people adapt to the format, less time will be needed.

Other teams only hold retrospectives at the end of a major project or after a milestone. These retrospectives tend to be longer, because they cover a longer time period and more issues will be raised. It is still important to make these retrospectives part of the routine and culture, but it's more difficult to do so because they happen less frequently.

11.4 Outsiders

Sometimes, it's useful to bring in outsiders to help. Outsiders, whether trainers, consultants, facilitators or others, can't replace your own learning, but they can be very effective at helping seed learning and speeding things up. There's a long history of consultants introducing change – from the time-and-motion men who typified scientific management to the *Business Process Re-engineering (BPR)* consultants.

Using consultants to bring about change in your organization is one model for creating change, but it's very different to the one considered in this book. This book focuses on how you can bring about learning and change within your own organization. Using consultants is different because consultants are by their very nature temporary. One day they won't be there, and you'll need to continue learning and changing without them.

Consultants aren't the only outsiders who can help your organization learn and there are a variety of reasons why you might want to make use of outsiders to help. This section considers some of the ways in which outsiders can help with learning and change.

In a large organization, the outsiders may actually work for the same organization. They may be dedicated *internal consultants* or they may be people from a different department. Small organizations may choose to build up a network of regular consultants, trainers and facilitators to create consistency. This approach will also benefit the outsiders, who will better understand the organization and issues involved.

11.4.1   Consultants

Many different types of consultants are available and they can play a valuable role in assisting your learning and change. Senior managers who want to create change but don't know where or how to begin may turn to outside consultants. When consultants arrive, they're largely free of history and legacy in a company. Since the consultants won't be around for long, there's less likelihood that they will get involved in the existing battles and politics present in organizations.

But using consultants isn't without problems. The presence of consultants and their role can itself be the subject of such disagreements. Nor are consultants always impartial. Someone has to invite consultants into the company and cynics may see consultants as proxies for those paying their fees. The fees themselves also pose a problem: some companies may simply be unable to afford consultants.

Consultants may bring specialist knowledge that is lacking within an organization. Some consultants will use their knowledge directly to perform a task, while others will transfer their knowledge to you or to someone else in the organization.

Even without specialist knowledge, consultants can be useful as an external pair of eyes to assess your current position. Sometimes we can be too close to a situation to step back and take stock of what's actually happening. Even if we are capable of doing this, we may find that time pressures prevent us. So, consultants can play the role of an extra pair of hands or a fresh pair of eyes.

While consultants rarely know our business as well as we do, they do benefit from seeing many problems in many different organizations. This can lead to greater experience of problems and solutions than most of us tend to have. Not only will they see a larger variety of problems, but they will also see the same problem again and again. A consultant may see a problem once or twice a year that we only see once or twice in a career. (Unfortunately, this can lead to them recommending the same solution each time.)

Seeing many different problems, solutions and companies can increase the consultant's knowledge of change. However, consultants often depart from a company before change is complete and don't have to live with the result of the change. Therefore, their experiences will be different to our own.

When consultants are experienced in a field, they speak with authority and legitimacy. This experience not only reduces the risk of change, because the consultant has experienced it before, but also demonstrates the importance that management place on the problem.

Expert consultants are also useful for seeding learning. They can introduce new ideas, directly or indirectly, to groups (say, in a TechTalk) and individuals (in one-to-one conversation.) Once the new ideas are on the table, they can talk through the alternatives and options that the organization faces and outline the possible outcomes. Describing outcomes is part of the process of creating aspirations and persuading people that there's a better way of doing things.

It is important not to see the consultant as the source of all knowledge, because if this happens it will be difficult to continue when the consultant is gone. Often, clients know the solution to their own problems and the consultant's role is only to help the clients recognize their solution. Gerry Weinberg[11] calls this the *Five Minute Rule*:

"Clients always know how to solve their problems, and always tell the solution in the first five minutes."

11.4.2   Training

Despite saying a lot about learning and knowledge creation, this book has said very little about training and more traditional classroom learning. The focus has been on action-based learning and the belief that we learn much through doing. So this section isn't a call to send people on courses.

One of the problems with sending people on courses to 'learn', and expecting them to come back to the office and act on the learning, is that we've separated the learning from the action. Direct training and courses need to be used to support existing ideas of learning and change rather than as a substitute for them. Simply sending people on a SCRUM course won't turn them into practitioners. It can, however, play a role in introducing ideas or speeding up a change.

Like consulting, training works at two levels. The obvious aspect is to that people get trained in some new skill; the more subliminal message is that leaders and managers regard something as important enough to spend money on and take people away from their day jobs.

Giving people training both helps them directly improve a skill, or learn a new one, and allows them to practise and learn without fear. This reduces the risk of making a change; individuals aren't going to be thrown in the deep end. Training courses can be a good way of introducing new ideas, alleviating fear of the unknown, speeding up change programmes and showing commitment to actual learning and change. In addition, when training courses are run specifically for a particular team, it can help the team form and create a shared understanding.

[11] See Weinberg (1985).

Training is usually only the start of the education process. Many of the technologies that we use today, whether they be C#, Linux or AJAX, require actual hands-on use before we become proficient. A training course can give someone a good start, but hands-on experience is often the only way to really learn the tacit knowledge needed to master a technology.

The boundary between trainers and consultants is highly permeable. Many independent consultants run a healthy training business in addition to their consulting activities, while those focused on training can often be persuaded to do a spot of consultancy. It can be useful to follow up a training course with some consultancy to reinforce the message and answer the questions that people have as they use a technology.

11.4.3 Facilitators

Some of the techniques outlined in this chapter, and throughout the book, require someone to lead and facilitate a meeting. For example, retrospectives need someone to initiate the conversations, run the exercises and mediate in discussions. Often, it's better to bring in someone from outside the organization to run such sessions than use people within the firm.

At first sight, this may seem like an unnecessary expense, but there are good reasons why this is money well spent. Using someone inside your organization as a facilitator still costs money: the expenditure may be hidden, but it still exists. For larger exercises, the actual cost of hiring an outside facilitator is only a small part of the overall cost.

An exercise such as workout or a retrospective might be completely new to a company. It's entirely possible that nobody in the organization has ever attended such an exercise before. In such cases, the only way to see what this is like is to use an outside facilitator.

A good facilitator will bring both good facilitation skills and experience in running group sessions. He or she will know how to get people talking, how to stop people talking, how to deal with emotional issues that may arise and how to run exercises to help maximize learning.

Exercises such as retrospectives benefit from having a facilitator who has no previous connection with the project. He or she can talk to people impartially, find out what the 'unspoken problems' are and provide a safe person to confide in. It's worth quoting Norm Kerth's advice:[12]

> "A facilitator needs to be an outsider rather than a member of the team. Facilitators need to remain neutral during the retrospective – watching the process, building a safe environment, helping people participate, summarizing points as the story lines begin to weave, and encouraging the exploration of alternatives."

[12] See Kerth (2001).

There's simply far too much for facilitators to do to allow them to partake in the exercise as well. People who are both trying to lead the exercise and contribute their own opinions and experiences will be swamped. Not only will this mean that they can't fulfil the role of facilitator, but it also means that their own learning will be hindered.

11.4.4   Coaches

To make the most of the coaching techniques described in Chapter 10, it can be necessary to employ outside coaches. Agile development often makes use of directive coaching to introduce Agile practices and help teams improve. Hiring an experienced Agile coach to work with your team can be beneficial. Initially, the role of Agile coach is usually filled by a consultant who has a mandate to help the team change and to transfer his or her own knowledge. Over time, one of the team members may take on the coaching role themselves.

Non-directive coaching isn't specific to Agile, and the coach almost always needs to be an outsider. Using an outside coach allows the coachee to discuss events, people and issues in confidence, and more freely than they could with an internal coach. Most organizations are unlikely to be able to afford to give each individual his or her own external coach, so non-directive coaching is likely to be limited to a few individuals or for short periods.

Observing either type of coach at work can help improve both your own performance and your own coaching skills. These skills can help you improve your own team. In a learning culture, every manager needs to be able to coach his or her team and develop the team members' individual potential. Over the long term, this work can't be done by outsiders.

11.5   Conclusion

In previous chapters, we've looked at tools and ideas that are available for you to use immediately. You don't need approval from anybody else to start listening to your colleagues or to start writing a diary. The suggestions given in this chapter differ because they are group focused and more structured in their application.

This difference has two consequences. Firstly, these techniques are likely to cost you money. Secondly, you need other people to agree to use these tools, so you'll need to be clearer about what you are doing. If you hold a position of authority in your organization, these techniques might represent a good place to start your initiatives. For example, you could ask each team to hold a retrospective and report back.

Conversely, if you hold a more junior position these techniques won't be available to you until later in your initiative. Until you've shown a modicum of success, until you're trusted, until those with authority see the improvements that you've made, it will be hard to get buy-in and expenditure on facilitators and trainers. Don't let such blocks stop you from taking action and starting other initiatives – expect to start small.

Whatever your position, it's useful to know that these tools exist and to understand something of the philosophy behind them. There are more techniques not covered here that may also help; once you start looking around, you'll find many to choose from.

New Beginnings

"Here is Edward Bear, coming downstairs now, bump, bump, bump, on the back of his head, behind Christopher Robin. It is, as far as he knows, the only way of coming downstairs, but sometimes he feels that there really is another way, if only he could stop bumping for a moment and think of it."

A.A. Milne[1]

Often, people fail to change and improve simply because they're unaware of how things could be better. This doesn't stop them wanting things to be better, but the lack of a better example stops them from doing anything. The lack of a better way of doing things may be simply because we haven't taken the time to find a better way. We may be so busy doing *stuff* and then doing *more stuff* that there's no time to find a better way.

It is seldom possible to stop everything and find a better way. Instead, we need to find a way to improve things as we go. This is the reality of modern business.

The Agile manifesto and volumes of writing on Agile and Lean software development show that there is a better way. This book has tried to show how you can get from where you are today to where you want to be.

---

[1] See Milne (1974).

12.1 The Change Problem

The problem facing many software development organizations today is how to change. Teams know how to develop software, but some teams are more successful than others. For those who are less successful, there's an obvious imperative to improve. For those who are more successful, there's still a need to do better. Agile software development is a means of improving a development team's performance.

There's no mystery to Agile software development. There are plenty of books, conferences, mailing lists and even drinking clubs concerned with the subject. The basic ideas behind Agile aren't difficult to grasp. The difficult part is becoming Agile, moving from where the team is today to where it wants to be.

For those teams that are already practising Agile development, the problem is slightly different. The challenge for these teams is to stay Agile and to do even better; they need to improve on the success that they're already enjoying.

This book has proposed one solution to both problems: learning (Figure 12.1).

By learning, and the accompanying change, teams can become Agile, and once Agile they can continue to improve and move beyond current thinking and best practice. The rewards for such teams are great. The organizations for which they work will benefit and so too will the people. Individuals will enjoy

Where we are today ...

Today's challenge: *How do we get from here, to there?*

... want to go here ...

Tomorrow's challenge: *Keep going.*

Where next?

Figure 12.1 The change problem.

learning, the satisfaction of a job well done and the benefits of working for a successful organization.

In the long term, it's possible that the practices, processes and techniques developed within software development may spread well beyond the bounds of the development community. Software developers are at the leading edge of knowledge work. We can expect to see more knowledge workers follow our example.

12.2 Bottom-up over Top-down

This book has been mainly about bottom-up change. The kind of change that happens when the people who do the work set about changing the way in which they do what they do. Too many people think of change in terms of top-down change, the kind of change that happens to us.

Sometimes top-down change is needed. Perhaps companies need to restructure and people need to be told what to do. Sometimes solving problems requires changing the organogram: new people need to be hired and others need to be fired; new departments need to be created and others merged or closed.

But the need for top-down change is far less than we think. Waiting for top-down change to happen can be an excuse for not changing ourselves and taking action now. Waiting for someone else to fix things excuses you from acting yourself. This book has been about taking action yourself and creating change, wherever you are in the organization.

This also means working with the resources that you have available now. Rather than waiting for money to become available, or for new people to join the company, or for management to make a decision, look instead to the resources that you have available right now. Imagination and careful thinking will allow you to start making changes immediately.

You might not be able to solve all your problems with your current resources in a bottom-up fashion, but you can make a start and solve some. Most probably, you can do far more than you initially imagine. When making change is at its most difficult, even the smallest changes are an achievement to be savoured.

12.3 Begin with Yourself

Creating change starts with yourself: your outlook, your perspective, your approach. You're always empowered to change yourself. Rather than expecting others to do things differently or make change happen, start with yourself:

- Maybe you need to know more about some aspect of this book. Look at the Further Reading section and follow the references mentioned. Then consider what you can do differently.

- Maybe you need to change some aspect of your behaviour. Perhaps you can set a good example to the team, or perhaps you can experiment with a different way of doing things.

- Ask others how you could improve. What do others think that you could do better?

- Maybe you can pick one of the specific methods discussed here and put it into practice: keep your own diary, start a book study group, listen to people.

- If you don't know what needs doing, then seek out someone who does: your manager, your manager's manager, an expert in the field, an outside consultant, or just the people who you work with every day.

- Understand what's going on around you: watch and listen to what's happening in your organization and try to understand. Avoid cynicism when interpreting events. Instead, prefer the principle of Occam's razor: look for the simplest explanation possible.

Over time, you can expand your activities: you'll gain confidence in yourself and others will gain confidence in you.

12.3.1 Warnings

However, this advice doesn't come without warnings.

Changing yourself might not be easy; nor might it be comfortable. It's easy to fall back on your old ways of doing things. Those around you may feel uncomfortable when you change: it may take time for people to recognize and accept your personal changes.

Not everything that you try will be successful. Some decisions will go against you, some initiatives will fail to attract support and others will start well but lose their momentum. At times like these, it can be hard to muster the energy to continue and persevere.

But persevere you must. Sticking with your initiatives will help you to establish credibility. Listen to what others say: try to understand why things happened, why some things succeed and others fail, and why each decision was made. Use this information to adjust your plans and initiatives.

Savour your successes and accept your defeats graciously – easier said than done. Seek to learn from everything you do – success or failure. It's a cliché to say 'learn from your failures', but remember to learn from your successes too.

12.3.2 Legitimacy

Before embarking on a change initiative, it's essential to check you should be doing so. Ask yourself:

- Have I been asked to do this?
- Do I have the authority to do this?
- Do I need to do this to achieve another of my stated objectives?

Kicking off change without legitimacy may not be the best career move you ever made. Fortunately, without some degree of legitimacy you're unlikely to get very far: sooner or later people will say *No* and you'll have problems acquiring resources.

On the other hand, you may be able to start a debate that eventually ends up as a change programme. The management guru Tom Peters[2] quotes the American comedian Roseanne Barr: 'Nobody gives you power … you just take it!'

12.3.3 In a Lonely Place

Introducing change can be lonely and demoralizing. In the beginning, it might only be you who can see the need for change or the opportunities. Sometimes – especially at first – you may be a lone voice for change and at times you'll feel isolated. Worse still, because change always takes longer than you think, this isolation may last for some time.

The best advice is to look for supporters and allies. Find people who are receptive to your ideas, people to whom you can talk. Like-minded individuals can help relieve the loneliness and share the burden. Having trusted colleagues with whom you can to share and discuss ideas is invaluable.

You're going to need other people on your change journey, because you can't do everything yourself. Nor can you be seen to be doing everything yourself. If you do everything yourself, or even if you're perceived as doing everything yourself, then you're not spreading the change. If change is dependent on you alone, then it isn't sustainable in the long run.

There are also times when you'll find your changes blocked. You need your allies to keep your spirits up, but you also need them to find a way around the obstacles. Sometimes the obstacles will be more about you than about your ideas, and in these cases you might need to use one of your allies as a proxy to further your goals. If you do so, remember that these people are still their own men and women – they aren't on remote control and they won't always do things the way you would have done.

Although you may begin the change journey on your own, you can't finish on your own. Change begins with yourself, but ultimately changing the way in which you develop software means helping the whole team, and your organization.

[2] See Peters (2003).

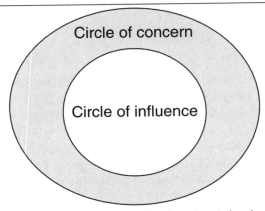

Figure 12.2 The circle of influence is smaller than the circle of concern.

Build Your Reputation – Circles of Influence

The *Seven Habits of Highly Effective People*[3] is a book that isn't to everyone's taste. You can argue with some of it, but it does contain a lot of good ideas that are useful. One idea is that we all have *circles of concern* and *circles of influence*, and normally the former is larger than the latter (see Figure 12.2).

According to this model, we're all concerned about a lot of things, which might include: the quality of our software code, our testing systems, our product requirements, the direction of the product, the strategic direction of the company and global warming. Ideally, we'd like to change all of these things – and certainly the guys in the pub or at the water cooler think that we should change them. This is our *circle of concern*, the things we worry about, and the things we talk about and even complain about.

However, whatever position we're in, there's little that we can do about many of our concerns. As a developer you may be in a position to improve the quality of the code, but you may be able to do little about the strategic direction of the company. Conversely, the new CEO may be able to change the strategic direction of the company, but can do little to improve the quality of the code.

Most people, CEO and developer alike, have *circles of influence* that are smaller than their *circle of concern*. Ideally we would like to grow our circle of influence to the point at which we can address all of the issues that we're concerned about, but how?

Stephen Covey's answer is for us to focus our attention inside our circle of influence, where we can improve things. By working within the circle, we can get things done and show how we can make a difference. Over time, our

---

[3] See Covey (1992).

success will lead to more people trusting us, our reputation will grow and so will our circle of influence, thus allowing us to address more concerns.

By not trying to change things that we're concerned about but can't influence, we save our time and energy, improve our success rate and avoid conflicts that may later hinder progress. Over time, we hope to see our circle of influence grow, and while it may never match entirely our area of concern, we can at least make more of a difference than we do now.

This is a great theory, but it has a couple of drawbacks. Firstly, it's difficult to know just where these barriers are. We don't always know when we have influence and when we don't. We may overstretch ourselves into the zone of *concern without influence* without knowing that we have. Alternatively, we may pass up possible opportunities to influence.

Secondly, this theory encourages us to stay within the realms of what we know and are comfortable with. Rather than grow our circle of influence, we could choose to shrink our circle of concern. Consequently we would never move out of our conform zone, and we would miss the experience, learning and growth that comes from pushing our boundaries.

Still, for anyone attempting to bring about change in his or her organization, it's worth keeping this theory in mind and working with it. This means choosing the battles that you fight: you might not win them all, but some battles are better off not fought at all.

12.4 Make Learning Happen

Once you've examined yourself, start to create change through learning:

- *Plant the seeds of learning:* Give people opportunities to learn, reflect and discuss. Create forums where people can talk openly and learn from others, where they have time to learn and to rehearse.

- *Remove barriers to learning:* Whether it's lack of time, materials or space, address the issue. You may not be able to remove the barrier completely at the first attempt.

- *Turn learning into action:* Help people to apply what they're learning – give them a chance to try new things and encourage them to continue.

- *Turn the action back into learning:* Help people examine and reflect on what the outcome of different actions might be and what they can learn.

- *Remove the barriers to further change:* Spread the news about success and address concerns about doing things differently.

Remember to feed the results and experience of learning and change back into your own learning. Learn from what others do and help others to learn from what they do themselves.

Don't Use Jargon: Don't Use These Words . . .

Throughout this book, we've used words such as 'learning organization', 'knowledge management', 'incremental change', 'tacit knowledge', 'mental models' and even 'change'. These words are jargon. We have used them here because they name ideas and concepts, and help connect with existing work on these subjects.

Don't use these words in public. Think them if you wish, but don't use them:

- Don't use them because they're jargon, and using jargon will separate you from the people around you. Such 'management speak' will separate you from the world that most software developers live in.
- Don't use these words because they're meaningless to most other people.
- Don't use these terms because they're meaningless in a day-to-day environment.

Eliminating these words will help you explain yourself better and focus on action over talk.

Instead of using these words, seek to apply the ideas. Rather than talking about creating a 'learning organization', look to see what you can do to enhance learning in the organization. Look for incremental changes that you can make to bring about more learning.

Most of all, don't use the 'C-word'. *Change* carries too much baggage: redundancies, management consultants, authority, disruption and failure. For understandable reasons, people may react badly to talk of change.

12.5 Create a Vision, Draw Up a Plan

Some people instinctively know what needs to be done. For others, it can be hard to see where to start. It's useful to think about how you can make change happen and draw up a plan. Before you can plan how to change, it helps to have an image of what an improved environment will look like.

Many of the stories about Agile and Lean software development, and about what such an environment looks like, seem very attractive. These stories are powerful motivators and help us imagine what the end result will look like.

Start by imagining what your final state will look like and how it will feel to work in. Feel free to change the picture painted by others, to make it your own. This will give you something to aim for and a story with which to motivate both yourself and others. This will create not just a personal vision but also one that you can share with others.

Once you have an idea of where you're heading, then you need to consider how you can get there. If you know you have a mandate for change, you might want to start by creating a change plan. If you're unsure of your mandate, then you might simply like to choose one of the ideas presented in this book and try it out. Introduce project retrospectives, form a book study group or start blogging. With a little experience, you might try another initiative or you may choose to create your own change plan.

Before starting a plan, examine the gap between how your organization works at the moment and your vision of how it could work. You might find that you're already achieving some parts of the vision, or you might find that it's simply a case of doing things better. Once you've examined the gaps, you can start developing your plan.

Creating a plan can help firm up your own ideas of what needs doing, as well as providing structure. The change models described in Chapter 8 can help you anticipate some problems and suggest actions. Kotter's model is particularly useful in this context.

It might help to write your plan down, perhaps as a description, or as story or a picture. You might be the only person to see the plan or you might want to circulate it to others – or your plan may exist only in your head and in the stories you tell other people. Just remember that you need to be able to explain where you're going, and perhaps how you hope to get there, to other people. If you can't explain where you're going, then it's hard for others to join you.

Remember too that the plan, and possibly the destination, will change. No plan will unfold exactly as imagined, but the exercise of planning it is useful in preparing your own actions. Better plans and more ambitious destinations will arise, and as you learn from others your own ideas will change. This is a sign of success, not failure.

Thinking Point: Start with Three Ideas

Write down three ideas that you've found in this book (or any other) that you think would benefit your organization. Now consider:

- How would your work benefit if these three ideas were adopted? Just assume that it happens tomorrow: How would your life improve? What would you feel?

- What would need to happen to implement these ideas? For each idea, visualize how it could happen and think about who you need to talk to, what resources you would need and what objections there could be.

- Share your ideas with some co-workers. Do they share your vision? Do they see the benefit that your ideas would bring? Can they see any other obstacles?

- Select the idea that looks most promising and start to make it happen: remove the obstacles, obtain the resources and talk to people.

Once you've succeeded with one idea, start over again. The two other ideas may still look good or you may want to start with a clean slate.

12.6 Three Interlocking Ideas

Behind the learning and change agenda laid out in this book are three key ideas:

- *Drive to do better:* No matter how well we're doing today, we can do better. In everything we do, there's always opportunity to improve. Problems are easy to find, but demoralizing: once we get past problems, we need to maintain our drive to find opportunities and repeat the process. We can always do better.

- *Systems thinking:* Although this book hasn't dwelt on systems thinking in detail – there are plenty of other books that do – it's key to helping us learn, change and improve. It isn't enough to improve single aspects of what we do. We need to look at what these aspects link to. This will help us to find new opportunities for improvement.

  There's a tension here: constantly applying systems thinking will lead us to examine bigger and bigger challenges. The bigger the challenge, the less is our ability to do anything about it. Some problems are so big that while we can make an improvement, it will have very little effect. It can be difficult to solve some big challenges because there are too many pieces (including people) involved.

  Sometimes we need to bound our changes in order to do anything. The danger is that improving one aspect of a system may impair a larger system.

- *Continual change:* The drive to do better should lead to continual improvement. But we can't solve everything at once, so change needs to be incremental.

Continual incremental improvement addresses the systems thinking conundrum. While we can't fix everything at once, we can fix one part provided that we're able to improve again. Continual improvement allows us to start with small changes and work up to bigger changes.

The combination of these three ideas allows us to tackle any problem. The drive to do better motivates our continual improvement: systems thinking allows us to find the opportunities for improvement; and continual improvement allows us to address small parts of a bigger challenge bit by bit (Figure 12.3).

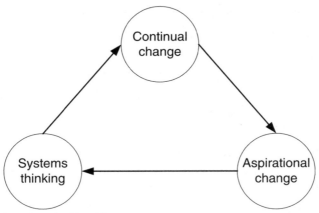

Figure 12.3 Three interlocking ideas.

12.7 Change Never Ends

As human beings, we continue to learn. Since learning never ends, neither does change. It's simply a question of how fast learning and change happen.

In part, change takes longer than you think because it's never done. As soon as we succeed in one field, more options and ideas open up. This is natural, because we're learning, problem solving and creating. It also takes longer than we think, because it involves people – many people – and each one needs his or her own time to change.

Savour every success, even the little ones: use them for your own inner strength and to recognize that change is possible. Don't expect people to say 'Thank you': some of them won't, some of them won't know it was you who initiated the change and some of them will just be too busy. Just remember to thank those who help you.

Spread the success, celebrate success, involve others and demonstrate that your ideas work and change is happening. This will reward your supporters and enthuse them. However, don't over-celebrate – remember that there's still work to do. Celebration is itself a double-edged sword: it's a reward and it can be an incentive when you're in the middle of change. But celebration can also be read as marking the end. By celebrating, you might send the message that success has been achieved, that change has ended or slowed down.

Start Today

I can't tell you what to do next. I don't know your organization, I don't know your problems and I certainly don't know what needs doing. Hopefully your list of *Three Ideas* from above can give you a starting point.

If you're still struggling, try this:

- Talk to the people around you and learn what they think needs to be done.
- Make time in your routine to think about what needs to be improved.
- Create a regular forum where you can seed learning. Allow people to express themselves, and together you can identify problems and suggest solutions.

Remember that things won't improve on their own; someone needs to make it happen. We need to learn how to make change happen: together, the learning and action create knowledge.

12.8 Conclusion

Hopefully, as this book draws to a close you have some idea of what to do next. Maybe you've even started to apply some of what you've read to yourself and your team. At this point, your learning from this book is finished and it's time for action and change.

The core idea contained in this book is very simple: learning is change; when we apply learning, we change; and when we change, we learn.[4] This happens for us as individuals, it happens to our team members as individuals and to teams as a collective, and it happens for our customers. Our products change our customers, who in turn learn and ask for more change.

This book has tried to show how ideas that are usually applied to management can equally be applied to software development. The work of software developers and corporate managers has much in common: both work to give ideas physical presence, both seek to create structures for abstract concepts and in the process reduce costs to improve efficiency – whether measured in financial terms or through performance.

Agile software development seeks to deliver better software by more closely matching business requirements. As the software development process takes on the characteristics of business and management, it will better meet these requirements. The divide between IT people and business people will narrow. While this will benefit both sides, a few people will feel uncomfortable with a narrower gap. Managers who are heard to declare 'I don't understand technology' must learn to understand; and developers who immerse themselves in technology and ignore the business will need to broaden their understanding.

Key to this change is the learning process. Businesses learn and change, so do development teams. Continual learning and change benefits everyone – the challenge is to direct and enhance this process.

---

[4] While I'm sure I read this theory explicitly in the work of someone else, I can't definitively trace the idea. Certainly, the idea that *change is learning and learning is change* is implicit in much of the literature cited throughout this book.

Further Reading

Many books, journal articles and other sources are referenced throughout this book. Some of these texts have been more influential than others. For anyone wishing to understand these subjects in more detail, the following short list of books is recommended:

On Agile and Lean software development, see Poppendieck and Poppendieck (2003), Coplien and Harrison (2004), Cockburn (2002) and Highsmith (2002).
On business in general, see de Geus (1997) and Mintzberg (1994).
On knowledge, see Nonaka and Takeuchi (1995).
On learning and change, see Manns and Rising (2005) and Senge (1990).
On other topics, see DeMarco (2001) and Covey (1992).

References

Adams, D. (1979) *The Hitchhiker's Guide to the Galaxy*, Pan Books, London.

Ang, K., Thong, J.Y.L. and Yap, C. (1997) IT implementation through the lens of organizational learning: a case study of insuror. International Conference on Information Systems. http://portal.acm.org/toc.cfm?id=353071&coll= portal&dl=ACM&type=proceeding.

Argyris, C. (1977) Organizational learning and management information systems. *Accounting, Organizations and Society*, **2**, 113–123.

Argyris, C. (1994) *On Organizational Learning*, Blackwell, Oxford.

Beer, M. and Nohria, N. (2000) Cracking the code of change. *Harvard Business Review*, **78** (3), 133–142.

Boehm, B. and Pappacio, P.N. (1988) Understanding and controlling software costs. *IEEE Transactions on Software Engineering*, **14**, 1462–1477.

Borchardt-Hume A. (ed.)(2006) *Albers and Moholy-Nagy: from the Bauhaus to the New World*, Tate Publishing, London.

Brand, S. (1994) *How Buildings Learn: What Happens after They're Built*, Viking, New York.

Brooks, F. (1975) *The Mythical Man Month: Essays on Software Engineering*, 1st edn, Addison-Wesley, Reading, MA.

Brooks, F. (1995) *The Mythical Man Month: Essays on Software Engineering*, anniversary edn, Addison-Wesley, Reading, MA.

Brown, J.S. and Duguid, P. (2000) *The Social Life of Information*, Harvard Business School Press, Boston, MA.

Busche, G.R. (1998) Appreciative Inquiry with teams. *The Organization Development Journal*, **16**, 41–50. http://www.gervasebushe.ca/aiteams.htm.

Cameron, E. and Green, M. (2005) *Making Sense of Change Management*, Kogan Page, London.

Changing Software Development: Learning to Become Agile   Allan Kelly
© 2008 John Wiley & Sons, Ltd.

Carse, J.P. (1986) *Finite and Infinite Games*, The Free Press, New York.

Cockburn, A. (2002) *Agile Software Development*, Addison-Wesley, Reading, MA.

Conway, M.E. (1968) How do committees invent? *Datamation*, **14** (4), 28–31. http://www.melconway.com/research/committees.html.

Cooperrider, D.L. and Srivastva, S. (1987) Appreciative Inquiry in organizational life. *Organizational Change and Development*, **1**, 129–169.

Coplien, J.O. and Harrison, N.B. (2004) *Organizational Patterns of Agile Software Development*, Pearson Prentice Hall, Upper Saddle River, NJ.

Covey, S.R. (1992) *The Seven Habits of Highly Effective People: Restoring the Character Ethic*, Simon & Schuster, London.

Crosby, P.B. (1980) *Quality is Free: the Art of Making Quality Certain*, New American Library, New York.

Davenport, T.H. (2005) *Thinking for a Living*, Harvard Business School Press, Boston, MA.

Davenport, T.H. and Prusak, L. (2000) *Working Knowledge*, Harvard Business School Press, Boston, MA.

de Geus, A.P. (1988) Planning as learning. *Harvard Business Review*, **66**, 70.

de Geus, A.P. (1997) *The Living Company*, Nicholas Brealey, London.

DeMarco, T. (2001) *Slack*, Broadway Books, New York.

DeMarco, T. and Lister, T. (1987) *Peopleware*, Dorset House, New York.

Denning, S. (2001) *The Springboard: How Story Telling Ignites Action in Knowledge-era Organizations*, Butterworth-Heinemann, Oxford.

Derby, E. and Larsen, D. (2006) *Agile Retrospectives: Making Good Teams Great*, Pragmatic Programmers, Raleigh, NC.

Downey, M. (2003) *Effective Coaching*, Texere, New York.

Drucker, P.F. (1969) *The Age of Discontinuity*, Heinemann, London.

Edberg, D. and Olfman, L. (2001) Organizational learning through the process of enhancing information systems. Paper presented at the 34th Hawaii International Conference on System Sciences, Maui, Hawaii, IEEE. http://csdl.computer.org/comp/proceedings/hicss/2001/0981/04/09814025.pdf.

Fahey, L. and Prusak, L. (1998) The eleven deadliest sins of knowledge management. *California Management Review*, **40**, 265–276.

Gladwell, M. (2000) *The Tipping Point*, Little Brown, London.

Goleman, D. (1996) *Emotional Intelligence*, Bloomsbury, London.

Grove, A. (1997) *Only the Paranoid Survive*, HarperCollins, London.

Hamel, G. and Prahalad, C.K. (1991) Corporate imagination and expeditionary marketing. *Harvard Business Review*, July–August, 81–91.

Hammer, M. and Champy, J. (1994) *Reengineering the Corporation: a Manifesto for Business Revolution*, HarperCollins, London.

Highsmith, J. (2002) *Agile Software Development Ecosystems*, Addison-Wesley, Reading, MA.

Holt, R. (2001) Software architecture as a shared mental model, Position paper to ASERC Workshop on Software Architecture. http://plg.uwaterloo.ca/~holt/papers/sw-arch-mental-model-020314c-1.pdf.

Huysman, M. (2000) Rethinking organizational learning: analyzing learning processes of information system designers. *Accounting, Management and Information Technologies*, **10**, 81–99.

Hvatum, L. and Kelly, A. (2005) What do I think of Conway's Law now? in 10th European Conference on Pattern Languages of Programs (EuroPLoP), UVK Universitätsverlag Konstanz GmbH, Irsee, Germany, pp. 735–750.

Ilavarasan, P.V. and Sharma, A.K. (2003) Is software work routinized? Some empirical observations from Indian software industry. *The Journal of Systems and Software*, **66**, 1, 1–6.

Kennedy, M.N. (2003) *Product Development for the Lean Enterprise*, Oaklea Press, Richmond, VA.

Kerth, N.L. (2001) *Project Retrospectives*, Dorset House, New York.

Kinni, T. (2003) *The Art of Appreciative Inquiry*, Harvard Business School Press, Boston, MA. http://hbswk.hbs.edu/archive/3684.html.

Kolb, D.A. (1976) Management and the learning process. *California Management Review*, **18**, 21–31.

Kotter, J.P. (1996) *Leading Change*, Harvard Business School Press, Boston, MA.

Levinson, M. (2006) *The Box*, Princeton University Press, Princeton, NJ.

Lewin, K. (1951) *Field Theory in Social Science*, Harper and Row, New York.

Linberg, K.R. (1999) Software developer perceptions about software project failure: a case study. *The Journal of Systems and Software*, **49**, 177–192.

Manns, M.L. and Rising, L. (2005) *Fearless Change: Patterns for Introducing New Ideas*, Addison-Wesley, Boston, MA.

McConnell, S. (1993) *Code Complete*, Microsoft Press, Redmond, WA.

Messerschmitt, D.G. and Szyperski, C. (2003) *Software Ecosystems*, The MIT Press, Cambridge, MA.

Milne, A.A. (1974) *The World of Pooh*, Methuen Children's Books, London.

Mintzberg, H. (1994) *The Rise and Fall of Strategic Planning*, FT Prentice Hall, New York.

Moss Kanter, R. (1999) The enduring skills of change leaders. *Leader to Leader*, **1**, 15–22. http://www.pfdf.org/leaderbooks/L2L/summer99/kanter.html.

Nonaka, I. and Konno, N. (1998) The concept of 'Ba'. *California Management Review*, **40** (3), 40–54.

Nonaka, I. and Takeuchi, H. (1995) *The Knowledge Creating Company*, Oxford University Press, Oxford.

Orr, J. (1990)Talking about machines: an ethnography of a modern job. Ph.D. thesis, Cornell University.

Peters, T.J. (2003) *Re-imagine!*, Dorling Kindersley, London.

Peters, T.J. and Waterman, R.H. (1991) *In Search of Excellence*, HarperCollins, London.

Pfeffer, J. and Sutton, R. (2000) *The Knowing-Doing Gap*, Harvard Business School Press, Boston, MA.

Poppendieck, M. and Poppendieck, T. (2003) *Lean Software Development*, Addison-Wesley, Boston, MA.

Poppendieck, M. and Poppendieck, T. (2007) *Implementing Lean Software Development: from Concept to Cash*, Addison-Wesley, London.

Raymond, E.S. (1996) *The New Hacker's Dictionary*, The MIT Press, Cambridge, MA.

Robey, D., Boundreau, M. and Rose, G. (2000) Information technology and organizational learning: a review and assessment of research. *Accounting, Management and Information Technologies*, **10**, 125–155.

Satir, V. (1991) *The Satir Model: Family Therapy and Beyond*, Science and Behavior Books, Palo Alto, CA.

Schaninger, W.S., Harris, S.G. and Niebuhr, R.E. (1999) Adapting General Electric's workout for use in other organizations: a template. *Management Development Forum*, **2**, 1. http://www.esc.edu/ESConline/Across_ESC/Forumjournal.nsf/web+view/C8C020477EE750CB852568FD0056CD61?opendocument.

Schwartz, P. (1991) *The Art of the Long View*, Bantam Doubleday Dell, New York.

Schwartz, P. (2003) *Inevitable Surprises: a Survival Guide for the 21st Century*, The Free Press, London.

Senge, P. (1990) *The Fifth Discipline*, Random House, New York.

Stroustrup, B. (1997) *The C++ Programming Language*, Addison-Wesley, Reading, MA.

Tichy, N.M. (1993) Revolutionize your company. *Fortune*, **128**, 114–118. http://money.cnn.com/magazines/fortune/fortune_archive/1993/12/13/78732/index.htm.

Truex, D., Baskerville, R. and Travis, J. (2000) Amethodical systems development: the deferred meaning of systems development methods. *Accounting, Management and Information Technologies*, **10**, 53–79.

Wastell, D.G. (1996) The fetish of technique: a methodology as a social defence. *Information Systems Journal*, **6**, 25–40.

Weinberg, G.M. (1971) *The Psychology of Computer Programming*, Van Nostrand Reinhold.

Weinberg, G.M. (1985) *The Secrets of Consulting*, Dorset House, New York.

Weinberg, G.M. (1997) *Quality Software Management: Anticipating Change*, Dorset House.

Weir, C. and Noble, J. (1999) Process patterns for personal practice. EuroPLoP 1999, UVK Universitätsverlag Konstanz GmbH, Irsee, Germany. http://www.charlesweir.com/papers/ProcessPatterns.pdf.

Welch, J. (2001) *Jack: What I've Learned Leading a Great Company and Great People*, Headline, London.

Whitmore, J. (2002) *Coaching for Performance: GROWing People, Performance and Purpose*, Nicholas Brealey, London.

Womack, J.P. and Jones, D.T. (2005) *Lean Solutions*, Simon & Schuster, London.

Womack, J.P., Jones, D.T. and Roos, D. (1991) *The Machine that Changed the World*, HarperCollins, New York.

Index